Table Of Contents

About The Author
A Very Unusual Background

Bill Way started his first business in 1972 with no money except a $300.00 finance company loan, while still in college. It was a simple sub-contract construction service, but he began making so much money that he dropped out of college, never to return. Within just 6 years he built a million dollar construction and land development company, building up to 50 homes per year, completing numerous remodeling projects, and employing up to 26 people!

He has a diverse and prosperous background as manager of many companies he has owned since 1972. . . including home building, land development, real estate dealer and property manager, mortgage investment, manufacturing, VENDING ROUTE OPERATOR AND EQUIPMENT DISTRIBUTOR, marketing, publishing, and Freedom Technology.

Bill enthusiastically proclaims that vending route operating is one of the MOST profitable and attractive businesses he's ever been involved in! And he's helped countless others get started in their own highly profitable vending business.

This book was written because Bill is very concerned about the many unscrupulous vending machine sales companies that are promoting 'blue sky' vending business opportunities with exaggerated profit claims. . . in order to sell overpriced, poor quality, or poor concept vending machines. There was virtually no reliable or complete information available regarding how to enter into the immensely profitable vending business, until now. Since he had the knowledge, he felt he should share it.

Bill is also one of the pioneers in the development and implementation of modern 'freedom technology' (which includes the vending business and much more). Since 1988, He has devoted much of his efforts in that direction.

Freedom technology has been defined as "the PRACTICAL means to live free, and prosper, in an increasingly unfree world". A little-publicized yet explosive new growth industry, freedom technology was born from strange parents: Invasive government. . . and the information revolution. It's important to note that it does not challenge or threaten the authority of any legitimate government or law.

After discovering that Americans are absolutely "starved" for freedom technology, but that it has been difficult to come by, Bill takes great pleasure in sharing this technology with others. He's always asking: "The rich have been doing much of this for years, isn't it about time we all started?"

The vending machine business is one of the best of the many freedom technologies which he has been very successful in developing, operating, and/or sharing with others. He is fully dedicated to sharing his knowledge of freedom technology with others. . . which most certainly includes his 'VENDING SUCCESS SECRETS - How Anyone Can Grow Rich In America's Best Cash Business'!

His company, Bill Way's FREEDOM TECHNOLOGY, is an authorized distributor for some of the largest and most respected vending equipment manufacturers in the U.S. These companies are very selective in who they choose to deal with.

Bill now runs his very profitable international business from his home, and he enjoys a very high degree of both personal and financial freedom: All as a result of his knowledge of freedom technology!

Born in 1951; Bill is the father of 3 and lives happily in a rural area in the foothills of the Rocky Mountains, US. His favorite activities are travel, flying, boating, and downhill skiing with his family and friends.

Warning - Disclaimer

Introduction

Congratulations on your decision to learn more about the INCREDIBLE opportunity that awaits you in the world of vending! You'll soon see why this is one of the best and most solid income opportunities available in America today!

If the prospect of becoming financially independent really motivates you. . . if you want to live 'the good life' in EVERY way. . . and if you can spare just a few hours per month to get started in your new business. . . then this is the opportunity you're looking for!

How would you like to make up to $200.00 gross profit per hour, or even more, in a very simple business where you could earn a 100% return of your investment back within as little as 4 months?!

I'm not kidding. I've done it myself, and I've helped countless others to do the same.

With some types of machines you can empty them just 2 times and you'll have your ENTIRE investment back! And listen to this. . . many machines require servicing only about ONCE every OTHER month!

I believe you'll find vending to be the HIGHEST profit business with the LEAST risk, the SMALLEST time commitment, and the SIMPLEST to operate. Perhaps equally as important. . . you can have FUN in the process! What more could you possibly want?

This is a book that can really change your life! With vending, many people JUST LIKE YOU are enjoying the lifestyle they've always dreamed of. . . short working hours and plenty of time and money for family, vacations, and special interests of all kinds!

Vending machines are like having little 'money-collecting ROBOTS' doing most of the work for you all day. . . while you kick-back and enjoy life! I think you can see why I call it "the ULTIMATE business"!

Each time you service your vending locations you'll feel like you just hit the JACK POT in Las Vegas. Believe me when I say. . . this business can be FUN!

And YOU can do it! In fact ANYONE can 'Grow Rich In America's Best Cash Business'. . . once you know the 'Vending Success Secrets'!

This book which you now hold in your hands is absolutely 'one-of-a-kind'. It was written by 'popular demand'. . . because very little reliable or complete information was available on the subject of entering into the immensely profitable vending business.

Who Really Is Getting Rich?

1st Group

Because vending is so profitable, it has attracted many unscrupulous promoters who find they can sell machines at up to 400% markup. (Machines with a factory cost of $250. are routinely selling for $750. to $1,000.) This first group of people are promoting concepts and machines that don't even work, at prices that are beyond belief, to people who just don't know any better. Beware. These people are getting rich at your expense!

Those without accurate information are often VICTIMIZED by these unscrupulous promoters who PRESSURE for quick decisions and make EXAGGERATED profit claims. . . in order to sell OVER-priced or POOR quality equipment.

But those who knew where the 'REAL MONEY' is kept their secrets to themselves. . . UNTIL NOW!

2nd Group

The second and largest group of people who are getting rich are vending route operators who know how to buy the RIGHT KIND of machines, at the RIGHT PRICE, and how to obtain PROFITABLE LOCATIONS. And this is not at all difficult to learn. This is the group you'll want to be in, and I'll help you in every respect.

This book is the result of over 20 years of research and actual successful experience. . . not just wishful thinking. It is substantive, yet concisely written (to make the best use of your time).

I am going to EXPOSE to you some of the most closely guarded secrets of the vending industry. Information that many people in the industry don't want you to know.

Secrets that can make you successful beyond your imagination. You will learn how to start small (or big) and become wealthy in vending.

You Will Learn. . .

How to get started on a shoestring. . . and with a money back guarantee!

How to make up to $200.00 gross profit per hour!

Your initial investment pay-back could take as little as 4 months!

You can earn up to 500% gross return on investment per year!

How to quickly turn $2,500.00 into at least $5,000.00 monthly income. . . working part-time only a few fun hours a month!

Do all this with no selling or selling experience required!

You'll learn how to buy ALL the BEST vending and amusement machines at the factory-direct WHOLESALE cost, and SAVE up to 75%.

Learn the pitfalls, risks and rip-offs in vending. . . yes, there are scams and fatal mistakes you must learn to avoid!

● Also, route management, machine selection, getting great locations (without selling), financing, getting started.

● You'll receive ready-to-use forms, and a simple route record keeping system.

● What trade magazines to get, what associations to join, what conventions and shows to attend. . .

● PLUS much, much more. PLEASE. . . take the time to read this carefully. It could be worth a fortune to you!

It is my sincere hope and belief that you will find this book to be a valuable and indispensable tool that you can use in evaluating the vending business; which area of vending you will enter into; and how to start up, manage, and expand your route to reach your personal financial goals.

I have freely shared my knowledge and experience as both a vending route operator and an equipment distributor. . . and added valuable general business information and 'freedom technology' that I have learned since I started my first business 'on a shoestring' in 1972 (more about my background is available at the front of the book, "About The Author"). I'd like to help you to create and expand a business that has been as successful as mine. In fact nothing would please me more than to see your success even surpass my own!

This book really IS just FULL of 'Secrets', 'how-to' information, contacts, surveys and statistics, EXPOSED rip-offs, and other valuable information not easily found elsewhere. With it, YOU really CAN achieve 'Vending Success'. . . the kind of financial success that can set you free!

And I believe you will find that I have 'simplified' the whole process for you.

You Can Do It!

Hundreds of people just like you are starting successful vending or amusement business every year. Regardless of your background. . . whether you're starting full-time or part-time. . . no matter if you have $50,000.00 to invest, or must start with just $500.00 borrowed money. . . YOU CAN DO IT!

An interesting note from the recent Vending Times Census Of The Industry: There are over 9700 vending route operators in the U.S. The majority of them (69%) are very small, employing 3 or fewer people. And 26% comprise the owner only. So as you can see, you don't need a big operation or a huge financial investment to be successful!

Most people find that this book answers most all their questions about vending, but some do have questions or need extra support. Please don't hesitate to contact us anytime we may be of service in any way.

In A Rush?

Doing business with us here at FREEDOM TECHNOLOGY? You'll be glad you did! But BEFORE you consider doing business with anyone else, please make sure you AT LEAST read the chapters titled "Pitfalls, Risks, and Rip-offs", "A Better Way" and "What's Best For You". They can honestly save you thousands of dollars, and a lot of aggravation!

Also see the last page of this book for FREE resources (reports, videos, etc.) including the "HOTTEST Vending Money-Makers" report!

TO YOUR GREAT SUCCESS!

Notes

Chapter 1
Why Vending?

Top 10 Profit Maker!

The Small Business Administration has released statistics ranking vending machines in the TOP 10% OF PROFIT-MAKING BUSINESSES, with profits increasing steadily since the early 1940's!

AVERAGE hourly income of OFFICE WORKER... $ 4.85
AVERAGE hourly income of FACTORY WORKER... $ 7.04
AVERAGE hourly income of SALESMAN... $ 8.16
AVERAGE hourly income of PLUMBER... $ 12.00

AVERAGE hourly income of SNACK VENDOR owner/operator.......................... $70.58

How does your present income compare with the above? Incomes of up to $200.00 gross profit per hour, and 4 month investment returns are not uncommon!

With income like that, it's NO WONDER the U.S. Department of Commerce reports that of those people starting a new vending business, a full 92% are successful and still in business after 5 years, 90% after 10 years!

BUSINESS SUCCESS RATE

INDIVIDUAL NEW START UP BUSINESS   VENDING BUSINESS

Vending Is NOT Small Change. . . It's BIG Business!

Last week alone, Americans plunked a staggering $600 million dollars into vending machines.

That's over $3 million dollars an hour. . . and more than enough quarters to circle the earth!

Vending (including amusement) is a dynamic $35 billion dollar industry that's growing at an impressive rate! And the vending concepts I'll share with you offers you among the highest profits available. . . and maximum market penetration. . . due to some very unique machines and management concepts!

Vending. . . The ULTIMATE Business Opportunity!!

You could earn an AMAZING return on a very SMALL investment!

Ask Yourself?

What other business offers you all the following. Be in a business with. . .

- HIGH income potential!
- LITTLE competition!
- AUTOMATIC repeat business!
- NOT Seasonal!
- NO fixed overhead!
- NO employees (unless you want)!
- IMMEDIATE cash flow!
- START full-time OR part-time!
- RECESSION PROOF!

- ● MINIMAL time investment!
- ● NO selling experience needed!
- ● NO technical experience required!
- ● NO advertising!
- ● NO trucks!
- ● NO franchise fees or royalties to pay!
- ● All CASH (no collections, financial privacy)!
- ● Comprehensive company support!
- ● INFLATION PROOF!

In fact, this business has almost NONE of the usual expense, risk, or hassles normally associated with a business venture! And it's FUN to operate! What else is there?

According to the recent Vending Times Census Of The Industry, there are over 9700 vending route operators in the U.S. The majority of them (69%) are very small, employing 3 or fewer people. And 26% comprise the owner only. So as you can see, you don't need a big operation or a huge financial investment to be successful!

No Selling Experience Needed

In the chapter titled "Getting GREAT Locations" I share many unique and effective ways to get the best locations with no selling or selling experience required. ANYONE can do it!

You can get good, profitable vending locations easily with the 'space donated' CHARITY CONCEPT. . . the free 'space provided' CONVENIENCE CENTER CONCEPT. . . or the SHARED REVENUE CONCEPT. And I will direct you to excellent sources of product supply.

Recession And Inflation Proof!

The whole vending and amusement industry is uniquely recession and inflation proof! For example:

The U.S. candy market is a multi-billion dollar industry that is virtually unaffected by the ups and downs of the national economy.

In tough times, people may put off buying a new car or clothes. . . they may eat less steak and lobster. . . but they won't do without their candy bar! It's a simple luxury that anyone and everyone can afford no matter what's going on in their world.

Americans eat over 20 pounds of candy per year each. . . and over half of that is chocolate!

It's interesting to note that the candy industry is growing, even though there is a perception that people should eat more healthy. They know they should, and many are, but they STILL want their candy.

Similar recession proofing is observed in other areas of vending and amusement. Various candy, snacks and games are viewed as an AFFORDABLE INDULGENCE. . . often bought on impulse.

The whole industry is INFLATION proof as well, because products are sold at consistent mark-ups based upon cost. When cost goes up, so does the sales price. And when the sales price goes up, YOUR PROFIT MARGIN GOES UP with it!

The Magic Of Compounding BIG Returns!

Surely you'd agree that when you have an opportunity to make up to 100%, or even as high as 500% annual return on your money, it doesn't have to take a lot of money to make a lot. Even a small investment compounded (reinvested) over a relatively short time can add up to a fortune!

The chart below shows how much money you'd have at the end of 1 through 5 years for each $1,000.00 you could invest at 10%, 50%, etc. Look at what you'd have after five years at 10% versus 100%. You sure can't get anywhere at bank rates, can you?

$1,000.00 Invested At Various Annual Rates Of Return

Year	10.%	50.%	100.%	200.%	500.%
1	$1,100.	$1,500.	$2,000.	$3,000.	$6,000.
2	1,210.	2,250.	4,000.	9,000.	36,000.
3	1,331.	3,375.	8,000.	27,000.	216,000.
4	1,464.	5,062.	16,000.	81,000.	1,296,000.
5	1,610.	7,593.	32,000.	243,000.	7,776,000.

I certainly can't guarantee any particular rate of return, and I certainly would not want you to expect to compound you money at a rate of 500% every year. . . but in this book you can read testimonials from people who are enjoying returns on their vending investments far in excess of 100%!

I'm sure you'd agree that AT LEAST 100% annual return is certainly possible and sustainable.

For EACH $1,000.00 you invest in the right machines. . . assuming you 'average' 100% annual rate of return or better on your money, and you reinvested all your profits in more machines. . . just look what you'd have in only 5 years. . . $32,000.00 worth of vending equipment making you $32,000.00 in cash per year!

Suppose (after you prove to yourself that this actually works, and it can) you invest several thousand more dollars? And what if you could average higher than 100% as others have done? It starts to get even more exciting, doesn't it?

The truth is you'd be doing FANTASTIC even if you only did half that well. . . yet there is a real possibility of doing even better!

You see, it IS possible to reach your dreams of financial independence even starting with a small investment.

If you're willing to do what it takes, and give it a little time, YOU CAN DO IT! Start big or start small, but START!

There's Opportunity With. . .

- Glass front snack vendors
- Hot food and popcorn vendors
- Hot and cold drink, and juice vendors
- Amusement machines
- Honor snack and drink systems
- Unique and 'hard to find' equipment

- Bulk vendors
- 'Fun-size' vendors
- Sticker and sports card vendors
- Personal Products
- Coin changers and bill (currency) acceptors
- Reconditioned used equipment

There's Nothing Like Owning Your Own Business!

You'll never tire of the prosperity and freedom that comes only with owning your own business. Being your own boss means that ONLY YOU have control of your time and your life. . . your destiny!

Besides all the obvious advantages of owning your own VENDING business in particular. . . a small business is generally recognized as the best:

Tax Shelter For The Common Man!

Are you tired of looking at the big chunk the government takes out of your paycheck?

40 years ago a middle class family paid about 2% of its earnings to pay all taxes (income and other). . . today you work past lunch time just to pay these taxes (which are in excess of 60%). Didn't we use to call involuntary servitude SLAVERY?

The TAX BENEFITS for people who own their own vending business is amazing!

You could enjoy enormous tax savings since many expenses may now be deductible: Car, telephone, office in home, travel and entertainment, etc.

One of the most FANTASTIC BENEFITS is the ability to expense equipment as allowed by section 179 of the I.R.S. Code. Normally, vending equipment is depreciated over about 7 years (even though the actual useful life can be up to 20 years or more). This means that 1/7th of the cost of your machines is tax deductible each year for 7 years!

But section 179 also allows you to expense (fully deduct) the cost of up to $10,000.00 worth of vending machines each and every year!

A $10,000.00 tax shelter! This means you can buy up to $10,000.00 in equipment each year and offset the tax you WOULD

have had to pay on $10,000.00 in OTHER business income or wages earned! What a BONANZA!

All CASH Business!

"All cash" means many things. . . and different things to different people. Primarily, it means:

- No collection problems or expenses (bad checks, uncollectible accounts, costs of billing and collection, etc.). This is a HUGE advantage.

- Financial privacy. . . to whatever degree you choose.

The financial privacy issue is controversial if you extend it to the point of not reporting income to tax collection agencies.

While I do not necessarily ADVISE anyone to pocket their vending cash profits. . . not reporting it on tax returns. . . it is a simple fact of life that most vending operators do not claim either part, or all of their income from vending machines. Many people consider this unethical. . . and many others consider this a big advantage of the vending business. You decide.

This is an all cash business, so what you report is a personal decision you will have to make based upon your own personal belief system. . . your views regarding the legitimacy (or lack thereof) of our government and it's tax laws. . . your personal assessment as to the risks of getting caught. . . and the consequences if caught.

Many books have been written on this subject alone, and a detailed discussion is beyond the scope of this book. See "Freedom Technology" below, and the chapter titled "Route Management" under the section titled "Handling Cash".

NOTE: The publisher and author are not engaged in rendering legal, accounting, tax or other advice or services for which a professional license may be required. The author is simply sharing his personal experience, beliefs and opinions. If required, the services of a competent licensed professional should be sought.

Freedom Technology

The term 'Freedom Technology' certainly INCLUDES the vending business and tax issues, which is why I'm mentioning it here. . . but so VERY MUCH MORE.

Definition

The PRACTICAL means to live free, and prosper, in an increasingly unfree world.

It has evolved primarily as a result of invasive government. . . and the information revolution. And although not highly publicized in the mainstream media, it is actually an explosive and exciting new growth industry! It's important to note that:

Freedom Technology does not challenge or threaten the authority of any legitimate government or law.

I have found that people around the world, and Americans in particular, are absolutely 'starved' for Freedom Technology, but that it has been difficult to come by until now.

The rich have been doing much of this for years. Isn't it about time we all started?

Freedom Technology will help you to increase your personal and financial freedom, privacy, and your wealth.

If you're not sure you understand the need for Freedom Technology, read the chapter titled "Getting Started" under the section titled "Your Business Organizational Structure". It's also discussed further in the chapter titled "Route Management" under the section titled "Handling Cash".

If any of this interests you, and you want to learn more (which I highly recommend to everyone) please contact my company (Bill Way's FREEDOM TECHNOLOGY) and ask for a complimentary copy of the 'Freedom Technology Report.'

Vending. . . The ULTIMATE Business Opportunity!

With the information in this book, almost anyone with a desire to succeed can expect to be successful in the vending business.

With the RIGHT EQUIPMENT. . . at the RIGHT PRICE. . . and in the RIGHT LOCATIONS. . . vending can be VERY PROFITABLE for you.

It's not uncommon to earn up to $200.00 gross profit per hour. . . 4 month pay-pack on start-up costs. . . and returns of 100% to even 500% per year!

With vending, many people JUST LIKE YOU are enjoying the lifestyle they've always dreamed of. . . short working hours and plenty of time and money for family, vacations, and special interests of all kinds!

Vending machines are like having little 'money-collecting ROBOTS' doing most of the work for you all day. . . while you kick-back and enjoy life! I think you can see why I call it "the ULTIMATE business"!

Each time you service your vending locations you'll feel like you just hit the

JACK POT in Las Vegas.   Believe me when I say. . . this business can be FUN!

Getting it "RIGHT" is the key, and with this book in hand you should be a giant step ahead.

Before we go on, lets take the time to learn about the pitfalls, risks, and rip-offs you must learn to avoid at all costs. . . then we'll take a close look at one of the most spectacular opportunities for financial independence ever!

Chapter 2
Pitfalls, Risks, And Rip-offs!

This is probably the most important part of this book. While there is TREMENDOUS OPPORTUNITY FOR SUCCESS in this dynamic, growing industry. . . there are ALSO some pitfalls and risks as with any business. The most important thing to look out for are the 'rip-offs'.

WARNING: The biggest mistake you can make would be to let any of this information scare you into not taking action. Be aware of this for your own financial well-being. . . but don't ever let it stop you from starting on the path towards financial success in the exciting vending business!

There is an old saying: "If something looks too good to be true, it probably is". That may OFTEN be a true statement, but it has caused a lot of people to pass on the best opportunities of their lives. Some things really ARE very good!

Regardless, I do want you to have balanced information. You should know the good and the bad. . . and THE BAD ISN'T SO BAD. . . ONCE YOU'RE INFORMED. Here it is:

It has been my experience that when people do fail in vending, more often than not, it is almost always one of these 4 reasons:

Most Common Reasons For Vending Failure

Biz-Op Scams

Being victimized by one of the unscrupulous biz-op (business opportunity) promoters which abound: Paying way too much money, being sold very poor quality machines, and sometimes a flawed and ineffective vending concept (that looked great to someone that does not know the business). Also, many of these companies just take your money and never ship you anything.

Locating Companies

Trusting a professional locating company. Most of these companies look good, but in all my years in this business I am aware of only a couple that I would recommend to you.

Spending All Funds Available

Investing too much money at first. When they did learn the truth about the vending business and could have corrected their mistakes and been successful. . . it was too late for them. They had already either spent all their money and/or borrowed all they could get a hold of. They were out of the game, and out of money too!

Used Equipment

Buying used equipment. Buying old technology and poor appearance does not help to get or keep locations. Besides, you spend too much time and money making repairs. It's no bargain. A bargain is new equipment at a big discount.

If you follow the instructions in this book, you will not make any of these mistakes. You will learn how to buy the right machines, at the right price, and how to get great locations regardless of your background (no sales required, unless you want to). You'll also be able to start small, without risking too much, until you feel comfortable expanding.

While most vending equipment manufacturers and distributors are ethical and honest. . . there are many unscrupulous promoters who use a variety of techniques to separate you from your money. Some of these techniques are downright dishonest and/or illegal (even involving fraud and theft) but most are simply misleading and deceptive. Many of these techniques are quite legal, operating in the GRAY areas of the law, and yet they are still 'rip-offs'.

I estimate that vending machine fraud runs between $50 million and $100 million in the U.S. each year!

This includes not only outright theft, but selling machines that will not perform their intended purpose. . . and even QUALITY machines that are sold at grossly inflated prices.

So is vending as good as it looks? It is BECAUSE vending is so profitable that it has attracted so many unscrupulous promoters. If you will just steer clear of these vultures, and learn the 'VENDING SUCCESS SECRETS', you can get started with the right machines for much less money and 'GROW RICH IN AMERICA'S BEST CASH BUSINESS'!

Let's take a quick look at some of the predominant pitfalls, the risks, and especially the rip-offs. . . that you will most certainly want to be aware of as you plan your exciting new business venture.

Are You The Entrepreneurial Type?

Webster's Dictionary defines entrepreneur as:

"One who organizes and directs a business undertaking, assuming the risk for the sake of the profit".

Entrepreneurs are made, not born. Anyone can learn the skills required. The big question is whether or not you're WILLING to learn the skills, exercising sufficient SELF-DISCIPLINE to implement them. . . and to ASSUME THE RISKS, to whatever degree they might be.

Are you really eager to be your own boss? To control your time and your life. . . your destiny? To experience the kind of wealth and freedom that comes only with running your own business? Are you willing to put in the time required to achieve your goals, and not be unduly discouraged by the inevitable little setbacks that may come to pass?

Hard though it may be to believe, I'm aware of some seemingly quite silly examples of failure in the vending business. For example: One of my own vending machine purchase customers failed when he never placed his 10 new snack vending machines in the locations that he had obtained. He just never quite got around to it, so there they sat (in his garage). Eventually, as a favor to him, I bought back all of his machines.

Most everyone would like to have a lot of money and the quality of life it can provide for themselves and their family. . . but not everyone is willing to do what it takes to get it! The fact that you have this book in your hands indicates that you are probably the kind of person who is willing to do what it takes. . . and that you're just looking for the right opportunity. If so. . . congratulations, you've found it!

The vending business is probably one of the least risky businesses you could ever become involved in. . . assuming, of course, that you buy the right machines, at the right price. . . and considering that if you start small you have so little to lose by giving it a try.

Consider this example: If you invested a lot of your money in a shoe store and it didn't do well, you may be in big trouble. But if you invested a lot of your money in (quality, fair priced) vending machines and they (or some of them) didn't do well. . . the worst thing that could happen is that you'd have to move them. . . right?

If you decide to get into vending, I recommend that you start relatively small, regardless as to your financial resources. Most vending biz-op (business opportunity) promotion companies insist on a MINIMUM order of $5,000. to $10,000. or even much more. This is for THEIR benefit, not yours.

For many people $10,000. to $50,000. IS a small investment, and that's OK if you can afford it, and do your homework first.

But you can start in this business on a shoestring if that's what you need or want to do. Besides, why invest a lot of money until you've had first hand experience in vending? It only makes sense.

If you start out with a small investment you're comfortable with and discover how great and profitable the business is, you'll feel equally comfortable expanding. But if you start out too big, you may not sleep nights.

I think the best advice I can give you is this: No matter how good this all looks to you, don't risk more than you can afford to lose. Start relatively small and your risk will be correspondingly small. THEN expand as fast as you want to.

One of the nice features of the vending business is that it doesn't require you to quit your present job (or business), or invest your life savings to begin, or to become successful. You can invest a 'comfortable' share of your savings (or take a small loan) and 'test the waters' with a PART TIME vending business. . . growing as you feel so inclined (as your confidence builds).

When you're through reading this book, you should take stock of yourself and what you've learned. . . and decide if you are willing to give it a try or not.

If you decide that you ARE willing to assume the minimal risks involved. . . the next step is to decide if you have the self-discipline to service your vending route as you are being advised in this book. There are some people who are just not willing and/or able to accept responsibility for the most simple management tasks required in this particular business. Nevertheless, you must believe in your ability to handle it, and be committed to achieving you financial goals, if you are to succeed.

Welcome to the world of entrepreneurs. If you really want to. . . you CAN do it!

Myths

Here are some commonly held misconceptions that you should not be taken in by.

"The Mafia Runs The Industry"

Nothing could be further from the truth. What probably perpetrated this myth is the old Elliot Ness movies in which gangsters laundered money through the vending business. . . but that's just 'show biz'. I suppose you could assume that organized crime has some involvement in virtually all types of businesses, but I've never seen any evidence that vending has been singled out in any way. Don't give it another thought.

"Too Much Competition"

There may be a lot of vending machines out there, but there is very little REAL competition. Most locations complain of poor service, machine breakdowns, and/or stale products from vending operators. If you care about your business and offer good equipment and service, you will find that there is a tremendous opportunity awaiting you!

Even in situations where there appears to be competition, there are new types of machines available that literally blows the competition away! I'm aware of one machine, in particular, that will get 8 out of 10 sales when placed right next to any competing machine!

In snack and drink vending, most of the competition is from the larger vending companies who want locations with at least 100 or more employees (or similar customer traffic). This is because they have so much overhead, and their equipment is so expensive, that they must have very, very high volume locations. You will find a huge opportunity open to you in locations with 20 to 100 employees (or similar customer traffic). . . and they eat just as much as the people in the bigger locations.

When in comes to games and impulse machines, much of the real competition is in the arcades and bars. Arcades only represent about 15% of all game machines located. About 45% are in taverns and bars. I don't recommend starting an arcade unless you have some experience with the business first, as they can be risky. The easiest locations for a beginner to get started with are restaurants, retail stores and shopping malls.

> There is no shortage of good locations for a well-managed vending operation. . . all geographical locations. . . all markets. . . all machine types.

Also keep in mind that the industry is growing at around 9% to 11% per year. . . creating a lot of new opportunities everyday!

B B B Report Reliability

It seems almost sacrilegious to say anything but positive things about the Better Business Bureau. They are almost an institution in America, and have certainly done admirable things for the promotion of ethical business practices in over 80 years of service. But there are some important, generally applicable facts that you should be aware of:

Each BBB office has some leeway as to how they may operate, so there are sometimes slight differences, but they are all under the same basic umbrella.

Whether negative OR even positive, you can NOT rely on BBB (so called) 'Reliability' Reports alone if you want to make a well-informed, reasonable, and prudent decision. Those who do so may well later regret either lost money, aggravation, or missed opportunities. Here's why:

In my opinion, the BBB is basically a 'complaint house'. So called 'Reliability' Reports are most often based upon the number and type of complaints filed (IF any) and whether or not those complaints are resolved. There are many reasons why you can not rely on these reports. . . REGARDLESS as to whether they seem negative OR even positive.

Each BBB is a non-profit corporation SUPPORTED by local BUSINESS OWNERS. Their By-Laws generally state that their purpose is the "protection" of the "vitality of the free enterprise system". Therefore, an argument could me made that they may have a conflict of interest as a consumer advocacy group.

They say that they attempt to encourage fairness in business and discourage deceptive trade practices, and yet they themselves engage in practices which one may question. Not the least of which is the very fact that they call themselves a "bureau". . . which has lead some unknowing people to believe that they are an agency of government, and they are not (which gives them added, but UNDUE credibility).

A common definition of 'bureau' is defined by Webster's Dictionary as follows: "A government department, or a subdivision of a government department". The BBB is neither.

Business 'Reliability Reports' are compiled by background information PROVIDED by the SUBJECT BUSINESSES THEMSELVES on a questionnaire. . . and are seldom investigated or checked out by the BBB. . . making the information provided dubious at best.

An adverse rating may be applied by the BBB if a company fails to respond to a customer complaint (s), if the company resolves complaints but fails to resolve the "nature" of a series of complaints, or if (in the infinite wisdom of the BBB) they feel the complaint was not resolved fairly.

Contrary to popular belief, however: No adverse rating is necessarily given a business simply because complaints have been filed against them. The BBB considers complaints a normal occurrence (which they are, of course) that most all businesses experience to varying degrees. The BBB does not necessarily require the business to meet the customers demands, but primarily to RESPOND to them. And NO INFORMATION regarding past 'responded to' complaints are provided to inquirers unless obvious unethical or abusive patterns develop.

Many unethical businesses can fall through the cracks of the BBB reporting system because they may communicate well with their 'unhappy' customers, so complaints never even get filed in the first place unless and until it's far to late to do any good, if ever. Or complaints are actually filed, but are adequately responded to (but not necessarily to the customers liking). So, a company with a GOOD-looking report COULD actually be someone you would definitely NOT want to do business with.

Even a 'GOOD-looking' Reliability Report is, at best, only a report of an ABSENCE of unresolved complaints filed. . . NEVER an endorsement by the BBB. That may seem sufficient for your needs until you're aware of the above details.

On the other hand, even a company with a 'BAD-looking' Reliability Report may not be so bad at all. The BBB generally will NOT TELL YOU the NUMBER OF COMPLAINTS filed, nor the 'NATURE' of those complaints, nor the NUMBER OF CUSTOMERS that particular company serves. . . making it IMPOSSIBLE for you to decide for yourself the degree of relevance of the adverse rating.

They expect you to defer to THEIR judgement ONLY, with NO INPUT as to the severity of the reported problem (which can and does vary widely). In America, all people are guaranteed the right to their opinions and free speech (under the First Amendment of the Constitution). Therefore, the BBB is entitled to express their opinions, but they are not necessarily valid or correct. . . and they give you VERY LITTLE OR NO INFORMATION with which to MAKE UP YOUR OWN MIND.

I'm not saying that the BBB 'Reliability Reports' are of no value. . . they are often of value. . . they're just not 'reliable'. I believe that to IMPLY that they ARE 'reliable' is in itself misleading. . . and is self-serving to the member businesses of the BBB (in the minority) who (good or bad) impose their beliefs and values on other non-member businesses (in the majority) and consumers.

To summarize: A seemingly 'good' report doesn't necessarily mean anything. . . and a seemingly 'bad' report doesn't necessarily mean anything. All reports, good and bad, provide information which adds to the big picture, and which can stimulate further investigation.

The moral: Whether negative OR even positive, you can NOT rely on BBB (so called) 'Reliability' Reports alone if you want to make a well-informed, reasonable, and prudent decision. Those who do so may well later regret either lost money, aggravation, or missed opportunities.

I suggest you call your local BBB and ask for a free copy of their brochure entitled "Tips On Automatic Vending Machines". The publication may be helpful, however, I believe you will find it quite pessimistic. For example: This chapter entitled "Pitfalls, Risks and Rip-offs" exposes much information you should be aware of, however, it is counterbalanced with a lot of positive information in the rest of the book. The BBB's brochure lacks this balance and leaves me with a generally negative (and unwarranted) feeling. DON'T LET IT GET TO YOU. It is not their role to promote any business or activity and, therefore, they have very little positive to say on the subject.

For very interesting details on the motivation behind this booklet, see the chapter titled "Trade Publications, Organizations, And Shows" under the section titled "A Note Of Caution".

I've dedicated a fair amount of space to this subject because it represents a particular myth which has proved an expensive lesson for many people. . . and equally so for missed opportunities as well as lost money and aggravation. Now that you know the truth. . . ask more questions, get more references, listen to your gut (your intuition is usually right) and make up your own mind.

"We'll Get Your Locations For You"

Virtually all vending equipment distributors and promoters contract with professional vending machine locating companies to provide locations for their customers. . . although many of them are not very 'up front' about it.

Many who sell you equipment promise you that "OUR locators will get you your locations" but they simply sub-contract to these professional companies. The only advantage they gain by misrepresenting this fact is that it may give their prospective customers a false sense of confidence in them. . . leading them to believe that they are a 'complete' service and supply source. This gives them added but undue credibility.

The companies who do work for many of these distributors and promoters are happy to work directly for you as well. And you'll generally have better control and get better service that way.

By the way, I want to make it perfectly clear that I recommend exercising CAUTION when considering working with ANY professional locating company. Look for more on this in the next section: "What To Watch For" under the subheading "Professional Locators", and also in the chapter titled "Getting Great Locations".

"It Takes A Lot Of Money"

This is a matter of personal choice. You can start with as little as 1 or 2 machines, and grow quite successfully from there (many have done just that). For $2,000.00 to $5,000.00 you can make a fairly aggressive start. Part-time, or full-time. . . $500.00 or $100,000.00 start-up. . . it's all up to you. Remember, as I said earlier, I do not recommend large investments until you are comfortable with what you are doing.

Surely you'd agree that anytime you have an opportunity to make up to 100% to 500% (or more) annual return on your money, it doesn't have to take a lot initially. Even a small initial investment compounded (reinvested) over a relatively short time can add up to a fortune. See the heading: "The Magic Of Compounding BIG Returns" in the chapter titled "Why Vending".

One thing to be careful of is that you are prepared for all costs you may incur. Don't forget that you will have freight costs, product inventory (except for games and impulse machines), and locating costs to name a couple. In addition, for some types of equipment, in some areas, you may need permits or licenses etc. (See the chapter titled "Getting Started" as well as individual machine chapters).

"Don't Tell Anyone"

Some promoters use this technique. They ask you to sign a 'Non-Disclosure Agreement' in which you promise not to tell anyone what they share with you regarding their vending equipment. They'd like you to believe that they offer something new and unique, not found elsewhere. This is only a marketing gimmick. If you look around a little you'll find the truth is that the same, or very similar equipment and opportunities are available from many other companies.

What To Watch For

Here's some of the misleading, deceptive or downright illegal marketing practices some unethical companies use to separate you from your money:

"Biz-op" Promoters

A biz-op promoter is any company that is in the business of promoting any income or business opportunity.

My advice to you is that you should exercise extreme CAUTION when considering doing business with ANY vending biz-op promoter. While there are a few good ones around, these companies are notorious for poor concepts, low quality, exaggerated profit claims and high prices. They typically put all their money into slick marketing and professional exteriors. . . but they rarely deliver.

Most of them charge high prices just because they have learned that they can get away with it. . . but many have no choice because they have set themselves up with such high overhead.

How can you recognize a biz-op promoter? They are companies which are obviously primarily sales and marketing organizations. You'll find them at the Business Opportunity and Franchise Shows. You'll find their ads in newspapers and magazines. And you'll receive their expensive information packets in the mail.

The point is, they spend so much money finding sales prospects with their expensive Madison Avenue marketing campaigns. . . even more on closing the sale. . . and 20% to 30% commissions for their salespeople. . . that they HAVE TO markup equipment 300% to 400% in order to stay in business.

The simplest way to describe this is just to say that it is a FLAWED MARKETING CONCEPT. Their overhead is just too high. I am intimately familiar with the economics of how they operate because (I must confess) I used to do business that way. When I learned the error of the concept I immediately made changes in an effort to provide an honest, valuable source for information and equipment. YOU can NOT pay the prices that these companies MUST charge and still make a good return on your investment.

In addition, they often sell poor quality equipment, and come up with poor vending concepts that they can make look good or unique, but just don't work in the real world.

Another important point to remember is this: The ONLY way they can get people to pay their high prices is to EXAGGERATE the profit potential. Don't believe it!

Technically speaking, I am still a biz-op promoter only because (after all) I DO promote the vending business. . . but that is where the similarity ends! This will become more apparent to you as you read on.

"Biz-Op" Shows

These are the business opportunity and franchise shows that come to your area one or more times per year. I prefer to call them a "den of thieves". You'll see them advertised on TV, radio, newspapers, etc. Yes, there are some well known and quite legitimate companies participating, but I believe them to be the exception. Most of the participants are the unscrupulous biz-op promoters mentioned above.

There are several show "circuits" (or show companies). Each one has a show going on almost every single weekend somewhere in the U.S. Many biz-op promoters participate in several shows in a given weekend. It is not uncommon to pay $10,000.00 per weekend, per show for booth space. It is also not uncommon to set up $50,000.00 displays. Consider all the related overhead like air freight to get their display moved each week, airline costs for staff, hotels, meals, etc. Add to that the 20% to 30% commission that they pay their salespeople.

> Can you see why their prices are so high? Do you really want to pay for all this? Again, this is simply a FLAWED MARKETING CONCEPT. YOU can NOT pay the prices that these companies MUST charge and still make a good return on your investment.

This book has been banned by the largest show promoter in the world. In fact, most all the shows have banned (or will ban) this book from distribution at their shows. I have been told that my open and honest method of distributing information and equipment is not welcome there. . . that I would cost the other exhibitors too much money in lost sales. If they let me in, they would lose too many of their other exhibitors.

There is very little "opportunity" at these shows. If you have time, you may find them interesting, but leave your checkbook at home.

Professional Locating Companies

One of the single biggest reasons why some people fail in the vending business is because they relied upon a "professional" locating company. Trust me. . . there is almost nothing "professional" about most of these companies, except their very convincing marketing tactics. In all the years I've been in this business, I can think of only a couple of companies that I would refer you to if you called me on the phone today (I don't even list them in the Appendix because I want to be in a position to withdraw their names quickly if their quality of service changed suddenly). Believe me, if you went through as many of them as I have, you'd feel the same way.

This does not mean that you should rule out a professional locating company. . . just exercise extreme CAUTION. And consider hiring a local individual to do locating for you (which can work

out great). There is more information and many very successful solutions which are covered in the chapter titled "Getting Great Locations".

Take The Money And Run

I REGULARLY run across people who tell me they have paid 'deposits' or 'full payments' of $2,000.00 or more (sometimes much more) to companies who never ship them anything. . . and subsequently disappear.

> Moral: Know who you're doing business with. Pay C.O.D. when possible and practical. And listen to your intuition. . . it's usually right.

Exaggerated Profits = High Prices

This is one of the most common rip-offs. High prices on equipment. Yeah, the equipment may (or may not) be good, and there is certainly a POTENTIAL for profit. The promoter may even have a couple of 'shills' who will say they are "making a fortune" with these machines.

> The bottom line: Beware of unscrupulous companies that PRESSURE you for quick decisions and make EXAGGERATED profit claims in order to sell you overpriced, poor quality, or poor concept equipment.

Remember: Exaggerating the profit potential of equipment is the ONLY way these slick operators can get anyone to pay 3 to 4 times what it's worth. They do it in very clever ways that keep them within the law. . . often it is not even in writing, or they get you to write it out on a worksheet yourself. Check around until you're comfortable that you know the true profit potential and value of the machines you're buying. (See "Established Routes" below).

References, Paid References, And Shills

It's 'business as usual' for biz-op promoters and even reputable equipment distributors to provide references of existing so called "successful" route operators, and other references as well. I've always advised to go ahead and check out these references (which may well be fine), but don't make a decision SOLELY on the basis of a couple of references.

Keep in mind that almost any company can come up with at least a couple of good references. . . and they certainly aren't going to give you the names of negative references, unsuccessful distributors, etc. Still, this is one (of many) reasonable and prudent ways to check them out.

It's also very common (almost standard practice really) to pay route operators for providing references. I believe you will find this is usually legal as long as the reference tells the truth. . . but if a cash commission payment (for example) is linked to your purchase, how impartial do you think the reference will be with the information provided? There's lots of room for abuse here. . . sometimes even involving 'shills' who outright lie.

Many people would like to talk with a successful route operator or two before making an investment. . . and that is fine. Also consider, though, that if you are a successful and busy route operator you have better things to do than take 10 or 20 calls a month (which almost always last 30 to 60 minutes each) from the prospective customers of your supplier. That's why it's almost impossible for equipment companies to get people to act as references unless they compensate them in SOME way. See the chapter titled "A Better Way" for more on this subject.

Be sure to temper the information provided from references with a little common sense, in light of the above. Question both the company (what their policy is) and the reference (what they're getting out of it). Of course, that doesn't necessarily mean you'll get the truth.

Just ask a lot of questions, consider other factors when checking them out, and rely heavily on your gut instincts (your intuition is usually right).

If possible, see if you can get the company to put their policy regarding reference compensation in writing. My own company policy is as follows:

FREEDOM TECHNOLOGY does not ask our customers to take phone calls as references. We often receive nice letters from satisfied customers, which I sometimes share in whole or in part (while protecting their privacy). But I do not offer any sort of compensation in exchange for these letters, as I consider such practices to be unethical in most cases (particularly if not disclosed).

By the way, you'll find that many companies limit their references to their bank, attorney, accountant, etc. While these are fine to list, these references will usually not provide you with any particularly useful information. You need to check with their suppliers, associates, and customers, etc. . . and ask if they offer a WRITTEN satisfaction guarantee of any kind.

While a written satisfaction guarantee is not very common in this industry, I do offer such a guarantee on machines purchased through my company, FREEDOM TECHNOLOGY (See "Satisfaction Guarantee" in the Appendix under "Forms And Miscellaneous" for details).

Promises, Promises

There's an old saying among attorneys that goes like this: "A verbal agreement is not worth the paper it's written on". Humorous, but nevertheless quite true.

No company will object to putting any promise or agreement in writing if they are reputable, and if they really intend to perform. IF it's important to you, get it in writing. Don't rely on anything the promoter or distributor does not (or will not) put in writing. Enough said.

'Weasel' Clauses

A weasel is an agile 'slippery' animal known for it cunning and slyness. Hence, a 'weasel clause' is a provision in an agreement which is designed to let one or more parties 'slip out' of a responsibility which was otherwise thought to be agreed upon.

Weasel clauses are commonly used in all areas of business, which means you have to read agreements carefully. It's always good advise to consult with an attorney if you are unsure of your ability to read and understand any agreement.

'Help Wanted' Ads

These ads appear in many forms. A sales company runs a 'thinly disguised' ad trying to create the illusion that you'd be "practically" working for them. . . that the whole route is already "set up", etc. These ads often run under 'Help Wanted', 'Sales Help Wanted', 'Business Opportunities', 'Established Businesses For Sale', etc. The goal is almost always to sell you overpriced equipment, and to make you believe that there is "little or no risk". To the best of my knowledge, there are no legitimate opportunities of this kind.

"Representing Frito-Lay, M & M Mars"

Many unethical promoters will mention in their ads that you will be representing Frito-Lay, M & M Mars, Coca-Cola, etc. This serves to improve their image, and it sounds good to you, but it's nothing more than a lot of hot air. All it means is that you'll be buying these products and selling them in your vending machines.

The whole purpose of the misrepresentation being to raise their image by association, and give you a false sense of confidence in them.

"Established" Routes

There are some legitimate established route deals available (see below), but Biz-op Promoters and Distributors almost never sell truly "established" routes. Why many of them actually do, however, is advertise that they are established and then they establish them AFTER you buy them. This way they can get away with charging you 3 to 4 times more money than it's worth! Some 'turn-key' promoters do essentially the same thing, packaging what 'appears' to be established routes (see the section on "Turn-Key Vending" below).

As you may know, a 'WELL-established' business is valued NOT according to the value of the assets it holds (which are sometimes insignificant) but RATHER by the INCOME it can produce. The length of time in business is extremely important, because (for example) you would not want to pay much more than the value of assets for a business that was established only one month ago.

A vending business should be established an absolute MINIMUM of several months to a year before you should consider it 'well-established' and value it by the income approach (above). Otherwise, compute the 'real' value by totaling the equipment value, basic locating costs, freight paid, product inventory, etc. This is just one of the ways some slick promoters devise to charge you 3 to 4 times what the equipment is worth. Don't fall for it.

As a general 'rule of thumb', a truly 'well-established' vending route with QUALITY equipment will sell for AT LEAST the equivalent of the annual net profit and sometimes up to 3 or 4 times that amount depending upon other factors. For example, if a route was producing an

annual net profit of $10,000.00, the sale price may range from $10,000.00 to $40,000.00 or more. If you could purchase such a route for only $10,000.00 (which you probably can not) you would be receiving a return on investment of about 100% A.P.R. (Purchase at $10,000.00, receive $10,000.00 annual return = 100% A.P.R.). If you paid $40,000.00 for such a route (which is more likely) you would be receiving a return of about 25% (Purchase at $40,000.00, receive $10,000.00 annual return = 25%). The cost of the equipment is irrelevant and is generally much, much lower. For these reasons, buying established routes is usually no bargain. You can set one up yourself for much less money!

But on the other hand, if you should ever decide to sell your own route you can see that there is an opportunity to make a lot of money! In fact, some people (just like you) establish routes over and over just to sell them later for a huge profit.

There are occasionally some 'well-established' routes for sale from individual operators (not promoters). They are rarely a bargain, however. If the route is doing real well, you will pay a very high price for it. If it's doing poorly, there's often a reason you can not fix (i.e. poor quality, worn out equipment).

Also, many so called "established" routes are sold by people who where mislead by Biz-op Promoters into paying 3 to 4 times what it was worth in the first place. . . they couldn't make it and you can't either. They want to unload it on you.

Used Equipment

I have been able to get good deals on used equipment from time to time, but it is rare. It takes a lot of 'know-how' to recognize the good deals from the bad. You also run the risk of excessive breakdowns and repair costs when you don't know what you're getting. Also, used generally = older designs and technology which makes locating more difficult.

You may think you're saving money on used equipment, but any such savings can be quickly LOST (and then some) through repair costs, and lost profits (plus lost locations) due to frequent breakdowns.

LATE MODEL used equipment which has been properly RECONDITIONED can sometimes be a good buy, and there are a few reputable companies that specialize in this (they advertise in the trade magazines). Quality reconditioned used (late model - 3 to 7 year old) machines are priced at about 10% to 40% less than similar new machines. Due to popularity, availability is very limited on many of these machines. . . particularly small glass front snack machines.

The vast majority of used equipment that you'll find for sale in the newspaper is poor quality, poor concept, and/or overpriced machines owned by people who have been ripped off by the biz-op vending promotion companies. They pay $1,000.00 for a machine they could have bought for $500.00 or less. Then they discount them to $600.00 or $800.00 and try to sell them as some sort of a bargain.

I've found that most people would rather have new equipment when they discover they can buy it at up to 75% off from discount distributors like my company, FREEDOM TECHNOLOGY. Besides, new, quality, well-managed vending equipment has the potential to pay for itself in less than a year anyway (if purchased at a fair price). . . and it's more attractive (making it easier to locate).

I no longer offer used machines through my distribution company. Primarily due to the problems mentioned above: Poor appearance, old technology, locating difficulties, frequent breakdowns, etc. Instead, I concentrate on offering the best machines at the lowest possible price. . . which makes locating much easier and keeps maintenance to a minimum. I think it's a mistake for a beginner to buy used machines. . . once you have a little experience. . . it may make sense in some situations. In my own routes, however, I prefer to stick with new equipment only.

'Turn-Key' Vending

Here, the promoter sells you a 'package' which is supposedly complete. You buy the vending machines and the locations (which the promoter usually secures AFTER your purchase), the promoter often delivers the equipment to the locations for you, uncrates them, sets them up, and stocks them with product. . . then hands you the keys (all ready to go). Hence, "turn-key".

In principal, this doesn't necessarily sound like a bad idea. . . but in practice it is usually not desirable. This is generally the same scam we've already discussed. . . a method of selling poor quality and/or poor concept machines at 3 to 4 times what they're worth.

If you want to evaluate such an offer, just try the following. Look up the desired equipment on my FREEDOM TECHNOLOGY wholesale price list in the Appendix (or check prices elsewhere). Add the cost of freight and initial product inventory. Then add the cost of getting your locations (see "Getting Great Locations").

The only other service that they sometimes provide is that they may physically place the equipment and stock it for you. It's easy to find people with a truck or van to do this for you at a cost of about $10.00 to $15.00 per hour, or a flat rate of around $10.00 to $50.00 per location (depending upon type of equipment). For the sake of comparison, estimate that cost and add it on. In actual practice you would almost surely not use this particular service since it is so simple to place and stock machines yourself, and it's a good opportunity to get to know your equipment and locations anyway.

It is inconceivable that after completing the above exercise you would ever agree to such a turn-key plan. Sure, they can make it look mighty attractive with a lot of fancy brochures and glowing promises. . . but it's nothing more than a lot of hot air!

> They put together the same package you can easily do for yourself. . . then they triple or quadruple the price!

The only way they can convince anyone to pay these outrageous prices is by misrepresenting and exaggerating the profit potential of the business. Forget it.

Lease-Back Deals

Some promoters offer to lease you the equipment for a fixed or variable monthly payment, and then they contract to service the machines for you (including collecting the money). Often, the money turned in is not sufficient to cover the payments.

A lease in and of itself is not necessarily a bad idea. Just evaluate the true cost and terms of the lease carefully. And watch out for any service contract.

"We're The Manufacturer"

This one may seem harmless. A promoter tells you that THEY are the manufacturer of the vending equipment. Of course, sometimes they are, but usually it is not true.

> The whole purpose of the lie being to raise their image and give you a false sense of confidence in them.

The truth is that there are actually relatively few well established, quality vending manufacturers in the U. S. Many of these manufacturers offer what is known as 'custom manufacturing'. This equates to simply making the machine and putting the promoters name on it. They are not the manufacturer. They SUBCONTRACT to the manufacturer, therefore, it is often legal (though misleading) to state that they are in fact the manufacturer.

One of the problems with this is that if the Biz-op Promoter goes out of business you may not know who the real manufacturer is. Making it difficult or impossible to get parts, etc.

Furthermore, very few of the reputable, well-established manufacturers will sell direct to the route operator. Almost without exception, they sell through distributors like myself (FREEDOM TECHNOLOGY). By the way, buying direct does not necessarily mean you save money. For example: A couple of my suppliers will sell direct to route operators, but my pricing to you is lower than you would pay from those manufacturers because distributors get a large discount. . . and my markup is relatively tiny.

Usually, if you are actually dealing DIRECT with a true manufacturer, it is some small operation. These little companies come and go with the seasons. Would you like to take a chance on owning some 'orphan' vending machines that you can't get parts for? This is not to imply that all small manufacturers are bad. Just watch out for the little unstable operations. Check them out.

> My company, FREEDOM TECHNOLOGY, is an authorized distributor for some of the largest and most respected vending equipment manufacturers in the U.S. These companies are very selective in who they choose to work with. I also deal with some small, but very reliable manufacturers who offer very

unique equipment. And I don't put my name on them. . . I leave the manufacturers name on and let you know who they are.

'Apply' To Buy

This one really insults my intelligence. . . and I know it will have the same effect on you too. Yet it is so very prevalent among vending equipment promoters! Yes, you must actually fill out an application to get them to take your money (or so they will have you believe).

They make it seem almost reasonable sometimes. Telling you things like: "We offer PROTECTED TERRITORIES so we only accept the best applicants", or "We need to see if you QUALIFY for our program, since we only accept those with the qualities (and enough cash) to succeed", etc., etc.

The application always request personal information like how much money you earn, how much you have in savings, and questions to determine if you could likely qualify for a loan. The other questions are just 'fluff'. . . only there to make it appear like they care about you and your chances for success.

It doesn't matter who they are or what they tell you, there are only three reasons for the application:

> To find out enough about you and your personal business (like how much cash you have or can borrow) so that they can determine if they want to spend any time on you (Known as: 'PRE-QUALIFY the sales prospect').

> Armed with this information they can make a more convincing sales pitch to you. . . attempting to 'manipulate' you into doing something that you may later regret.

> They figure (and they're usually right) that if they can get you to 'apply to buy'. . . that they've got you where they want you (psychologically speaking). They don't have to sell you on the true merits of the proposal. YOU have to SELL THEM on why they should accept you! After all, you APPLIED!

Isn't that just preposterous? Do you really want to give them the upper hand by providing such information? Would you truly want to do business with a company like that? Think about it. It's ludicrous!

Protected Territories

Generally, the only way you're going to get a protected territory 'of any value' is if you're purchasing a legitimate franchise. . . AND if you're buying a very, very UNIQUE vending or amusement machine. But then you're going to be paying franchise fees. Undoubtedly, there are a few (not many) such deals around. . . but take note that:

> Many slick promoters use this technique to entice you to "buy now before your territory is gone". It is USUALLY no more than a HIGH PRESSURE sales tactic, sometimes used with the 'apply to buy' marketing approach.

Often they never actually put it in writing in any way that is enforceable. If they do, they get around it with some sneaky provisions (weasel clauses) they slip into the agreement, or they simply set up a new business entity and start selling all over under a new name.

Besides, protected territories are of little or no value unless your equipment is very, very unique. Even if you actually had an ENFORCEABLE protected territory (or franchise) agreement on a particular machine, that doesn't mean that a competitor can't put another similar machine in your area.

Beware of paying extra for a protected territory or franchise deal. . . and don't let them pressure you into a quick decision that you may later regret, just because "your territory may be gone later".

Limited Time Offers

We are all used to seeing limited time offers. Most all retailers have short-term 'sales', etc. There are many legitimate reasons for limited time offers, like clearing out an overstock, improving sales in a seasonally slow month, etc.

The problem comes when the limited time offer is designed only to get you to make a MAJOR decision in an UNREASONABLE amount of time. . . like now, today, or tomorrow. This may be okay if you're buying a toaster on sale at Walmart,

but it's not reasonable when investing large amounts of money in a new business opportunity.

My advice to you is that you run, don't walk, from such offers! Usually companies that pressure you for quick decisions sell poor concept, poor quality, and overpriced equipment or have something else to hide that they don't want you to take too long to think about it because they're afraid you'll come to your senses!

You're the kind of person who is not afraid to make a business decision once you have all the facts required to do so intelligently. Don't let anyone rush you.

Consider this: The only legitimate motivation to get started fast is to avoid the loss of the income you could be earning by delaying unnecessarily. Just be careful that an IRRATIONAL fear is not getting the best of your usual good judgement. . . causing you to put off making a decision at all. If you don't make a decision reasonably promptly, you probably never will. And you don't want to cheat you and your family out of a good thing, do you?

Scam Financing

I regularly come across people who regret having been duped into paying 3 to 4 times too much for vending machines when some slick promoter convinced them that their special financing added value to the equipment offer.

> The way this works is: The promoter offers financing that sounds extremely attractive. It's almost never available at the initial purchase, however. . . only for later expansion, or after buying a minimum number of machines first. Usually it involves no interest (or very low interest) and very low or no down payment. Sometimes the down payment is on a sliding scale (i.e. so many machines at 50% down, so many at 25%, and a certain number thereafter at NO down payment).

While this may sound great on the surface, there are many pitfalls.

These companies are usually 'fast buck artists' who go for the quick 'one-time' sale. They don't expect you to ever buy from them again, although they will make glowing statements about how "this is the start of a long and prosperous association".

They make their living by preying upon ignorant buyers. . . making one quick, profitable sale. . . and then going on to the next poor sucker.

Consider this outrageous example:

Option #1:   Buy a machine at guaranteed lowest factory-direct wholesale price of $1,000.00 from a discount distributor like FREEDOM TECHNOLOGY. Obtain 100% (no down payment) financing for 36 months at high finance company rate of 20% A.P.R. (much lower rate is often available). Monthly payment is $37.16 for 36 months. Total of payments is $1,337.76.

Option #2: Buy the same machine from a slick promoter for $2,000.00 to $4,000.00. Whether bought now, or using their proposed financing later, your total of payments is at least $2,000.00 to $4,000.00 (more if they charge you interest)!

Obviously, this is a very bad deal. But some people take part anyway because they are ignorant as to the true cost of equipment, financing, and

vending profit potential. . . and they're very enthusiastic about expanding and don't believe they can obtain expansion financing elsewhere.

What they fail to realize is that they would be doomed to failure if they paid these kind of prices just to get the promise of some future 'lousy' financing. If they do make such a deal they will not BE expanding. . . in fact they may well fail altogether.

Surely you'd agree that it's better to SAVE up to 75% on price, and then get your own 'legitimate' financing without suffering through one of these rip-off financing scams. You can't really expect to make a good profit if you pay 3 to 4 times the fair price of your machines.

See the chapter on "Financing" for more information on this subject.

Company Stability

Obviously, any promise, agreement, or guarantee is only as good as the company behind it. You'll want to make sure that you're dealing with a well established company.

Summary

Where Does This Leave You?

We started out by looking at all the reasons why the vending business is so great, and now you've read a long chapter which covers a lot of negative subjects. Remember the warning I gave you at the beginning of this chapter?

WARNING: The biggest mistake you can make would be to let any of this information scare you into not taking action. Be aware of this for your own financial well-being. . . but don't ever let it

stop you from starting on the path towards financial success in the exciting vending business!

Because vending can be so very profitable. . . it has attracted a lot of con artists. Now that you know their tricks, and the other risks connected to this business, you are in an excellent position to proceed.

See chapter titled "Other Opportunities - And Mistakes!"

Notes

Chapter 3
A Better Way

Now that you have a good understanding of the mistakes you must avoid making, lets take a look at a better way to do business:

The Right Way To Learn

No matter what type of business opportunity you are interested in, you will find that you can learn a lot by doing the following:

Research

Go to your public library reference section and ask for help with the directories. There are directories for everything. Look up trade associations and trade publications for the business you are interested in. Try these two directories:

National Trade And Professional Associations Of The United States and Canada, and;

Ulrich's International Periodicals Directory.

Contact these associations and publications for more information. Join trade associations, go to their meetings and conventions, and order their informative materials available on a variety of subjects (free or low cost). Also, subscribe to the association's publications and other trade publications available. Call or write to those associated with the industry and ask for guidance. You will be amazed at how much you will learn.

You won't have to bother doing this for the vending business and will save a lot of time by reading the chapter titled "Trade Publications, Organizations, And Shows".

Search book stores and libraries for books on the business you are interested in. If you can't find any, check a directory called:

"Bowker's Books In Print".

Bowker's (available at libraries and bookstores) lists all books which are available and your bookstore can order them for you. . . or you can order them yourself directly from the publisher.

If you research books about the vending business you will most likely be disappointed to find that both your library and bookstore will have nothing available. Bowker's does have a couple of listings which I have researched, but they are very superficial and I would not recommend any of them to you. That is why I wrote this book. There are a lot of people interested in vending and not much information available.

Contact Route Operators

You might want to try looking for vending machines in your town which are the type you are interested in. . . look on the side or back of the machine for the phone number of the operator (which is almost always there unless the machine is owned by the location). . . and give them a call. Occasionally they will be helpful. Most of the time, however, they will say and do almost anything to keep you from getting into the business (or if they're not doing well, they'll talk it up and try to sell you their machines).

Remember. . . you would be their new competition! If you decide to try this, it usually works out better if you contact route operators in a distant town where you would not be competing with them. . . tell them this up front. . . and that you won't take much of their time. Go there, or get their phone numbers from a trade association or the phone book (Note: Many small operators are not listed in the phone book, and many trade association membership lists are confidential).

Better yet, attend a trade show and talk to route operators from all over the country. They are usually most helpful in that environment since they are usually on vacation in a relaxed atmosphere. . . and will certainly not view you as competition (unless you happen to be from their area).

Contact Distributors

See below "Sources For Vending Machines" for information regarding what type of distributor may prove helpful to you. Also, once again, consider going to a trade show. Most of the exhibitors there will try to be helpful and you can learn a lot from them (just remember that their main motivation will be to sell you something).

Sources For Vending Machines

There are basically 5 primary sources for new vending equipment:

Biz-Op

Biz-op (business opportunity) promoters. Least attractive. Up to 400% markup. High marketing costs. Little or no support.

Traditional

Traditional distributors. Okay. Sell at 10% to 50% markups. Usually maintain equipment showroom and warehouse. Little or no support. Costs more than buying through a discount distributor.

Factory

Deal directly with factory. Okay, but very few factories sell this way. Little or no support available, except machine warranty. Costs more than buying through a discount distributor (see below).

Discount Clubs

Discount clubs like Sam's Warehouse. Sometimes okay, but very limited selection and little or no support, except machine warranty. Often offer inappropriate, or low quality "off-brand" machines. Prices are fair, but usually higher than discount distributor.

Factory-Direct Discount Distributor

Factory-direct discount distributor like FREEDOM TECHNOLOGY. Best source. Buy at factory-direct wholesale prices (distributors discounted cost plus a relatively TINY mark-up). See Money Back Guarantee, and Lowest Price Guarantee. Shipped direct from factory to you. Consulting available at little or no cost.

Forget most biz-op promoters and their 400% markups.

Vending manufacturers typically offer distributors a discount that ranges from AT LEAST 10% to 50% or more. Honest, legitimate vending equipment distributors operate on this markup (or less). 10% to 20% would be a typical fair markup on a large and expensive single machine with a factory cost of at least $2,000. to $3,000. 20% to 40% would be more typical on machines with a factory cost of a few hundred dollars. These distributors are used to working with established vending route operators and are generally not very interested in working with new operators, nor are they very helpful. Information and support is almost nonexistent, except for basic machine service and warranty backup.

Most factories sell only through distributors, although some will sell direct to route operators, but at a higher price than distributors get. For example:

> One factory I deal with will sell direct to you, but gives FREEDOM TECHNOLOGY a large distributor discount. You'd have to buy 150 machines to get their very best price, and it would still be higher than our regular price! No kidding! Our pricing and marketing strategy is just a lot different. If you buy through us, you get our discounted price and actually pay a lot less!

Discount clubs like Sam's Warehouse have recently begun selling a very limited selection of vending machines. While some of their marketing efforts are directed towards vending operators, much of their marketing is directed to the business that wants to own their own vendor and fire their local vending service.

> The reason many businesses are willing to consider buying their own vending machines is usually NOT for the extra money they will make on just one location (their own). . . but rather, to control the

quality of machines and/or service, because they are dissatisfied with their current vending operator. It's really just another indication of the opportunity that awaits for someone who will do a good job. . . like YOU!

Typically, they may offer a counter-top snack vendor, glass front snack machines, canned drink vendors, and sometimes bulk vendors.

Often these machines will be inappropriate for your use, or low quality. Also, check the weight on their vendors. Most of the machines offered are not very mobile, weighing up to 1000 pounds, and requiring special equipment to move. This equipment is difficult for a new operator to work with. There is similar, good-quality equipment available that weighs much less (so you won't need a truck or special lifts) for a lot less money. And most of the bulk vendors I have seen available are very low quality.

Many discount clubs are now selling machines made by The Wittern Group, started in 1931 by F.A. Wittern. This is a very large and reputable company based in Des Moines, Iowa. They use several trade names, such as: Select-A-Vend, USI (U-Select It), Federal Machine, Fawn Vendors, etc. They offer 'no-money-down' financing for up to 48 months (only with excellent credit, and at high interest rates) which has made them one of the largest lenders in Iowa. The machines are good quality, but very heavy to handle, and selection is quite limited. Lighter machines of good quality are available at lower prices from other sources.

In this book I will direct you to a multitude of reputable sources to buy vending equipment. I encourage you to compare prices and service before buying any machines. However, you will find no better source than our discount distribution method which enables you to buy all the machines you want at our factory-direct wholesale price.

What Makes FREEDOM TECHNOLOGY Different?

I get asked this question a lot! "Your prices are way below everyone else's. . . and your service is so good. . . how can you do it?" We offer a very unique and creative concept. . . and it's something you should really understand fully. Here's how it works:

Rock-Bottom Prices

We negotiate great distributor discounts on the best vending machines. Then we add a relatively TINY mark-up. This makes it possible for you to buy at the lowest possible factory-direct wholesale price and save up to 75%. Nobody can beat our prices. And this is one of the most important elements of success in vending.

Factory-Direct

We ship nationally, direct from factory to you for almost any type of vending machine that you might want, but we actively promote what I have found in my experience to be the most profitable and lowest risk vending concepts, and the highest quality equipment.

Pay For What You Take

We're a "pay for what you take company". What does that mean? You pay only for what you need from us in the way of printed support material (like this book) vending machines, and private consulting services, etc. By the same token, we do not give much away for free. . . so YOU are not subsidizing the cost of our marketing or supporting OTHERS who may drain our resources. And YOU are NOT paying for products or services that you do not use. There's more:

Very LOW Overhead

At FREEDOM TECHNOLOGY we no longer use toll free 800 numbers, accept credit cards, or have a sales staff, all of which raises costs. And we send out relatively little FREE information which use to cost us a lot of money. Nor do we run large expensive ads or use other costly promotional methods.

All orders are shipped direct from the factory to you by special arrangement with the manufacturer. We do not maintain an equipment showroom or warehouse. As a result, we save showroom, shipping, handling, and warehousing costs.

Our fixed overhead is very low because I have created a cottage industry. I work mostly (but not entirely) out of my home. And I work with others who also work out of their homes. As a result we require only very little commercial space. This all works out well through the magic of 'Centron' (telephone call transfer and management software), e-mail, FAX, Federal Express, U.S. Postal Service, United Parcel Service, various freight companies, and very supportive manufacturers. If I hadn't just told you, you would probably never know that we are doing such a huge volume of business in this way.

These huge savings are all passed on to you.

Low Sales Costs

Here's the best part: At FREEDOM TECHNOLOGY we have very low 'cost of sales' tied to vending machine sales. This is the biggest single expense most of our competitors must pay. . . THE COST OF FINDING CUSTOMERS. . . you! And we pass the savings on to you.

We maximize the use of (free) media releases, radio talk shows, coop advertising (with the media and others), internet marketing, and by running only inexpensive and highly effective advertising promotions.

Most of this marketing effort is directed towards distributing this book (Vending Success Secrets). While I don't make very much money on the book (after deducting the high cost of producing a 'short-run' (low print run) book, promotion, distribution, shipping costs, etc.) I usually recover most of my marketing costs and develop a very loyal and informed customer base. This brings me buyers for vending machines without having to pay the traditional costs of advertising (or other forms of expensive promotion) to find those people (you).

Vending Success Secrets

Information is dispensed inexpensively through this book, which generally informs our clients of most everything they need to know to get started in vending, usually without having to pay for consulting. It is my goal to answer all your questions in this book and eliminate your need to spend any more money on consulting. When we get questions that are not answered in this book, I modify the book and include the answer. We print in low numbers, so we can keep the information current. For most people, the book is enough. . . with little or no private consulting required. If you do need consulting, it is available by e-mail, FAX, regular mail, or telephone appointment, for little or no cost (NO CHARGE for initial or brief consultations, at our discretion).

Most of our new clients simply read this book and find they are comfortable getting started in vending at that point. They choose what type of vending interests them most. They order one or more machines (following the simple instructions in the Appendix on "Ordering Factory Direct"). Next, they locate and service their machines as I advise in this book. They find that things work out about like they expect, so they are very happy. Then they continue ordering more machines on a regular basis. It's that simple. Little or no consulting is usually necessary.

This method keeps our cost so low that nobody can beat our prices. . . and the material in this book makes it all possible because otherwise it would be too time consuming and expensive for you to learn what you need to know (it's not easy to find accurate information). My business is supported by a lot of people who order a little bit each month or two.

Small Staff

Because of our low costs, we must keep all overhead very low. For this reason we have a small staff.

Small staff means that if you phone us, you may get voice mail at busy times. If this happens, please do not hang up. . . leave a detailed message. . . and we'll call you back as soon as possible.

I invite you to contact us with your questions not answered in this book, specific machines, or how to order. Also, we'd be glad to go over your personal objectives and help guide you as you get started. And if you feel you need more in-depth consulting (which is usually not even required) it is available as well (see "Consulting Services" in Appendix).

Above all else, please remember that we're here to serve you. So feel free to communicate in whatever manner best meets your needs (phone, fax, email or mail).

Bottom Line

This marketing strategy eliminates much of our direct marketing costs. . . the need for sales staff. . . encourages prudent use of the telephone. . . eliminates a showroom, warehouse, and double shipping of orders. . . and lowers all our costs dramatically. . . which means we can PASS HUGE SAVINGS ON TO YOU. This is what makes it possible to sell at such low, discounted factory-direct wholesale prices. You may not even need any consulting services if you pay attention while you're reading this book!

My goal is to do a large sales volume and help a lot of people get into vending, become successful, and then reorder many times. . . NOT to make a big profit on each individual sale.

Full Line Of Machines Available. . .

ONLY the BEST Profit Opportunities PROMOTED!

We do have access to a full line of machines which are available to you. But in order to make our discounted marketing concept workable, I negotiate the best discounted distributor prices on a limited line of equipment which we actively promote. You will find that we offer among the highest quality and most profitable machines available anywhere. Proven winners as well as new concepts. . . but no gimmicks. . . only what really works. If I believe in it, we recommend it and sell it.

If you are interested in any other type of vending machines which are not on our price list, please contact us. We have sources for most everything and can probably either get it for you or direct you to a good supplier.

NO Minimum Order!

Order a sample if you'd like. Then get started with as few or as many machines as you like. After you PROVE to yourself that you are doing the RIGHT thing. . . then EXPAND at whatever rate you are COMFORTABLE with (even one machine at a time).

As a practical matter, if you're just getting started, I'd suggest you start out with at least 5 machines if you can (3 minimum). Some people want to try only 1, but that's really not a very good market test. Whether the experience is good or bad, 1 is just not a good representative sample.

Money Back Guarantee!

In an industry where virtually nobody offers any type of satisfaction guarantee (except product warranty) we offer a Money Back Satisfaction Guarantee! This has proven to give a lot of peace of mind to our clients, particularly those new to the business. (See "Satisfaction Guarantee" in the Appendix under "Forms And Miscellaneous" for details).

LOWEST PRICE Guarantee - Or DOUBLE The Difference Back!

As a national factory-direct discount distributor of vending and amusement machines, we strive to offer the absolute LOWEST PRICES possible on QUALITY machines - or DOUBLE the difference refunded! (See "Satisfaction Guarantee" in the Appendix under "Forms And Miscellaneous" for details).

Factory-Direct Wholesale Prices

Due to our unique marketing method you can buy any quantity of the machines you want at our factory-direct wholesale price and save up to 75%!

Total Support!

You will find us to be TOTALLY COMMITTED to our customers! And we offer you well-trained and talented Vending CONSULTANTS to help assure your success in the vending business.

We simply present the facts to you. . . help you determine if vending is right for you. . . which vending program is right for you. . . and then you make a decision.

Please contact us for a free consultation, and feel free to contact us at any time if there is anything at all that we can do to assist you! (See "Consulting Services" in Appendix).

The Golden Rule!

No exaggeration of profit potential. . . no embellishment or misrepresentation of the opportunity. . . no B. S. . . period! JUST STRAIGHT TALK! I am absolutely 100% totally committed to your success and satisfaction in the vending and amusement business. Our business policies, operations, support services, and marketing all reflect this. I think you can see already, just from the above (Money Back Guarantee, Lowest Price Guarantee, etc.) that at FREEDOM TECHNOLOGY we flat "PUT OUR MONEY WHERE OUR MOUTH IS"!

Our motto is simply the GOLDEN RULE. "Do unto others as you would have them do unto you."

Not real clever or slick. . . not Madison Avenue marketing genius. . . but that's us. It's served us and our clients well for over 20 years.

NOTE: ALL PROFIT ILLUSTRATIONS are in keeping with our 'STRAIGHT TALK' policy and SATISFACTION GUARANTEE. This means that profit illustrations are VERY conservative and you should be able to do AT LEAST this well or potentially much better (while the information is deemed reliable it, of course, can not be guaranteed).

Be In Business For Yourself. . . But Not By Yourself!!

What other company offers you this kind of security and support? We at FREEDOM TECH are committed to your success It's very rare to find an opportunity this good! If you can find one, do it.

With FREEDOM TECH and VENDING SUCCESS SECRETS you're joining a team that has the potential to launch MORE vending operators on MILLION-DOLLAR careers than

ALL the others! Join us part time or full time in this DYNAMIC . . . GROWING industry and you could have ALL the money you need. . . AND have the TIME to enjoy it.

FREEDOM TECH: Serving you since 1972. Written Satisfaction Guarantee!

I invite you to join us!

Chapter 4
What's Best For You?

There are many very profitable types of vending and amusement systems. And there are many factors to consider when making a decision as to 'what's best for you'. Earning potential is not the only consideration. For example:

Time Constraints

If you're looking for a part-time commitment and you have a job that requires you to work from 9 to 5 Monday through Friday, you would probably not want to get involved in office snack vending... no matter how profitable it is (since you would not be available to service your locations during office hours). If you have at least a half day free each work week, then you could consider office snack vending. There are many choices in this area, ranging from the low cost honor snack tray system to sophisticated electronic snack and cold drink vending equipment.

Low On Cash - Lots Of Time

If you don't have much capital to invest, but you have a lot of time, or are out of work... an excellent option is the very popular honor snack tray mentioned in more detail below. Start up costs are very low and this system is INCREDIBLY profitable RELATIVE to the start-up cost... but MUCH more LABOR INTENSIVE than other types of vending. If you have the time, but your financial resources are strained, this is an excellent way to get started. If you're laid-off, you could 'make yourself' a job this way.

Low On Time - Lots Of Cash

If, on the other hand, you have sufficient capital to invest, but you're VERY, VERY busy... you'd probably want to consider something that is very low labor. Let the equipment do more of the work for you.

For lowest time commitment: A couple of the most profitable areas to consider would be bulk snack vending, or impulse (game) machines. Both require servicing only about once every month or two.

Bulk vending pays you the HIGHEST PROFIT MARGIN in the snack vending business and you only have to stock a couple of products.

And, of course, with amusement machines there is no product to stock so servicing generally amounts to a quick check-over and money collection.

BOTH are relatively easy to find good locations for, and can be placed in locations that will be accessible to you whenever you have time to service them.

Other Situations

The other types of machines fall somewhere in the middle, as far as time and cash commitments, and will be covered in more detail elsewhere in this book.

As mentioned earlier, a couple of the most overlooked areas that should concern you are;

Equipment SUITABILITY

QUALITY

PRICE Paid

If you end up with the wrong TYPE of equipment (or a poor vending CONCEPT), or poor QUALITY machines that break down constantly, it can be very disruptive and expensive. And of course, if you pay too much for equipment, you may never receive a good return on your investment.

When considering profitability, keep the following often-overlooked item in mind:

The biggest expense you will have, next to equipment cost (and possibility product cost) will be your time (or that of a helper). Since most people starting a vending business are one-person operations, they often tend to discount the value of their time far too much. If a machine looks very profitable relative to purchase price, but takes too much of your time, it may actually not be very profitable at all.

Profitability - Main Considerations:

● RETURN OF INVESTMENT. How fast can you earn your initial investment back?

● INCOME PER HOUR. How much do you earn per hour for your time?

With some vending equipment you will experience a very fast return of investment, such as honor snack trays which can pay-back in as little as 1 month. But when you consider your TIME investment, you may find that you're only making $15. gross profit per hour.

In other cases, like bulk vending or impulse (amusement) machines, you may find that it may take 4 to 10 months to earn your investment back. . . but you're making $100.00 to $200.00 gross profit per hour for your time.

I take these two main factors into account whenever I evaluate any machine opportunity mentioned in this book. My approach is simple and easy to understand, as you will soon see in the forthcoming chapters.

You will find it important to understand the difference between 'gross profit' and 'net profit'.

Gross profit = sales revenue less commission (if any), and less the cost of the product being sold. Example: .55¢ candy sale, less .06¢ commission (10%), less .24¢ cost of candy equals .25¢ gross profit per sale.

Net profit = gross profit less any other costs or overhead (such as machine cost, freight, sales tax, locating, telephone, vehicle expense, or other miscellaneous costs, if any).

There are methods of evaluating business opportunities and profitability that are more accurate, and more complex than what I use in this book. This involves treating your time as an expense (as if you had to hire someone to do the work for you) and deducting it from the NET profit.

When all cost information is available you can calculate the 'internal rate of return' which makes it possible to compare your rate of return with A.P.R. (Annual Percentage Rates) offered by banks, mutual funds, etc. You can even take it a step farther and consider the 'after tax' and 'after inflation' rate of return.

This is very interesting if you are the analytical type. But it is UNNECESSARILY COMPLEX for most people, and beyond the scope of this book. I've found that a simplified analysis is close enough for our purposes. If you think you need or want this type of analysis and you don't know how to do it yourself, I suggest you contact a certified public accountant.

In doing this type of analysis, be careful not to compare your opportunity with large vending operations which post profits on the stock exchange. They have huge expenses and overhead and are not doing business at all similar to you.

Hired Help

Another option you have, of course, would be to hire someone to service your route for you. This is usually an option only for those who have significant start-up money to invest, or who have built up their routes over a period of time and want to lay back a little.

This can dramatically increase your profit since you can often hire others at a relatively low cost compared to your profit. . . freeing you up for handling expansion and management duties only. There are many ways to handle this, which are covered in the chapters titled "Route Management" and "Getting Great Locations".

Summary

This brief chapter is not designed be all-inclusive, but rather to get you to start thinking about some of the factors that might be important for you to start considering. There is a lot of 'cross-over' between chapters with this theme of 'What's Best For You', and many other related points will be raised relative to each type of machine discussed.

We'll take a closer look at each of these points in other chapters. And if after reading this book you feel you need a little extra help, our consultants will be happy to help you determine what's best for your particular situation, your needs, and your wants.

Almost anyone with a desire to succeed can expect to be successful in the vending business.

With the RIGHT EQUIPMENT. . . at the RIGHT PRICE. . . in the RIGHT LOCATIONS. . . vending can be VERY PROFITABLE for you. It's not uncommon to earn returns of up to 100% to even 1,000% per year. Each time you service your vending locations you'll feel like you just hit the JACK POT in Las Vegas. Believe me when I say. . . this business can be FUN!

Getting it "RIGHT" is the key, and with this book in hand you should be a giant step ahead.

Now let's take a look now at some of the best areas of vending that you will want to consider:

Notes

Chapter 5
HONOR Snack And Drink Systems

Absolutely nothing makes more money for the dollar invested than honor snack tray systems! And you can get started for UNDER $500.00.

Essentially, for every dollar you invest, you make about a dollar a month! Want $5,000.00 monthly income? Invest $5,000.00. . . earn it back the first month. . . then continue making $5,000.00 per month. It's that simple!

Make up to $500.00 per month or more on a maximum total start-up investment of under $500.00. . . working only about 3 to 5 hours a week! And that's with just 25 honor snack trays serviced every OTHER week (or 13 per week). . . imagine your income if you expand to 100, 200 or more?

There's no reason you couldn't get started with 25 honor snack trays for under $500.00. . . start making up to $500.00 per month. . . and grow from there!

Definition

An honor snack tray is usually small. . . usually cardboard (sometimes plastic). . . and it's most distinguishing feature is that buyers may take any items they want and voluntarily pay for it by dropping their money in a cash box (hence, "honor" is a big factor). Obviously, they could take all the snacks and drop nothing in the cash box. . . or even take the cash box itself (and they do). Nevertheless, they can be very profitable IF well managed.

Honor System VS Machines

Remember, the name of the game is: "Get the job done for the LEAST equipment cost". Sure, there are MANY situations where honor snacks are NOT appropriate. . . but use them where you can in small businesses, OR STAY OUT of those locations (machines won't pay there).

As you read on in this book, you should note that I make recommendations regarding number of product selections in a vending MACHINE. . . and regarding coin changers and bill acceptors. Honor systems meet all these requirements:

> You can offer as many different products as will fit.

> Also, since customers often have access to the coin box, they can deposit any combination of coins or bills, and make their own change.

> These are advantages that you will come to appreciate. While honor systems have their disadvantages, they are ALWAYS better than an INFERIOR designed machine that offers too little selection, or too many restrictions on payment options.

Many, many locations just are not large enough to justify anything other than honor snacks. They are usually all that makes sense in a location with under 15 to 20 employees.

Market Saturation?

There are probably 100's of great locations for snack trays, close to your home. This has been an often over-looked area of vending which has very little GOOD competition. And what little competition there is tends to be poorly managed.

What About Product Theft?

Shrinkage (theft) is certainly a big problem with honor snacks. . . but it is a potentially MANAGEABLE PROBLEM!

The truth is that, in our modern society, there is less and less 'honor'. The honor sales concept worked much, much better 50 years ago than it does today. And I don't mean to sound too pessimistic, but I'll bet that it'll be measurably worse 10 years from now. Knowing this, many people simply rule out honor snacks without giving it much more thought.

Even if you decide against honor snacks yourself, you should understand what type of locations they are right for. This is a prerequisite that will make the following chapters more clear. SO PLEASE READ THIS CHAPTER ANYWAY!

Differences in locations makes a huge difference in results. Shrinkage can literally range from 10% (no, not zero %) to 100%. If you are careful what type of locations you seek, you will find that it is possible to keep shrinkage between 10% and 30% per location, with an average of about 20%. To achieve this you can, under NO circumstances, accept any locations that the general public has access to. . . as a group they have no conscience and they will steal you blind!

Public Access = Big Loser

A good rule of thumb is this: In any location where the general public has access to your products, you MUST place a COIN-OPERATED machine. Otherwise, you can count on 50% to 100% shrinkage. With 50% shrinkage you would have to have a VERY high profit margin on your products to make it. And as a rule of thumb, product cost is usually about 50%. So with 50% shrinkage you would just break even. . . over 50% you lose money. . . and this doesn't even consider your other overhead costs.

In this "What About Theft" section it is appropriate that I should point out that there has been a proliferation of CHARITY honor systems in the past few years. The charity does not own them, but rather licenses the use of their name, which is fine (more on this in the chapter titled "Getting Great Locations"). They usually sell ONLY ONE product (which in itself discourages sales) like Tootsie Pops™, or York Peppermint Patties™, etc. Almost always you will find them placed in locations where the public has access.

Some people have tried lower cost products, like Pearson's Mints™ instead of York Peppermint Patties™, because they cost about half as much (they also taste about half as good and are about 25% smaller) and they can get product cost down to 25%. . . making 50% shrinkage livable. But people resent being asked to pay so much for inferior quality and if they do pay. . . they will often take 2 while paying for 1.

I don't know of anyone that is doing well with this type of route (public access charity trays) or any public access type honor route. I advise people to stay away from these all the time, and some just won't listen. If you don't believe me and want to give it a try anyway, just remember. . . "I warned you"!

This is one of those 'flawed, or poor concepts' discussed earlier. Public access honor snacks just don't work.

Small Group Access Works Best

It does take good management to keep your shrinkage at or under 20%. This is possible only in locations that are fairly intimate, such as a small office with few employees and no exposure to theft from the public. These employees will often protect 'their' honor tray.

The ONLY honor snack tray system that can work is the wide-selection tray that is placed in small businesses with NO PUBLIC ACCESS.

It's impossible to eliminate shrinkage ENTIRELY. . . but who cares? When your equipment cost is so low, you can afford it. Successful honor snack route operators know that it's much cheaper to accept a 20% average loss, than to invest in equipment. If you have a good location and shrinkage is high, you can always install a coin-operated machine later. . . or simply move the tray. But try 'talker cards' before you give up on the location.

Talker Cards

After careful location selection, one important success secret is the use of 'talker cards'. These cards communicate to your customer (in a polite way) that their cooperation (and honesty) is necessary if they want to continue enjoying the benefits of their honor snack tray. They work very well in locations where you have customers with a conscience, and a vested interest in the tray (they want it to stay) like a small businesses private break room.

Westgate Systems (listed in summary below) offers a nice line of 'talker cards' that are easily changed and fit in a slot at the back of their tray. They feature attractive, 2-color artwork and communicate very effectively with phrases like:

"You're a winner! Thank you for being our customer"

"Thank you, for being honest"

"Oh-oh, I'm short. Please pay for what you take"

Or a host of others (some have much stronger wording) appropriate for ALL SITUATIONS. There are about 15 different ones in all.

Profit Potential

This is a typical example of the profits you could experience with an honor snack tray route. It is based upon only 5 employees with NO outside customer traffic, EACH employee buying an average of just .75 snacks per day (some won't buy any, and some will buy 2 or more). See the chapter titled "Location Targeting And Analysis" for survey results indicating the daily averages.

Here's how many $ $ $ you could be making with honor snack trays!

Products: Snacks (cookies, candy, bagged snacks, etc.).
Sale Price: Vend at .55¢ (to .65¢ or more), less 20% shrinkage = .44¢ net sale.
Cost: .10¢ to .30¢, average = .24¢.
Gross Profit: Average .20¢ per vend after shrinkage (.44¢ net sale - .24¢ average cost).
Based Upon: 5 employees X .75 snacks per day each (average) X 5 days per week = 19 vends per week.
Service Requirements: 25 locations once every 2 weeks = about 5 to 10 hours work every other week, or service 1/2 each week at just 3 to 5 hours per week!!

Description	Weekly Volume		Gross Profit		Weekly Gross Profit				Monthly Gross Profit	
1 Honor Snack Tray	19.	X	.20¢	=	$ 3.80	X	4.	=	$	15.20
25 Honor Snack Trays	475.	X	.20¢	=	$ 95.00	X	4.	=	$	380.00
100 Honor Snack Trays	1900.	X	.20¢	=	$ 380.00	X	4.	=	$	1,520.00

See chapters titled "Location Targeting And Analysis" and "Getting Great Locations"

NOTE: This is provided for illustrative purposes only. It does not include tray cost, freight, sales tax, locating, or other miscellaneous costs not specifically listed, if any. Figures may vary according to type of business, geographical location, fluctuations in customer traffic, and many other factors which can not be predicted. Therefore, the actual results achieved may vary and can not be guaranteed.

The above is fairly typical. $15.00 gross monthly per tray is, in my opinion, a conservative average you could plan around. It has been my experience, and other route operators confirm, that you can generally expect a low of about $10.00, to a high of about $20.00 gross monthly profit per tray.

Imagine the profits you could achieve in locations with 10 or more employees. . . or with 200 or more honor snack trays! You probably won't have an honor snack tray in a location with more than 15 to 20 employees (that type of location usually justifies a larger capacity coin-operated machine).

There's not a lot of guess work here. You will find that you can approximately predict how well one of your honor snack trays will do if you know the number of employees in a location. This is covered in more detail in the chapter titled "Location Targeting And Analysis". The 'shrinkage factor' is the big unknown.

Commission

No commission is generally paid to the locations on honor snack trays. Small business establishments (up to 30 to 50 employees) are just happy to have someone offer quality vending services to their people and usually do not expect a commission. Besides, the 10% to 15% commission you might pay them on a small volume vending operation is not enough money to motivate them. Convenience is their first priority.

Profit Summary

Based upon the above figures in locations with just 5 employees, if you had just 25 snack trays averaging about $15.00 to $20.00 monthly gross profit each. . . you could earn about $375.00 to $500.00 monthly gross profit.

You should be able to make at least $15.00 to as much as $50.00 gross profit per hour depending upon the various factors mentioned above.

Since the total set-up cost for a stocked honor snack tray, is only about $15.00 to $20.00 each, your gross return on investment could be well over 1000% per year (that's 1000%, not 100%)! This means that you could recover your entire investment within just 1 month!

I think you can see that the profit potential is absolutely incredible! Where else can you start with such a small initial investment ($375.00 to $500.00) and then earn up to $375.00 to $500.00 per month or more in about 3 to 5 hours per week of EASY and FUN work?

Based upon the above illustration, after properly located. Of course you'll also have to plan on spending some time buying product, counting money (too bad), keeping simple records, etc. (this could run at least 15 minutes to 1 hour for every hour of actual route servicing time, depending upon various factors).

Service Requirements

It takes most average people from 5 to 10 hours to service a 25 location honor snack route (depending upon how fast you work, and how far apart the locations are - keep as close together as possible). If, on average, you service your locations once every OTHER week, this means that you could service all 25 trays once every other week working a 5 to 10 hour week (and take a week off in-between) or service 13 EACH week working a 3 to 5 hour week.

Since the trays will hold about 100 items, according to the above example (19 sales per week) you would actually need to service the tray only every 3 to 4 weeks. In 4 weeks your tray may be almost empty (when you include shrinkage). Don't let the tray get too empty or lack of selection will cost you sales.

In reality you'll find that you'll need to service some locations each week, and some you'll service once a month. My own rule of thumb is that I like to have at least $10.00 gross profit available when I service an honor snack location (this figure is higher for more expensive coin-operated machines) so I divided my routes up according to frequency of service (weekly route, every other week, every third week, monthly, etc.) and it takes a little time to figure this out. So in the beginning service your route at least every other week.

See chapter titled "Route Management".

Suggested Honor Snack Tray Start-Up Checklist:

✓ 25 honor snack trays with divider and coin box

✓ 5 Snack tray stands (for those locations with no available counter-top space)

✓ 25 honor snack tray labels

✓ 25 Business card holders (mounts your business card on snack tray)

✓ 100 Tray liners (protects tray bottom, extends life)

✓ 60 Most popular 'Talker Cards' (about 15 different ones available)

✓ 1 Pack-line blue print (plans for high production packing system you can set up at home)

✓ Initial inventory of about 1250 snack items

✓ See chapter titled "Getting Started"

Product Inventory And Set-up Requirements

Much of the above items can be purchased from several different sources, however, ALL the above items are available from Westgate Systems (see "Summary" below) except for snack tray labels and product inventory. See chapter titled "Products And Inventory".

You may want to consider having some snack tray label stickers printed up at your local printer. These make the trays look more attractive and professional. . . and give you a place to advertise and offer instructions (such as price and payment instructions). Some operators print the price on this label, while others put it on the lower front part of the tray.

Typically, it may look something like this:

Honor Snacks .55¢

Please Pay Here, Thanks! ⇨⇨⇨

To get started, you can get by with (neatly) hand written instructions printed right on the tray with a felt tip marker. . . or on a piece of card-stock that you tape on the tray. At some point, you will want to get tray label stickers because they do look a lot more attractive and professional.

Also, as an additional option, you may want to consider ordering price stickers that you can place on the lower front of the tray in front of each column. This gives you the option of having a different price for each column if you want. Price stickers are available from WICO:

WICO Corporation
6400 West Gross Point Road
Niles, IL 60714
1-800-FOR-WICO (800-367-9426)
847-647-7500
MO-FR, 7:30am-5:00pm, CST

The trays will cost you a total of about $4.00 to $5.00 each depending upon quantity purchased, 'talker cards' purchased, type of sticker you may have printed and applied to each one, etc.

While the trays will hold about 100 items, many people start by loading them with about 50 (they won't look half empty either). This means your initial product inventory will cost about $12.00 (50 x .24¢ each).

You can set up a 25 location route yourself for under $500.00 ($15. to $20. each) and make up to $375.00 to $500.00 per month!

Honor Cold Drinks

Some honor snack tray route operators expand into honor cold drinks at some point. You could AT LEAST double your profit in locations where you offer cold drinks.

While this can be very profitable, in some locations it is often not AS practical, or AS profitable as snack trays.

There are 2 primary reasons for this:

Small businesses often have their own microwave oven and compact refrigerator. It is more convenient (than snacks) for them to put together their own honor system for cold drinks since they would only be buying a couple of products, and the shelf life on canned drinks is quite long.

And you will have considerably more cost in equipment since refrigerators obviously cost much more than cardboard trays.

Still, in some locations, they can make sense. . . and a lot of money. Since you can buy a small compact refrigerator for as little as $100.00 at your local appliance distributor, you could pay for it in as little as 4 months (in a 5 employee location as illustrated above).

This may be something you may want to consider offering at some point. . . at least for your best snack tray locations. . . as a convenience to them, and to increase your profits.

Typically, you would put a coin box of some type inside (or on top of) the refrigerator. This could be a metal box obtained from an office supply store, fastened to the shelf, and locked. Or it could be as simple as a cardboard box. You could even ask they they simply deposit payment in your snack tray coin box (put it on top of the refrigerator).

Talker cards can also be used very effectively here, as with the snack trays.

In general, you will do better if you prepare some sort of graphics for the front of the refrigerator to attract attention. . . although some locations may object if not in very good taste.

A colorful 'Cold Drinks" sign would suffice. You could have something made up at a local quick printer, and laminate it for durability. Or talk to a local sign company. Also, sometimes a local Pepsi™ or Coke™ bottler will have something they can offer you for free.

You can set your honor snack tray on top of the refrigerator (use it as a stand) for a nice little low-cost honor snack and drink combo center! They can pay for snacks AND drinks using the coin box in the honor snack tray.

I'm not going to go into a lot more detail on this here in this chapter. But if the idea of increased profits offering cold drinks on the honor system appeals to you, see the chapter titled "Packaged Snack And Cold Drink Vending" for more information. That information is easily adaptable to honor drinks, together with the above.

O C S (Office Coffee Service)

This is a natural 'go-together' for the honor tray business. In an O C S (Office Coffee Service) route, you would supply your clients with coffee brewing equipment (usually on a monthly fee basis) plus sell them coffee and any other related supplies they would need. Many OCS operators expand into honor trays later. And visa-versa, many honor tray operators get into OCS.

Having said that, I want to point out that there is MUCH more profit in both the honor snack tray and honor cold drink businesses. So "those who know" (or find out) often drop the OCS at some point.

Also, it is relatively convenient for small businesses to obtain and maintain their own brewing equipment, buy coffee, etc. In some markets you may find competition, but the biggest competition is the clients own willingness to provide this service for themselves. They are much less likely to be willing to set up and maintain their own honor snacks (or vending machine, for that matter).

Some very service-oriented honor snack operators offer OCS simply as a convenience to their locations, even though it is not nearly as profitable. It is beyond the scope of this book to get into OCS in any depth, particularly since I would not recommend it to you until you have already developed your successful honor snack (and possibly honor cold drink) route. When you get to that point and if you're still interested, I suggest you contact Coffee-Inn's™ and ask them for their free guide titled "Operators Guide For Entry Into The OCS Market". It is very well done and should be a big help. They also carry a nice line of new 'coin-operated' OCS coffee equipment, so you'd want to ask for their catalog as well.

Coffee-Inns™
Automatic Marketing Industries, Inc
2362 West Shangri-La Road
Bldg. 200
Phoenix, AZ 85029
800-528-0552, 602-944-3396
MO-FR, 8:00am-4:00pm, MST

For NON coin-operated OCS equipment you may want to try Westgate Systems, or check out the ads in the trade magazines.

Summary

You can easily start this business part-time with 25 to 100 honor snack trays and build it up by reinvesting profits in more honor snack trays or in other vending equipment. One person can service up to about 200 to 300 honor snack trays without having to hire help.

Based upon the above figures in locations with just 5 employees, 200 honor snack trays could net you up to $3,000.00 to $4,000.00 monthly gross profit as a one-person business! You should be able to make at least $15.00 to as much as $50.00 gross profit per hour depending upon the various factors mentioned above.

● FAST 1 month pay-back on your initial investment!

● OVER 1000% gross return on investment per year (that's 1000%, not 100%)!

● $15.00 to $50.00 gross profit per hour!

● Service every 2 weeks!

● Easy to locate!

Based upon the above illustration, after properly located. Of course you'll also have to plan on spending some time buying product, counting money (too bad), keeping simple records, etc. (this could run at least 15 minutes to 1 hour for every hour of actual route servicing time, depending upon various factors).

As good as the honor system business may sound to some people, you will find that (while initial investment will be more) your hourly income will go through the roof with MACHINES. They just make you MUCH more efficient.

Vending MACHINES are like having little 'money-collecting ROBOTS' doing most of the work for you all day. . . while you kick-back and enjoy life! I think you can see why I call it "the ULTIMATE business"!

I, personally, no longer operate honor routes for that reason, although I do know of many very successful honor route operators. . . some as big as 4000 tray operations! Many start out this way and grow into machines later. It just depends upon what you like, and what your resources are. It seems there is something for everyone in this business!

At this time my company, FREEDOM TECHNOLOGY, does not carry honor snack tray systems. There are many suppliers for snack trays, most of whom you will find advertise in the trade publications (see chapter titled "Trade Publications, Organizations, And Shows"). My favorite is the cardboard snack tray line manufactured by Westgate Systems. They are very inexpensive and offer many different styles of trays, stands, 'talker cards', and accessories. All of the above items are carried by Westgate (except the food items). They also carry a nice line of reconditioned OCS (coffee) equipment. You may want to call or write for their brochure and price list:

Westgate Systems, Inc.
323 Dewey Street North
P.O. Box 0203
Eau Claire, WI 54702
715-832-6013
MO-FR, 8:00am-5:00pm, CST

See chapters titled "Packaged Snack And Cold Drink Vending" and "Products And Inventory".

Also see the last page of this book for FREE resources (reports, videos, etc.) including the "HOTTEST Vending Money-Makers" report!

Notes

Chapter 6
Bulk Vending

Bulk-vending may not be as glamorous as some other types of vending, but WOW. . . it sure beats most of them when you look at the bottom line! Little else in the vending industry can net you as high a return on your investment of both your money AND your time!

Your profits will amaze you! Empty these machines just 2 times and you'll have your ENTIRE investment back! Many operators report earnings of up to $200.00 gross profit per hour! It's actually possible to receive a 100% return of your investment within just 3 to 6 months! And consider this. . . these machines require servicing only about ONCE every TWO MONTHS!

Definition

A bulk vending machine is one which sells snack items in 'bulk' (loose handfuls) rather than packaged. While most packaged vended products are marked up from 50% to 100%. . . bulk vending enjoys one of the highest mark-ups in the vending industry at 200% to 300% and more.

The most visible example of bulk vending is the large racks that greet you at the entrance of virtually every grocery store in America. They sell loose candy, toys and stickers in capsules, etc. . . at prices typically ranging from .10¢ to .50¢. For the purposes of this book, I will refer to these as 'bulk racks.'

You will also find various styles of candy and nut bulk vendors in restaurants, offices, retail stores, etc. . . typically featuring from 1 to 4 selections (some as many as 8). For the purposes of this book, I will refer to these simply as a 'bulk vendor', or a '1, 2, 3, 4, or 8 selection (etc.) bulk vendor'.

Another advantage of bulk vending is that you only have to service the machines about once every two months! And you only need to stock a few products. It's a very simple and highly profitable business.

Grocery Stores VS Other Locations

It is my experience that there is far more profit and far less competition if you stay away from the bulk racks seen in grocery stores (and other bulk rack locations). Bulk racks are outside the scope of this book (although a bulk vendor can do great in those same locations). If you have an interest in bulk racks, I recommend that you first establish your route with bulk vendors, and grow from there.

The largest bulk vending operator in the world is probably Folz Vending. This large national company has bulk racks in grocery stores from coast to coast, as well as bulk vendors in other types of locations. It was started from very modest beginnings by Roger Folz. . . a very nice 'down-to-earth' man whom I enjoyed the privilege of meeting at a convention in Orlando, Florida. He had flown there in his private plane.

I know others who own hundreds, even thousands of bulk vendors. . . who make lots of money. . . and have no interest in ever getting into the bulk rack market. At some point, you may have to decide for yourself.

Market Saturation?

Because bulk vendors are so visible in lots of retail locations, most vending novices are of the opinion that the market is already saturated with bulk vendors. . . but nothing could be further from the truth. Those in the business are happy to have you believe that, and they're laughing all the way to the bank!

Sure, there are a lot of them around. . . it's nothing new. . . its simply a proven concept that has past the test of time. But there are still plenty of profitable locations available. One of the most overlooked, and yet very profitable type of location, is offices and businesses - OTHER than retail.

Also, even though you may have other machines next to yours in a given location, you can still do very well with a high quality, attractive machine (MANY bulk vendors are not high quality, and MOST of them are not attractive).

I know of some machines that absolutely steal all the business away from the competitors. I'll refer to this type of machine as a "HOT bulk vendor" (See section on "Machine Recommendations" below).

Obtaining locations for bulk-vending machines is often easier using the charity licensing approach (more on this below under "Commission") detailed in chapter titled "Getting Great Locations".

I have done as well or better with bulk vendors than with any other types of machines I have owned. And I know people who are successful route operators who started off with the more 'sophisticated' electronic machines. . . then included or switched entirely into bulk vending after they 'discovered' it. I strongly recommend you seriously consider bulk vendors for yourself.

High Profit - Low Labor!

This is a typical example of the gross profits you could experience with bulk vendors. It is based upon operating 3 selection bulk vendors in locations yielding only 4 to 8 vends per day, which

is well within the range of the national averages. See below for survey results indicating the national averages.

Here's how many $ $ $ you could be making with bulk vendors!

Products: Bulk snacks (candy, nuts, etc.).
Sale Price: Vend at .25¢.
Cost: .80¢ to $5.00 per pound, average cost per vend = .07¢ (adjustable vend amount).
Gross Profit: .18¢ per vend (.25¢ net sale - .07¢ average cost).
Based Upon: 6 days per week in operation, 4 weeks (or 24 days) per month in operation.
Service Requirements: Approximately once monthly! * The total monthly time required to service 100 locations is usually about 3 to 4 days (15 to 20 minutes per machine).

Daily # of Vends	1 Vend	4 Vends	8 Vends
Daily gross profit per location	.18 ¢	.72 ¢	$ 1.44
Monthly gross profit per location	$ 4.32	$ 17.28	$ 34.56
Monthly gross profit - 10 locations	$ 43.20	$ 172.80	$ 345.60
Monthly gross profit - 100 locations	$ 432.00	$ 1,728.00	$ 3,456.00

Monthly donation to Charity Sponsor is about $1.00 to $2.00 per machine location (IF applicable).

National average is about 2.5 vends per candy selection (X number of selections) per day, per location.

See chapters titled "Location Targeting And Analysis" and "Getting Great Locations"

NOTE: This is provided for illustrative purposes only. It does not include machine cost, freight, sales tax, locating, or other miscellaneous costs not specifically listed, if any. Figures may vary according to type of business, geographical location, fluctuations in customer traffic, and many other factors which can not be predicted. Therefore, the actual results achieved may vary and can not be guaranteed.

According to a recent Vending Times Census Of The Industry, bulk vending is a 276 million dollar industry, and the .25¢ bulk vend accounts for 60% of the bulk vend market (.10¢ = 5%, .50¢ = 27%, other = 8%). The national average for candy and nut bulk vending is $200. gross per year, per individual machine product segment. Based upon .25¢ vends and a 6 day operating week, this would equal an average of approximately 2.5 vends per day, per individual machine product segment.

Since most machines have 3 or 4 product segments, this could amount to an average of 7.5 to 10 vends per machine location.

In my own experience, and in talking with route operators around the country, I have found that for well-managed routes using quality, attractive machines which offer at least 3 selections: That an AVERAGE (for all your locations) of 4 to 8 vends per day is quite achievable and reasonable.

With 3 selection bulk vendors, you should be able to anticipate an average of AT LEAST 4 vends per day, and enjoy a gross profit of AT LEAST $15.00 (to as much as $35.00 or more) per machine, per month... MUCH MORE for HOT bulk vendors (See section on "Machine Recommendations" below)!

Commission

Obtaining locations for bulk-vending machines is often easier using the charity licensing approach (detailed in chapter titled "Getting Great Locations"). No commission is generally paid to the locations on bulk-vending machines. The 10% to 30% (10% typical) commission you might offer a location is often not enough money for them to get enthused about, and that won't usually motivate them to let you install a machine.

What WILL motivate locations is the ATTRACTIVE CONVENIENCE of the snack machine for customers and employees. . . and/or HELPING OUT A WORTHWHILE CHARITY. Your monthly donation to the Charity Sponsor is usually about $1.00 to $2.00 per machine location.

These are essentially 'licensing' agreements. The charity gives you permission to use their name and/or trademark(s) in your vending operations in return for a royalty (donation) payment. . . usually a flat rate. This is completely legal and ethical in every way.

The charities love the program because they NEED the money. . . they don't have to do ANYTHING to get it . . . and they like the FREE ADVERTISING they get from their name being on the machines.

And it's great for you too, because it COSTS LESS than paying commission. . . and it makes it EASIER to get locations!

Furthermore, I know operators with hundreds of machines that DON'T PAY either commission OR charity donations. If you offer quality, attractive, late model equipment many locations will accept it as a convenience to them with no compensation.

Great retail locations, offices and other non-retail locations are readily available. Please see the chapter titled "Getting Great Locations" for details on this.

Profit Summary

Based upon the above, if you had 100 3 or 4 selection bulk vendors averaging from 4 to 8 vends per day, you could earn about $1,728.00 to $3,456.00 monthly gross profit. Assuming that you serviced them ONCE every OTHER month, taking 3 to 4 days per service, you would be working a total of up to 4 days (or 32 hours) every OTHER month. . . or an AVERAGE of only 16 hours per MONTH.

This equals about $108.00 to $216.00 gross profit per hour!

Since a high quality 3-select bulk vendor can be purchased for around $200.00, your gross return on investment could be about 100% to 200% gross return per year. This means that you could recover your entire investment within about 5 to 12 months!

Based upon the above illustration, after properly located. Of course you'll also have to plan on spending some time buying product, counting money (too bad), keeping simple records, etc. (this could run at least 15 minutes to 1 hour for every hour of actual route servicing time, depending upon various factors).

Consider HOT bulk vendors for even BETTER potential results! See "Machine Recommendations" below.

Service Requirements

Most bulk vending operators service their machines every 1 or 2 months. A typical 3 selection bulk vendor holds about 700 vends (at 4 to 8 vends per day = 3 to 6 month capacity)! Good quality equipment is so reliable. . . holds enough product. . . and has a big enough coin box that you can easily go 2 months between servicing in most all locations. Also, the product shelf life is long enough that this is not an issue. For the purposes of the above illustration, I am assuming every OTHER month servicing.

Servicing amounts to simply dumping the product into the top of the canisters. . . dumping the coin box into a bag. . . wiping off the machine. . . and making a couple of notes in your route record book. See chapter titled "Route Management".

Bulk vending is a relatively SIMPLE business. There's only about 3 major pitfalls to be concerned with, and they're EASY to handle:

Concern	Solution
Poor servicing: Dirty machine, out of product, etc.	Keep it CLEAN, filled, and working properly.
Selling the wrong candy/snack product.	Offer NAME BRANDS. Try other selections.
Poor location	Simply RELOCATE if/when necessary.

There's little question that you'll be able to handle these simple management requirements. And locating these machines is NOT difficult at all. There's just NO EXCUSE for not succeeding in bulk vending. It's not easy. . . but it's not hard either. It is a business, and should be treated as such. It works if you do.

You will find that it is sometimes difficult to predict in advance how well any one of your bulk vendors will do in a particular location. They will generally do well in retail and office locations but you really have to just try each location and see how it does. . . moving the machine if necessary. This is covered in more detail in the chapters titled "Getting Great Locations" and "Location Targeting And Analysis".

The bulk vending business offers you one of the most spectacular opportunities for financial independence ever! And for a relatively small investment of your time and money.

Suggested Bulk Vend Start-Up Checklist:

✓ Purchase 10 or more bulk-vendors

✓ Purchase at least 3# to 5# candy/nuts per machine product selection

✓ Low-cost postal scale

✓ Set-up charity licensing agreement
(Details in chapter titled "Getting Great Locations")

✓ See chapter titled "Getting Started"

Product Inventory Requirements

Depending upon the type of vendor, and product vended, it generally takes from 3 to 5 pounds of product to fill each cannister. If your budget is tight, do not hesitate to fill the machines only about half full. This will not affect sales and, in fact, may even offer a psychological advantage (a machine that is kept too full, too often, looks unused to regular customers and could actually decrease sales).

Suggested bulk vend products are listed in the chapter titled "Products And Inventory". Also see "Machine Recommendations" below for product tips.

Machine Set-up

Your bulk vendor is adjustable as to the amount of product it will vend. Simply adjust it to vend the proper amount by weight. Use a low cost postal scale to measure. You will want to keep your cost per vend at around .07¢. To compute this simply follow this example for a candy costing $2.00 per pound:

$2.00 per pound divided by .07$ vend cost = 28 vends per pound.

16 ounces (1 pound) divided by 28 vends = .57 ounces per vend.

In the above example, you would want to adjust your vending mechanism until it is dispensing a little over 1/2 ounce (.57 ounce) as indicated above.

It's really very simple. And it doesn't matter what the product cost is. If you're selling something that is expensive (like pistachio nuts, or Jelly Bellys™) you simply vend a smaller amount compared to something that is very low cost (like Hot Tamales™, or Runts™). Your customers will have a strong sense for value, and expect the portion to be adjusted according to product cost.

A typical 3 selection bulk vendor will have a capacity of about 700 vends. On average, you will vend around 2/3 ounce per vend, and each product segment can be filled up to about 10 pounds with most products. 10 pounds = 160 ounces. 160 ounces divided by 2/3 ounce = 242 vends. 242 vends X 3 product selections = 727 vends.

At only 4 vends per day, it would take about 181 days (or 6 months) to empty the machine. . . half that (or 3 months) at 8 vends per day. It's easy to see why every other month servicing is no problem.

If you're using brand name products (which I recommend, since they increase sales substantially) it may be helpful to apply a product label signifying so. Sometimes you can find printed labels (for M&M's™, Runts™, etc.) from suppliers, but most route operators just cut up a candy package and tape the logo on the inside of the canister.

There is very little preparation required for bulk vendors. Do the above, fill with product, apply your price sticker (usually come with machine) and your done. Place them on location and start making money!

Machine Recommendations

There are many very high quality bulk vendors on the market. Unfortunately, however, many of them are downright ugly! To get and keep the best locations, I advise you consider not only function, but appearance (and adequate product selection, of course).

If you had a business with 2 or 3 different bulk vendors in the entry, and you needed to cut back due to space limitations. Which vendor would you definitely keep. . . the ugly one. . . the cheap one that never works right. . . the limited-selection one... or the attractive multi-selection one that looks great and always works? Get my point? As I've said, I will refer to the later type of machine as a "HOT bulk vendor."

We've done tests where we placed a HOT bulk vendor next to other bulk vendors in a business. Then we handed out quarters at the door and asked people to help themselves to a free snack.

8 out of 10 times they purchased out of the HOT machine. Think about it. . . which one would you put your money in?

See why I like it so much?

When you compare bulk vending, IN GENERAL, to other types of vending you will see why it stands out. By the time you finish this book you will understand. I sell a lot of different types of vendors, but bulk vendors are one of THE simplest and MOST profitable vending routes to operate. . . and have always been one of my personal favorites!

If you're interested in getting into bulk vending and want to make big money fast, my suggestion is this: Operate only HOT bulk vendors. For more information get a free copy of my 'HOTTEST Vending Money-Makers' report (See last page for details).

Fill your bulk vendors with ONLY the following top-selling products. You won't know what to do with all the money you'll make!

The following products are listed in order of my preference (top-seller listed first).

See chapter titled "Products And Inventory".

M&M Peanut™, 1/2" Chicle Tabs™ gum (or Chiklets™, or gumballs), Hot Tamales™, Runts™ (or Skittles™), M&M Crispy™, M&M Plain™, Jelly Belly™ mixed flavor jelly beans (or Starburst™, or Jolly Rancher™ jelly beans) Reeses Pieces™ (or M&M Peanut Butter™) and nuts (pistachios, dry roasted salted peanuts, or mixed nuts).

Summary

Nationally, two-thirds of the bulk candy/snack vending machines are owned by small independents with an average of 107 machines each. Many operators have started small and built up routes of hundreds, even thousands of machines.

At a conservative average of just 4 to 8 vends (only $1.00 to $2.00) per-day per-location, 100 inexpensive 3 selection bulk vendors could earn you up to $1,728.00 to $3,456.00 monthly gross profit. . . working just 3 or 4 days every OTHER month! Make even more with HOT bulk vendors!

● Empty just 2 times and earn your ENTIRE investment back!

● 3 to 6 month pay-back on your initial investment!

● 100% to 300% gross return on investment per year!

● $100.00 to $200.00 gross profit per hour!

● Service every OTHER month!

● Easy to locate!

Based upon the above illustration, after properly located. Of course you'll also have to plan on spending some time buying product, counting money (too bad), keeping simple records, etc. (this could run at least 15 minutes to 1 hour for every hour of actual route servicing time, depending upon various factors).

Consider HOT bulk vendors for the BEST potential results! See the last page in the book for 'HOTTEST Vending Money-Makers' report!

Where else could you invest your money that offers this kind of potential return with so LITTLE work? Bulk vending has always been one of my personal favorites!

For machine sources, costs, and ordering information, please refer to the Appendix.

Also see the last page of this book for FREE resources (reports, videos, etc.) including the "HOTTEST Vending Money-Makers" report!

Notes

Notes

Chapter 7
'Fun-Size' Snack Vending

This dynamic new segment of the vending industry is so important, that a chapter dedicated to it is certainly justified! While less profitable than some other vending opportunities, the potential for the fun-size snack vendor is nevertheless astronomical!

There are MORE potential locations available NOW than for any other vending machine I know of! This is a real 'ground-floor' opportunity.

While there are similarities to both traditional packaged snack vending and bulk vending. . . I find fun-size vending MOST comparable to bulk vending. If you skipped over the chapter on bulk vending, you will find it helpful if you read it before continuing.

Definition

The fun-size snack vendor is a VERY unique, compact snack vendor that vends candy, nuts, and other snacks in fun-size (or 'bite-size') packages for about .25¢.

Up until the early 1990's you would almost never see fun-size candy sold except around Halloween or special holidays. You're familiar with the little versions of Snickers™, Hershey™ bars, Reese's Peanut Butter Cups™ etc., aren't you? Don't confuse these with the miniature's, which are smaller.

Fun-size candies are a FAST growing segment of the candy market. At .25¢ it's the PERFECT SIZE and PRICE, and it enjoys a VERY HIGH PROFIT MARGIN, second only to bulk vended products. All the best selling candies are now available in a fun-size, plus many non-candy snack items.

Market Saturation?

Not even an issue!

Why Fun-Size?

Recently, since the early 1990's, fun-size candies and snacks have caught on as a hot-selling year round item. One reason is that smaller portions appeal to dieters and to parents who think their children should eat less sweets. Even people who would not normally buy a large candy bar WILL often buy a fun-size bar (or 2, or 3).

It's the PERFECT SIZE and PRICE!

Fun-size candy currently retails for about .25¢, yet costs you only about .10¢, making it one of the highest mark-up food items in the vending industry, second only to bulk vended products (which average about .07¢)

It takes awhile for vending equipment manufacturers to respond to changes in the market, and they have recently begun making machines to vend these new fun-size products.

You may have noticed all the bulk vending machines which seem to be everywhere. These machines sell snack items in 'bulk' (loose handfuls) rather than in packages. Bulk vendors are everywhere because they are very, very profitable (I've sold and operated them for years). .

. but the fun-size snack vendor offers some important advantages over bulk vendors.

Compare To Bulk Vendors:

● Sanitary packaging appeals to many more people!

● Often greater selection (8 or more items instead of 1 to 8)!

● Can sell many best-selling snacks that can't be vended in bulk (like candy bars)!

● Easier inventory control!

● Does GREAT alone or placed right next to bulk vendors!

● Plentiful locations, not yet developed!

The fun-size snack vendor can be placed anywhere a bulk vendor can.

Compare To Full-Size Snack Vendors:

They also do very well anywhere conventional snack vending makes sense, even if there is already a full-size snack vendor in place. People just love the fun-size! It's the perfect size and price!

● Smaller .25¢ fun-size vend may = higher gross sales!

● Does GREAT alone or placed right next to 'full-size' vendors!

● Many more potential locations!

This all means HUGE sales and a TREMENDOUS new ground floor opportunity for you! There is a seemingly UNLIMITED number of GREAT locations for the fun-size snack vendor!

Other Benefits Of The Fun-Size Snack Vending Concept:

● Best selling FUN-SIZE (bite-size) candies and snacks results in the highest gross sales! The perfect SIZE and PRICE!

● One of the highest profit margins in the industry (about 250%) second only to bulk vending!

● Compact fun-size snack vendor takes less than 2 square feet of floor space!

● More potential locations at this time than any other vending machine!

● High capacity (up to 250 item) machines now available!

● Association with Charity makes locations even easier to obtain!

Fun-size candies and snacks are a fast growing segment of the market and are here to stay. They are readily available from many sources.

FUN Profits!

This is a typical example of the gross profits you could experience with 'fun-size' snack vendors. It is based upon locations yielding only 6 to 12 vends per day, which is only 50% more than the national averages for bulk vendors (which they are most comparable to). See the chapter titled "Bulk Vending" for survey results indicating those national averages.

Here's how many $ $ $ you could be making with 'fun-size' snack vendors!

Products: Snacks (candy, nuts, bagged snacks, etc.).
Sale Price: Vend at .25¢.
Cost: About .04¢ to .13¢, average = .08¢. to .12¢, use .12¢ for this illustration.
Gross Profit: At least .13¢ per vend (.25¢ net sale - .12¢ maximum average cost).
Based Upon: 6 days per week in operation, 4 weeks (or 24 days) per month in operation.
Service Requirements: About once every two weeks, 15 to 20 minutes each!

Daily # of Vends	1 Vend	6 Vends	12 Vends
Daily gross profit per location	13 ¢	78 ¢	$ 1.56
Monthly gross profit per location	$ 3.12	$ 18.72	$ 37.44
Monthly gross profit - 10 locations	$ 31.20	$ 187.20	$ 374.40
Monthly gross profit - 100 locations	$ 312.00	$ 1,872.00	$ 3,744.00

Monthly donation to Charity Sponsor is about $1.00 to $2.00 per machine location (IF applicable).

See chapters titled "Location Targeting And Analysis" and "Getting Great Locations"

NOTE: This is provided for illustrative purposes only. It does not include machine cost, freight, sales tax, locating, or other miscellaneous costs not specifically listed, if any. Figures may vary according to type of business, geographical location, fluctuations in customer traffic, and many other factors which can not be predicted. Therefore, the actual results achieved may vary and can not be guaranteed.

I have found that a fun-size vendor will do about 50% to 100% more in gross sales than a bulk vendor (for the reasons stated above). In the chapter on bulk vending we based our projection on only 4 vends per day, which is very conservative. If we increase that projection by only 50% for a fun-size vendor, that would be only 6 vends per day.

I have also found that for well-managed routes using quality, attractive machines which offer at least 8 selections: That an AVERAGE (for all your locations) of 6 to 12 vends per day is quite achievable.

Based upon the above figures in locations with just 6 vends (only $ 1.50 in sales) per-day per-machine, each fun-size vendor could net you about $18.72 gross profit per month.

Compare To Bulk Vendors

Now, when comparing this to bulk vendors: You will note that only 4 vends per day netted you a gross profit of $17.28 per month for a bulk vendor. The reason the gross profit is about the same, in spite of the fact that the fun-size vendor will generally do at least 50% more in sales. . . is because the profit margin is less on those increased sales. Remember, both machines vend products at .25¢, but with bulk your cost per vend is only .07¢ compared with .10¢ to .12¢ for fun-size.

It would seem that, in spite of increased sales, your gross profit would be about the same as with a bulk vendor. But there are other considerations:

A fun-size vendor will cost a little more than a bulk vendor. The machine I usually recommend and sell holds more than most other fun-size vendors, about 250 items, and costs about $100.00 more than a bulk vendor (bulk vendor = about $175.00, fun-size = about $275.00). Since they cost more, it takes more time to earn your investment back. In this example, it would take about 7 to 15 months to earn your money back, compared with only 5 to 10 months for a bulk vendor.

Also, since the fun-size vendor we are talking about has a capacity of only about 250 vends compared to about 700 vends for a 3-selection bulk vendor. . . it's obvious that it needs servicing AT LEAST twice as often. At just 6 vends per day, the fun-size vendor would be completely empty in 41 days. As a practical matter, it would need to be serviced at least once every 2 to 4 weeks, compared with every 2 months for a bulk vendor. This LOWERS your INCOME PER HOUR compared to bulk vending.

Commission

Like bulk vending machines, obtaining locations for fun-size vendors is easier using the charity licensing approach (detailed in chapter titled "Getting Great Locations"). No commission is generally paid to the locations on fun-size vendors. The 10% to 15% commission you might offer a business establishment is not enough money for them to get enthused about, and that won't usually motivate them to let you install a machine.

What WILL motivate locations is the ATTRACTIVE CONVENIENCE of the snack machine for customers and employees. . . and/or HELPING OUT A WORTHWHILE CHARITY. Your monthly donation to the Charity Sponsor is usually approximately $1.00 to $2.00 per machine location.

Furthermore, I know operators with hundreds of machines that neither pay commission nor use the charity approach. If you offer quality, attractive, late model equipment many locations will accept it as a convenience to them with no compensation.

Locations for the fun-size vendor are readily available. Please see the chapter titled "Getting Great Locations" for details on this.

Profit Summary

Based upon the above, if you had 100 fun-size machines averaging from 6 to 12 vends per day, you could earn about $1,872.00 to $3,744.00 monthly gross profit. Assuming that you serviced them once every two weeks, taking 3 to 4 days per service, you would be working a total of up to 8 days (or 64 hours) per month.

This equals about $30.00 to $60.00 gross profit per hour. Compare to bulk vending, which is about $100.00 to $200.00 gross profit per hour (in the similar example).

Still, that's up to $1,872. to $3,744 monthly gross profit. . . $30.00 to $60.00 gross profit per hour. . . as a one-person business. . . working only about 4 days every OTHER week (OR about 2 days EACH week) servicing your machines!

Since a high quality fun-size vendor can be purchased for around $300.00, your gross return on investment could be about 80% to 160% per year. This means that you could recover your entire investment within 7 to 15 months!

Based upon the above illustration, after properly located. Of course you'll also have to plan on spending some time buying product, counting money (too bad), keeping simple records, etc. (this could run at least 15 minutes to 1 hour for every hour of actual route servicing time, depending upon various factors).

While this is not as profitable as bulk vending, the profit is still very, very good. . . and the machines are especially easy to locate.

Service Requirements

Since your time is valuable, service calls are expensive. You'll always want to minimize the need for service calls.

Many fun-size vendors on the market offer 8 selections or more, but a capacity of only about 100 vends.

The fun-size vendor I usually recommend and sell has a capacity of about 250 vends. At just 6 vends per day, this fun-size vendor would be completely empty in 41 days. . . at 12 vends per day it would be empty in about 20 days. You shouldn't let it get more than 75% empty, so as a practical matter, it

would need to be serviced at least once every 2 to 4 weeks depending upon how busy your location is.

Servicing amounts to simply loading the product into the machine. . . dumping the coin box into a bag. . . wiping off the machine. . . and making a couple of notes in your route record book (see chapter titled "Route Management").

Fun-size vending is a SIMPLE business. There's little question that you'll be able to handle these simple management requirements. And locating these machines is NOT difficult at all.

Suggested Fun-Size Start-Up Checklist:

✓ Purchase 5 or more fun-size snack vendors

✓ Video (loading instructions)

✓ At least 200 candy/nut items per machine (about $24.00)

✓ Set-up charity licensing agreement (if applicable)

✓ See chapter titled "Getting Started"

Product Inventory Requirements

If you can, start off with at least enough product to fill each machine. If your budget is tight, do not hesitate to fill the machines only about half full. This will not affect sales and, in fact, may even offer a psychological advantage (a machine that is

kept too full, too often, looks unused to regular customers and could actually decrease sales).

In my experience, the hottest products to offer in fun-size vendors are as follows:

The following products are listed in order of my preference (hottest seller listed first). See chapter titled "Products And Inventory".

Snickers™, M&M Peanut™, Doublemint™ gum, M&Ms™, Reeces Peanut Butter Cups™, Runts™, Hot Tamales™, Jelly Belly™ mixed flavor jelly beans (no other jelly bean brand). Kit Kat™, Hershey™ bar, Nestles Crunch™, Butterfinger™, Baby Ruth™, Boston Baked Beans™.

Of the above, only 4 are not available in fun-size packaging. You could just offer something else if you want (which many people do). . . but they just happen to be among the best sellers. . . and they also have the highest profit markup! These are Runts™, Hot Tamales™, Jelly Belly™, and Boston Baked Beans™.

The easiest way to deal with this is just to package them yourself in food grade poly bags, sealed with a heat sealer. It's really very quick and easy to do, and they vend just fine. (No, a 'Seal-A-Meal™' from your local Wal-Mart store will NOT work. . . don't waste your time trying).

To do this, you'll need a supply of poly bags and a commercial grade 8" heat sealer, which you can obtain from AR-BEE Transparent, below (call for a catalog):

AR-BEE Transparent
1450 Pratt Blvd.
P. O. Box 1107
Elk Grove Village, IL 60009
800-621-6101, 847-593-0400
MO-FR, 9:00am-5:00pm, CST

The 2" x 3" multipurpose poly bags work best, and cost only about a penny (.01¢) for 3 bags (in quantities of 1000).

An 8" heat sealer will cost around $100.00, and will do the job fine until you build up a large operation. When that happens, you can either purchase a high speed packing machine, or have a local packaging company do it for you (check your Yellow Pages, or check with local food suppliers for a referral).

Machine Set-up

There are 3 basic types of fun-size machines, and set-up is different for each:

The horizontal helix coil dispenser looks like a coil spring, and the products are simply placed between each coil. When the coil rotates, the last product drops off the end. This is the fastest and easiest to load, but usually does not have a very large capacity.

The 'flip-down' shelf holds each product vertically and dispenses it by dropping the shelf (and product). It is loaded by placing each product on an individual shelf This is almost as fast and easy to load as the helix coil, but also does not usually hold very much.

The vertical stacking dispenser simply stacks all products vertically, and has a little 'pusher' arm that knocks the bottom item off the stack. It is loaded by stacking the products up in a column, one at a time from the top. This is a little slower to load than the other two types, but the capacity is much larger.

All of the above are okay if quality made. I prefer the vertical stacker only because it generally holds much more than the others, and capacity is so important in order to reduce the number of location service calls.

The only drawback to the vertical stacking dispenser is that they can be a little tricky to load at first. Each column must be adjusted to fit the product being vended. But once you know what you're doing it's no problem.

If you buy a machine with a vertical stacking dispenser, I recommend that you obtain a 'loading instruction video' if available. It will save you a lot of time and frustration.

Summary

At a conservative average of just 6 to 12 vends per day, 100 fun-size vendors could earn you up to $1,872.00 to $3,744.00 monthly gross profit.

Assuming that you serviced them once every two weeks, taking 3 to 4 days per service, you would be working a total of up to 8 days (or 64 hours) per month. This equals about $30.00 to $60.00 gross profit per hour.

 7 to 15 month pay-back on your initial investment!

● 80% to 160% gross return on investment per year!

● $30.00 to $60.00 gross profit per hour!

● Service every 2 to 3 weeks!

● Especially easy to locate!

Based upon the above illustration, after properly located. Of course you'll also have to plan on spending some time buying

product, counting money (too bad), keeping simple records, etc. (this could run at least 15 minutes to 1 hour for every hour of actual route servicing time, depending upon various factors).

Fun-size snack vending represents one of the best new opportunities I have seen in recent years. While not AS profitable as some other types of vending, the profit is good. . . plus locations are plentiful and acceptance is high.

For machine sources, costs, and ordering information, please refer to the Appendix.

Also see the last page of this book for FREE resources (reports, videos, etc.) including the "HOTTEST Vending Money-Makers" report!

Chapter 8
Packaged Snack And Cold Drink Vending

Coin-operated packaged snack and cold drink vending is also a VERY highly profitable area of vending. Since the machines are coin-operated there is much greater security than with honor snack trays (which is the ONLY option for the smaller locations). They are more work to service than 'fun-size' vendors, and much more work and responsibility than bulk-vending. . . but the profits make it worth it for many people!

There is a TREMENDOUS opportunity awaiting you in business locations with 20 to 100 employees (or similar customer traffic). Most large operators have such high overhead that they need locations with at least 100 to 150 employees to make the kind of profit they want. These locations are usually overlooked by the large operators so there is MUCH LESS competition for them. . . yet incredible profit potential as illustrated below! Please see the chapters titled "Location Targeting And Analysis" and "Getting Great Locations".

Definition

These are the vending machines that you are probably most familiar with. They vend packaged snacks and canned cold drinks, and come in a variety of sizes and styles.

Market Saturation?

It does 'seem' like these machines are everywhere. . . and of course, they really are! But don't let that discourage you. This is a not a new vending concept. It is 'time proven', and is VERY profitable (as is bulk vending). As I have said, there IS a lot of competition for the LARGE locations. . . and yet (in spite of that) many of my clients who started small are very successful with these large locations. Nevertheless, the best way to get started is with the smaller locations.

Locations in the 20 to 100 employee size range are plentiful. The competition that exists is sparse and (for the most part) not very professional. While most (not all) of these locations will ALREADY have vending machines, you will be amazed how many of them will tell you they are "not happy" with their vendor and are ready to do business with you TODAY!

Biggest complaints:

● Old, unattractive and/or poorly functioning machines.

● Inadequate product selection.

● Stale or out of date products in machine.

● Poor service.

● No coin changer. No dollar bill acceptor.

● Don't have room for large machines.

If you keep the above in mind. . . build your new route with quality equipment and offer good service. . . there is no reason why you should not be VERY successful!

COMBO Snack And Drink Profits

This is a typical example of the profits you could experience with a COMBO snack AND drink vendor (a single machine) or 2 separate vendors (1 snack and 1 drink).

It is a summary of (and is based upon) the 2 detailed profit illustrations shown later in this chapter. The 'bottom-line' figures from those 2 illustrations have simply been noted below and added together to quickly summarize for you what you could make if you vend BOTH product lines in each or your locations.

These illustrations are based upon only 20 employees with NO outside customer traffic, EACH employee buying an average of just .75 snacks per day, .20 pastries per day, 1 soda per day, and .25 juice per day (some won't buy any, and some will buy 2 or more)

See the chapter titled "Location Targeting And Analysis" for survey results indicating the daily averages.

Here's how many $ $ $ you could be making with combo vendors!

Based Upon: 20 employees, no outside customer traffic
Service Requirements: Generally once a week depending upon location and machine capacity. Servicing time about 20 to 30 minutes per location.

Description		Weekly Volume		Gross Profit		Weekly Gross Profit			Monthly Gross Profit
Products: Snacks		75	X	.25¢	=	$ 18.75	X 4	=	$ 75.00
Products: Pastries		20	X	.32¢	=	$ 6.40	X 4	=	$ 25.60
Products: Sodas		100	X	.24¢	=	$ 24.00	X 4	=	$ 96.00
Products: Juices		25	X	.34¢	=	$ 8.50	X 4	=	$ 34.00
						Total Monthly Gross Profit		$	230.60

See chapters titled "Location Targeting And Analysis" and "Getting Great Locations"

NOTE: This is provided for illustrative purposes only. It does not include machine cost, freight, sales tax, locating, or other miscellaneous costs not specifically listed, if any. Figures may vary according to type of business, geographical location, fluctuations in customer traffic, and many other factors which can not be predicted. Therefore, the actual results achieved may vary and can not be guaranteed.

This is for just 1 location! Imagine the monthly gross profit you could enjoy with 10 to 100 locations!

Unlike other types of vending and amusement, you will find that you can predict approximately how well one of your snack or drink vendors will do if you know either (1) the number of employees in a location, or; (2) the customer traffic flow. This is covered in more detail in the chapters titled "Location Targeting And Analysis" and "Getting Great Locations".

Vending sales (per person) can be dramatically affected by:

● Inadequate product selection. At least 15 to 20 snack/pastry products, and at least 5 cold drink/juice products are best.

● Availability of nearby fast food restaurants and convenience stores.

● Lack of a coin changer and dollar bill acceptor: See chapter titled "Coin Mechanisms And Bill Acceptors".

Some of these factors are beyond your control. . . but do what you can about the others!

Commission

No commission is generally paid to the locations on packaged snack machines unless they have a high number of employees or customer traffic. Small business establishments (up to 20 or so employees) are just happy to have someone offer quality vending services to their people and usually do not expect a commission. Besides, the 10% commission you might pay them on a small volume vending operation is not enough money to motivate them. Convenience is their first priority.

In locations with a high number of employees or customer traffic, the volume of sales may warrant paying a commission and you will not mind doing so because your profits will be high. You'll have to decide what (if any) commission should be paid on a case by case basis. Customarily, commission runs between 5% to 15% (typically averaging about 10%) and is negotiable.

In locations where commissions are expected, there are 2 options:

Pay the commission: Usually the company won't be interested in the money for themselves, but will use if for employee parties, or some other employee benefit.

Offer a discount: If you would have paid them 10% commission, instead offer to discount the prices of items sold in the vendors by 10%.

You will find that many (even most) companies will prefer that you simply lower the prices in the machine. This makes your life easier, and route servicing faster, since you won't have to bother taking the time to pay and account for the commission. Try it. . . it works!

Profit Summary

If you refer to the "Wholesale Factory-Direct Price List" in the Appendix, you will see that you can purchase vendors to handle a location like this (20 employees) for around $2,000.00. And of course, you COULD put them in locations with 30 to 50 employees (or more).

Based upon the above example, if you started out with only one location, with 20 to 40 employees, you could earn about $230.00 to $460.00 total monthly gross profit!

A 4 to 12 month pay-back, or 100% to 300% gross return on investment, is quite achievable!

You would only be working about 20 to 30 minutes per week, or 1-1/2 to 2 hours per month servicing your location. This equals about $100.00 to $300.00 gross profit per hour!

Multiply that out x 10, 50, or 100 locations and the profits really start to get exciting!

Based upon the above illustration, after properly located. Of course you'll also have to plan on spending some time buying product, counting money (too bad), keeping simple records, etc. (this could run at least 15 minutes to 1 hour for every hour of actual route servicing time, depending upon various factors).

Snack Profit Potential

This illustration was summarized earlier in this chapter, in the section titled "COMBO Snack And Drink Profits".

This is a typical example of the profits you could experience with a packaged snack vendor. It is based upon only 20 employees with NO outside customer traffic, EACH employee buying an average of just .75 snacks per day, and .20 pastries per day (some won't buy any, and some will buy 2 or more).

See the chapter titled "Location Targeting And Analysis" for survey results indicating the daily averages.

Here's how many $ $ $ you could be making with packaged snack vendors!

Based Upon: 20 employees, no outside customer traffic
Service Requirements: Generally once a week depending upon location and machine capacity. Servicing time about 15 to 20 minutes per location.

Description	Weekly Volume	Gross Profit	Weekly Gross Profit	Monthly Gross Profit

Products: Snacks (cookies, candy, bagged snacks, etc.).
Sale Price: .55¢ average (.40¢ to .65¢ typical)
Cost: .24¢ average (.15¢ to .30¢ typical)
Gross Profit: .25¢ average (.55¢ sale - .06¢ commission, and - .24¢ average cost)
Weekly Volume: 75 sales (20 employees X .75 snacks per day each (average) X 5 days per week)

75	X .25¢ =	$ 18.75	X 4 =	$ 75.00

Products: Pastries (sweet rolls, brownies, pie, etc.)
Sale Price: .70¢ average (.60¢ to .75¢ typical)
Cost: .31¢ average (.25¢ to .40¢ typical)
Gross Profit: .32¢ average (.70¢ sale - .07¢ commission, and - .31¢ average cost)
Weekly Volume: 20 sales (20 employees X .20 pastries per day each (average) X 5 days per week)

20	X .32¢ =	$ 6.40	X 4 =	$ 25.60

Total Monthly
Gross Profit $ 100.60

See chapters titled "Location Targeting And Analysis" and "Getting Great Locations"

NOTE: This is provided for illustrative purposes only. It does not include machine cost, freight, sales tax, locating, or other miscellaneous costs not specifically listed, if any. Figures may vary according to type of business, geographical location, fluctuations in customer traffic, and many other factors which can not be predicted. Therefore, the actual results achieved may vary and can not be guaranteed.

Cold Drink Vending

Cold drink vending is much more competitive than many other types of vending. Coke™ and Pepsi™ bottlers, in particular, make very attractive offers to even the small business locations to provide them with equipment and product. They'll even service the equipment. So, is there an opportunity in cold drink vending? There sure is!

In all locations people want product variety. Pepsi™ will only allow their products in their machines. Coke™ and others are the same. Since space is usually a consideration. . . businesses are interested in a single machine that can offer all the products they like. You can provide this and compete well with the giants. . . particularly in small to medium sized locations.

Also, fruit juice based products are fast becoming a significant and growing segment of the cold drink vending market. While sales are still way behind Coke and Pepsi products. . . they do sell very well. Soda sales are usually slower in the mornings, but fruit juice based drinks sell great in the morning and all day long . . another opportunity for you.

I do not suggest a machine dedicated solely to juice, unless it is in a VERY high traffic location, because the percentage of sales compared to Coke™ and Pepsi™ will be much smaller. However, some operators are very successful by specializing in juice sales in just such locations! See the chapter titled "Location Targeting And Analysis" for juice sales information.

One of the few drawbacks I've found to the cold drink vending business is the mere bulk and weight of the product. You will need a dolly and a small van, truck, or trailer (or at least a station wagon or mini-van) to haul around the cases of drink cans.

You can do very well in cold drink vending if you seek out the right type of locations, offer a flexible and complete product selection, offer juice, and provide top notch service.

Here's what you may expect to earn in a typical small business establishment:

Cold Cash Expectations

This illustration was summarized earlier in this chapter, in the section titled "COMBO Snack And Drink Profits".

This is a typical example of the profits you could experience with a cold drink vendor. It is based upon only 20 employees with NO outside customer traffic, EACH employee buying an average of just 1 soda per day, and .25 juice per day (some won't buy any, and some will buy 2 or more).

See the chapter titled "Location Targeting And Analysis" for survey results indicating the daily averages.

Here's how many $ $ $ you could be making with cold drink vendors!

Based Upon: 20 employees, no outside customer traffic
Service Requirements: Generally once a week depending upon location and machine capacity. Servicing time approximately 15 to 20 minutes per location.

Description	Weekly Volume	Gross Profit	Weekly Gross Profit	Monthly Gross Profit

Products: Sodas (12-oz. can cold drinks)
Sale Price: .55¢ average (.50¢ to .65¢ typical)
Cost: .25¢ average (.15¢ to .30¢ typical)
Gross Profit: .24¢ average (.55¢ sale - .06¢ commission, and - .25¢ average cost)
Weekly Volume: 100 sales (20 employees X 1. soda per day each (average) X 5 days per week)

	100	X	.24¢	=	$ 24.00	X 4	=	$ 96.00

Products: Juices (12-oz. can)
Sale Price: .75¢ average (.70¢ to .80¢ typical)
Cost: .33¢ average (.25¢ to .38¢ typical)
Gross Profit: .34¢ (.75¢ sale - .08¢ commission, and - .33¢ average cost)
Weekly Volume: 25 sales (20 employees X .25 juice per day each (average) X 5 days per week)

	25	X	.34¢	=	$ 8.50	X 4	=	$ 34.00

Total Monthly
Gross Profit $ 130.00

See chapters titled "Location Targeting And Analysis" and "Getting Great Locations"

NOTE: This is provided for illustrative purposes only. It does not include machine cost, freight, sales tax, locating, or other miscellaneous costs not specifically listed, if any. Figures may vary according to type of business, geographical location, fluctuations in customer traffic, and many other factors which can not be predicted. Therefore, the actual results achieved may vary and can not be guaranteed.

Service Requirements

If you operate bulk vendors, fun-size vendors, or amusement machines, you will find that you can be very flexible as to when you service your machines. In fact, if a machine was empty, dirty, or not working, it is unlikely that you would receive a call from the location. They just don't depend on them, and if they notice all all, they won't care enough to call you. Not so with snack and drink vendors!

If it's morning break-time and your vendor is out of pastries, you may well receive a phone call asking how soon you can get over to fill the machine. People tend to rely on these vendors more than others, so you can't let them down. If they can't count on their snacks and drinks being available when they want them, they'll make other plans rather than run the risk of doing without. . . and you'll lose a lot of business. And if it happens too often, they may even be looking for another route operator. Service is very important in this business.

Servicing amounts to simply loading the product into the machine. . . dumping the coin box into a bag. . . removing the currency from the bill stacker (if applicable), wiping off the machine. . . and making a couple of notes in your route record book. See chapter titled "Route Management".

It takes close to the SAME amount of TIME to service ANY location. While it's true that some machines may take more or less time to load (due to size and capacity), the bulk of your time will be spent handling duties that have similar time requirements.

> For virtually every type of machine, you will spend about the same amount of time driving to and from, wiping off the equipment, bagging and counting the money, and keeping records. This is the biggest reason why the large operators want locations with 100 to 150 employees or very high traffic. Their overhead is high, and it costs them just as much to service the smaller locations. As a small, low overhead business, you have an advantage that makes it very profitable to service these locations, but I want to make sure that you are clear on this point anyway, because it will affect your business. For example:

When you look at how much you can make snack vending. . . and then look at how much you can make vending cold drinks. . . and you consider the time and expense of servicing your locations. . . you will want to offer BOTH snacks and cold drinks in all your locations whenever possible. Many of my clients will turn down locations if they can't handle both product lines.

This is important to you, but usually doesn't matter too much to a location. Often, you may find a location that already has a cold drink machine that was supplied by their local Pepsi™ or Coke™ distributor, and they (think they) only want a snack machine. If you offer a first class snack vendor, but ONLY if you can have the drink business. . . they will very often say okay. They can have the other vendor picked up with a quick phone call.

> There are other ways to sell this to them as well. For example, Coke™ and Pepsi™ will only put their own products in their machine, but you can offer your locations both Coke™ and Pepsi™ products if they do business with you. Overall, this will make sense to most locations and you'll get the snack AND drink business if you'll just ask for it.

Service Schedule

I suggest you plan on servicing your SNACK vendors on a weekly basis:

> Since your time is valuable, service calls are expensive. . . MORE than once a week is expensive and unnecessary. Also, some locations consider it disruptive and will complain if you come in more often than once a week.

> You might be able to 'get by' servicing some locations once every two weeks if your machines have enough product capacity, but there is a potential problem with this. Some of the best selling items (like pastry) is perishable and has a short shelf life. You can't load up for 2 weeks in advance or you'll have stale items in your vendor (and you'll be hearing complaints).

> If you feel a location doesn't warrant a weekly service call, you could try every

other week, and leave out the perishable items. . . but it'll cost you. I'd either service the location right, or upgrade to a better location.

Weekly servicing just makes sense for snack vendors.

COLD DRINK vendors are another story. Since drinks are not perishable you can work out a service schedule relative to the product capacity of the vendor (but not more often than weekly). Obviously, if you have a cold drink vendor in the same location as a snack vendor and you're there anyway, you may as well service both machines at the same time.

Machine Capacity

Make sure your vendors have the product capacity to provide for your anticipated service schedule. If you expect to sell 100 items between servicing, and your vendor holds 100 items, you've got a problem. You can't let it get too close to being empty, or your selection will suffer (and the complaints will roll in).

You should plan your servicing around you machines being no more than 75% empty (25% full).

Suggested Snack And Drink Start-Up Checklist:

✓ Purchase 2 or more COMBO snack and drink vendors

✓ Purchase at least enough product to fill each machine once

✓ See chapter titled "Getting Started"

Product Inventory Requirements

If you can, start off with at least enough product to fill each machine. If your budget is tight, do not hesitate to fill the machines only about half full. This will not affect sales and, in fact, may even offer a psychological advantage (a machine that is kept too full, too often, looks unused to regular customers and could actually decrease sales). Suggested products are listed in the chapter titled "Products And Inventory".

Machine Set-up

Most all snack and drink vendors come fully assembled. Some may require some very minor assembly, such as installing shelves or product helix coils.

Helix coils look like a stretched out spring. Although there are some other dispensing systems on the market that are used for snack vendors, helix coils are by far the most common, and the best system. The items to be vended are placed in the horizontal coil, and when the coil rotates, the end product simply drops off the front of the shelf (and the next product moves into the end position).

Cold canned drink vendors typically employ one of two types of dispensing systems. A simple vertical column stacking system. . . or a serpentine system.

In the serpentine system, the cans are stacked in a 'S' shaped pattern. . . zig-zaging back and forth. . . like a serpent, or snake. Both systems are fine, and easy to load. Generally, neither require any assembly.

In some machines you may have to affix price labels, usually on the coin mech or the product shelf. Price stickers typically come with the machine and can be reordered from the manufacturer. You can also obtain price stickers, and a multitude of other vending and amusement parts and accessories from WICO. A catalog is available upon request:

WICO Corporation
6400 West Gross Point Road
Niles, IL 60714
1-800-FOR-WICO (800-367-9426)
847-647-7500
MO-FR, 7:30am-5:00pm, CST

All cold canned drink vendors require product labels that are placed under the selection buttons, or in a display area on the vendor. These are the color labels that display the product logo for items like Pepsi™, Diet Pepsi™, etc. They often come with the vendor, but if they do not, you can pick them up from your local bottler (or phone them and they'll usually mail them to you) at no charge. See the chapter titled "Products And Inventory".

Machines with adjustable price mechanical coin-mechs come pre-set at the most common settings. In some cases you may need to reset them to a different price, however, this is a very quick and easy process.

With electronic machines you will have to program the price for each item, which is also very quick and easy.

There are too many different type of machines to go into much more detail on this subject. Suffice it to say that machine set-up is a relatively quick and easy task. All machines will come with an owners manual which will clearly explain that machines set-up, operation, and maintenance requirements.

Machine Recommendations

For my own vending routes, my requirements (and recommendations) are as follows:

● Packaged snack vendor must offer at least 15 selections.

● Cold drink vendor must offer at least 5 selections.

● Must have a coin changer.

● Prefer a DBA (DOLLAR bill acceptor) or at least the ability to add-it-on later. . . but in small locations may do without.

● Use SLAVE machines whenever possible to save money. See chapter titled "Coin Mechanisms And Bill Acceptors" under section heading "Slave Machines".

● Product capacity large enough so that service calls ar not required more often than once per week.

None of this, of course, would apply to bulk vendors or 'fun-size' vendors.

YOU may be willing to consider servicing your machines more than once a week in order to save money buying smaller machines. . . but keep in mind that SOME locations won't want you disrupting their business more than once per week, and MAY consider it an inconvenience. Besides, service calls cost money. You'll do better planning on once weekly service calls.

Some route operators will install 2 smaller snack/drink combo vendors in 2 different spots within a location. . . rather than install 1 larger combo vendor. This costs more for equipment, but sometimes makes sense if there is more than 1 logical spot for vendors within a location. More convenience and better availability = higher sales.

In my machine distributorship, FREEDOM TECH, I do sell the mechanical 'exact change' snack and drink machines. . . I even sell machines with less than my recommended number of selections. . . even though I personally really do not recommend them. This is because they do have a place, and a lot of people want them. If my reorder rate is any indication, however, most people learn (at some point) that the machines with coin changers, BAs (bill acceptors) and more product selection and capacity are better 'long-term' investment options.

They're just a better investment in the future, and they really don't cost all that much more (see the "Wholesale Factory-Direct Price List" in the Appendix). Besides, it's easier to GET, and KEEP locations when you can offer 'first class' machines with coin changers and BA's. If you have 'second class' machines and a competitor comes around offering 'first class' machines. . . there is a very high probability that you are going to lose your location, even if you've been doing a good job in every other way.

> See chapter titled "Coin Mechanisms And Bill Acceptors" for very IMPORTANT information regarding machine selection.

You'll just have to make up your own mind on these issues. No matter what you decide to try, you can't go wrong if you start small. Once you're 'at it' for awhile, you will develop strong opinions as to what's best for you.

If you're starting with small MECHANICAL coin-operated counter-top snack vendors and mini drink vendors, I suggest a minimum of 10 employees (not for use with outside customer traffic). With the larger MECHANICAL coin-operated floor model vendors I suggest a minimum of 15 to 20 employees (not for use with outside customer traffic). If you're getting into the ELECTRONIC floor machines with coin changers and optional dollar bill acceptors, you'll need a minimum of 20 employees (or outside customer traffic to make up for less employees) to make a good profit (see chapter titled "Location Targeting And Analysis").

Regardless of the brand of snack or drink vendors, QUALITY machines will typically use the same major components. For example; there are only a few major companies that manufacturer coin changers and bill acceptors (such as Coinco and Mars). These major manufacturers all produce high quality components.

If your vendors are mechanical, there is little to wear out, and it is not unusual to go 10 to 20 years without a single repair.

With electric or electronic vendors, there is more complexity, and a higher possibility of repairs, however, they are typically very reliable. Most repairs you can do yourself very economically. If the problem is not obvious, usually a call to the manufacturers customer service department will result in a quick diagnosis. And the repair will usually amount to replacement of a relatively low cost component, such as a coil motor (these motors have a typical life of about 10,000 vends per motor, so you won't have to replace them very often).

See the chapters titled "Coin Mechanisms And Bill Acceptors" and "Route Management" for more information on maintenance and repairs.

Summary

Based upon the above illustration, using conservative survey figures, an average location with just 20 employees could bring in $230.00 in monthly gross profit, vending snacks, pastries, sodas, and juice. If you specialize in locations serving from 20 to 100 employees, and your average location has at least 20 to 40 employees, you could expect up to $230.00 to $460.00 monthly gross profit per location.

When you have 10 such locations established, you could be earning $2,300.00 to $4,600.00 per month, working only about 3 to 4 hours per week! This equals about $100.00 to $300.00 gross profit per hour!

● 4 to 12 month pay-back on your initial investment!

● 100% to 300% gross return on investment per year!

● $100.00 to $300.00 gross profit per hour!

● Service once each week!

● GREAT opportunity exists in locations serving 20 to 100 employees!

Based upon the above illustration, after properly located. Of course you'll also have to plan on spending some time buying product, counting money (too bad), keeping simple records, etc. (this could run at least 15 minutes to 1 hour for every hour of actual route servicing time, depending upon various factors).

Combo snack and drink vending is a very profitable and proven winner! The small to medium sized location market is a great opportunity for someone new to the business who does not mind the increased responsibility (compared to other types of vending and amusement machines) that goes along with this type of vending operation.

For machine sources, costs, and ordering information, please refer to the Appendix.

Also see the last page of this book for FREE resources (reports, videos, etc.) including the "HOTTEST Vending Money-Makers" report!

Notes

Chapter 9
Products And Inventory

Naturally you want to offer only the hottest, best-selling products so you can make as much money as possible with your vendors. This is a subject worthy of careful study. . . and it's also a lot of fun to watch your sales jump when you've made a new product 'discovery'. Luckily, there's not a lot of guess work involved in picking the winners.

There are studies, surveys, and statistics regarding what products sell the best. They typically indicate such information as:

> **The Product Ranking:** #1, #2, #3, etc. best-selling chocolate candies, non-chocolate candies, snacks, drinks, etc.

> **The Market Share:** The percentage of the total market that a particular product makes up.

For example: Snickers™ (made by M&M Mars) is the #1 best selling chocolate candy, with about 16% of the market share. M&M Peanuts™ is a close second with about 15% of the market. M&M Plain™ is 3rd with about 7% of the market. Items #4 through 10 are all close, with about 3% to 5% of the market.

> These top 10 products represent about 65% of the entire chocolate candy market!

Once you know this, you certainly understand how important it is to offer these top 3 chocolate products at all times, and as many of the other 7 as space in your machine allows.

These statistics are very interesting, and important, but an in-depth discussion of them is beyond the scope of this book. The exact figures change too often and would be difficult to keep up with. Beside, the EXACT figures are not important.

My "Vending Product List" which follows takes these statistics into account, together with plain old experience with what sells best in what type of machine. While it is not all-inclusive nor perfect. . . it WILL help you get started on the right track.

As you get a little experience in this business, you'll understand more about how I developed this list. . . and you'll develop your own.

Also, when you subscribe to the trade publications I recommend, you will be kept up to date on the statistics mentioned above. See chapter titled "Trade Publications, Organizations, And Shows".

Trust me! Just use my list for now.

Markup. . .
What Should You Charge?

In general, charge whatever the market will bare. Simply look at other vending machines. . . note what they offer. . . and the sale price. . . and COPY THEM.

> You can also get average price information from the "Census Of The Industry", or the "State Of The Industry" (but simply checking local machines works just fine). See chapter titled "Trade Publications, Organizations, And Shows".

For bulk and fun-size vendors, refer to those chapters for information on standard markups. The markup on these items is higher than for most other vended items.

For snacks, pastries, sodas, juice, and most other non or low perishable items, I have a formula that works pretty well in practically every market:

> Multiply your product cost X 2. Then add 10% to that for commission (whether you're actually paying it or not). That's your sales price.

Fast-Selling
Name Brand Products!

You'll make more money by offering only fast-selling name brand products. You may lower your product cost a little by selling off-brand products, but I don't recommend it. Brand names enjoy higher customer recognition and often taste better. They usually sell much better. High sales volume is much more important than a little higher profit margin.

You can purchase off-brand products cheaper, and have a larger profit margin. However, you'll find that your sales volume will usually be less than with name brands.

There are exceptions to this rule so experiment a little Even with the name brand products you'll want to experiment with different products from time to time.

What To Offer. . .

Most of the BEST-SELLING items are listed on my "Vending Product List" below. I suggest you choose your initial inventory from this list.

Keep in mind that hot-selling items come and go all the time, so it's hard to make a list like this and keep it current. Also, some locations prefer certain items, and not others, in seemingly total disregard for what national best-sellers are SUPPOSED to be!

As a practical matter, you just have to pay attention to your local market, ask your customers, and test new items.

Ask your customers what they'd like in the machine (or post a product 'Want List' on the machine). Even though you're stocking your machine with quality, name brand products, you will sell more if you 'custom pack' the machine according to the individual likes and dislikes of each location.

Also, notice what other route operators put in their machines. And check with your product suppliers for suggestions (See "Securing Suppliers" below).

Another 'gauge' of what sells is simply to notice what's on the shelf at the discount retail stores. Space is at a premium there. . . they only stock what sells well. If they've devoted a lot of space to a product you're not offering in your machines, it's PROBABLY selling well. . . and something you MAY want to try out (but not always).

Health-Oriented Products

Some locations are interested in health-oriented snacks and drinks. . . particularly medical centers, health clubs, etc. While, most people have good intentions about eating healthy, the truth is that the health-oriented items really do not sell very well in most all locations. For example:

I obtained a great snack and drink machine location from a very large medical clinic not long ago. The board of doctors that ran the clinic insisted that if they were going to have a snack machine in the building, it should sell healthy items. I knew they wouldn't sell, but to get the location I agreed to offer about 50% relatively healthy items with the understanding that if they did not sell, I would switch to something that did.

In less than a month it was obvious that the candy, bagged snacks, and pastry is what they were buying. . . and remember, these were doctors, nurses, and other medical personnel (who, of all people, you'd think would eat healthy). Needless to say, they finally agreed to offer what was selling and we removed most of the health-oriented items.

I've found that it often helps to offer 20% to 30% health-oriented items IN ORDER TO GET A LOCATION. But in most locations it will not sell as well as the other items. That may be changing slightly. Regardless. . . if it helps to get the location, offer some health-oriented items. If it sells, leave it in. If not, take it out.

Start out with my list, pay attention to your local market, ask your customers, and test. . . test. . . test!

Vending Product List

** = All around top sellers. * = Excellent choices. Others are good choices depending upon the location.

You may notice some listings below that seem like contradictions. They are not. For example:

Planters Salted Peanuts™ is the #1 best selling nut item, with about 23% of the market. Smokehouse Almonds™ is #2 with about 15% of the market.

There are several other nut products that are a close #3, including pistachio nuts.

When you look at the "Nut" category, below (NOT in the bulk vend or 'fun-size' category) you will see that I have given salted peanuts and Smokehouse Almonds™ a ** (2 star) rating, and pistachio nuts a * (1 star) rating, which corresponds with the product ranking and market share data mentioned above.

Now, when you look at the "Bulk Vending Items" category, below, under "Nuts". . . you'll see that pistachio nuts have been upgraded to a ** (2 star) rating, while salted peanuts and Smokehouse Almonds™ have been dropped to a * (1 star) rating. This is not a mistake. I've made allowances for the type of machines involved.

In bulk vendors, the shelf life of UNSHELLED and/or UNPACKAGED OIL roasted nuts is at least 30 days. Even though salted peanuts sell better than pistachio nuts, pistachio nuts are a little more attractive to vend in this situation since they have a longer shelf life (because no oil, and in the shell).

Also, peanuts are more maintenance to bulk vend since they are oil roasted, not packaged, and the oil needs to be cleaned off the inside of the canister with each service call (dry roasted peanuts aren't as messy, but don't sell as well). Similarly, Smokehouse Almonds™ leave a powder residue from their flavored coating.

Brand names are mentioned where important, and generic descriptions where unimportant, in my experience. For example: Jelly Belly™ brand jelly beans out sell all others by far, so I've specified Jelly Belly™, since brand name does matter in THIS case. On the other hand, I have found that most any QUALITY brand of salted peanut will sell about as well, so I haven't specified Planters™ necessarily, even though it IS the best selling brand of salted peanuts.

Bulk-Vending Items

* Boston Baked Beans™
  Gum
**   Chicle Tabs™ (1/2")
*   Gum balls
** Hot Tamales™
* Jelly Belly™ jelly beans
      (mixed flavors)
** M & M Peanut™
** M & M Plain™
  Nuts
*   Almonds (Smokehouse™)
      Cashews
*   Mixed nuts
      Peanuts (dry roasted)
*   Peanuts (salted)
**   Pistachio nuts
  Popped Wheat (salted)
      Nuts 'n' Stuff
      Onion & Garlic
*   Plain
      Sun Wheat
* Reeses Pieces™
** Runts™
* Skittles™ (similar to Runts™)
  Wheat Nuts™

'Fun-Size' Items

** Almond Joy™
  Baby Ruth™
  Bar None™

* Boston Baked Beans™
** Butterfinger™
  Caramello™
  Clark Bar™
* Corn Nuts™
  Dole Raisins™
  Gum (Wrigley™)
**   Doublemint™
*   Juicy Fruit™
*   Spearmint
      Sugarless
** Hershey™
** Hot Tamales™
* Jelly Belly™ jelly beans
      (mixed flavors)
* Junior Mints™
** Kit-Kat™
  Lemon Head™
* Lifesavors™ 5 flavors
** Lifesavors Beachnut Roll™
* Lifesavors™ (original)
** M & M Peanut™
** M & M Plain™
** Mars Bar™
  Mike & Ike™
** Milky Way™
  Mounds™
** Nestle Crunch™
  Nuts
*   Almonds (Smokehouse™)
      Beer Nuts™
      Cashews
      Cornnuts™

*   Mixed nuts
      Peanuts (dry roasted)
**   Peanuts (salted)
*   Pistachio nuts
** Pay Day™
  Red Hots™
** Reeses Peanut B. Cups™
* Reeses Pieces™
** Runts™
* Skittles™ (similar to Runts™)
** Snickers™
** Three Musketeers™
* Tic-Tacs™ (mints)
  Whatchamacallit™

Candy

** Almond Joy™
  Baby Ruth™
  Bar None™
* Boston Baked Beans™
** Butterfinger™
  Caramello™
  Clark Bar™
* Corn Nuts™
** Hershey™
** Hot Tamales™
* Jelly Belly™ jelly beans
      (mixed flavors)
* Junior Mints™
** Kit-Kat™
  Lemon Head™
* Lifesavors™ 5 flavors

** Lifesavors Beachnut Roll™
* Lifesavors™ (original)
** M & M Peanut™
** M & M Plain™
** Mars Bar™
Mike & Ike™
** Milky Way™
Mounds™
** Nestle Crunch™
** Pay Day™
Red Hots™
** Reeses Peanut B. Cups™
* Reeses Pieces™
Rolos™
** Runts™
Salted Nut Roll™
* Skittles™ (similar to Runts™)
** Snickers™
** Starburst™
** Three Musketeers™
Twix™
Whatchamacallit™

Cookies, Etc.

** Brownies (Plantation™)
F.L.™ Grandma's Cookies™
* Apple & Spice
** Chocolate Chip
** Choc./Choc
Oatmeal
* Peanut Butter
Raisin
Grandma's Cookies™ by:
Frito-Lay™
Nabisco™ Cookies
* Fig Newtons
** Lorna Doone
** Oreo's
* Vanilla creme
Quaker Oats™ Granola Bars
** Choc. Chip
Oats & Honey
PB/Choc. Chip
* Raisin/Cinnamon

Pastry

Dolly Madison™ - Hostess™
** Butter Pecan
* Cinnamon Rolls
Coffee Cake
Cup Cakes
Ding Dongs™
* Donuts
* Honeybuns

** Pies (fruit & pudding)
Zingers™
Little Debbie™
Banana Slices
Fudge Round
Oatmeal Cake
Peanut Crunch
Pecan Pie
Raisin Cake

Gum

Wrigley™
** Doublemint™
* Juicy Fruit™
* Spearmint
Sugarless

Crackers

** Cheese & Peanut Butter
** Cheese Crackers
** Cheese On Cheese
Rye Cheese Sandwich
* Toast & Peanut Butter
** Wheat Wafer
Above products made by:
Austin™
Frito-Lay™
Keebler™
Nabisco™
Sunshine™

Nuts

** Almonds (Smokehouse™)
* Beer Nuts™
Cashews
* Cornnuts™
* Mixed nuts
Peanuts (dry roasted)
** Peanuts (salted)
* Pistachio nuts

Snacks & Misc.

* Certs Mints™
Dole™ Raisins
Frito-Lay™
* B B Q Chips
** Cheetos™
** Corn Chips
** Doritos™
Funyion™
Munchos™
** Nacho Doritos™

Pork Skins
** Potato Chips
** Pretzels
Ruffles™
Tostitos™
Similar products made by:
Barrel-O-Fun™
Snyders™
* Popcorn
* Tic-Tacs™ (mints)

Cold Canned Drinks

Coke™ Products:
Cherry Coke™
Diet Cherry
** Classic Coke™
Caffeine Free
Diet
** Diet Caffeine Free
* Dr. Pepper™
* Diet Dr. Pepper™
Mellow Yellow™
* Sprite™
* Diet Sprite™
* Welches™ Grape
Juices
** Apple
* Apple, Orange, Pine.
Cran-Apple
* Grape
* Lemonade
** Orange
V-8™
Made by
Bluebird™
Campbell's™
Coke™
Hansens's™
Juice Bowl™
Ocean Spray™
Pepsi™
Tree Sweet™
Veryfine™
Pepsi™ Products
* Mountain Dew™
** Pepsi™
Pepsi Free™
Diet Pepsi™
** Diet Pepsi Free™
* Seven Up™
* Diet Seven Up™
* Slice™
* Orange Slice™
* Tea (Nestea™, Lipton™)

Product Inventory Requirements

For each machine you will need to plan an initial product inventory. The product capacity of each machine is listed on the machine brochure (also on my Wholesale Factory-Direct Price List in the appendix). Please refer to it.

Plan on having enough inventory available to fill all your machines at least 1/2 to 2/3 full initially. If your budget allows, have enough to handle the first service call as well. If not, at least have enough to service the first couple of machines. After you collect your cash, you can go shopping and get stocked up better.

It's okay to start out 1/2 to 2/3rds full until you know what your sales volume for each location will be, and determine what sells best in each location. This will also help keep your initial start-up costs down.

This will not affect sales and, in fact, may even offer a psychological advantage (a machine that is kept too full, too often, looks unused to regular customers and could actually decrease sales).

Take the average product cost and multiply times the capacity of each machine (or times the number of items you intend to stock initially) to compute your initial product inventory cost.

See the chapter covering the machines you are operating for more information.

A Word About Shelf Life

If you have the funds available, you may save money in SOME cases by buying large quantities of product inventory. . . or if you live far from a large town you may choose to stock up with periodic trips to a larger town for better pricing. . . but beware of shelf life limitations.

BULK ITEMS which are not packed in hermetically sealed containers (only boxes, plastic bags or placed in machine product canister) have a shelf life of AT LEAST:

30 days for OIL roasted nuts (3 months if DRY roasted or in-the shell, like pistachio nuts).

3 months for nuts if covered with candy.

Up to 6 months for other candies.

Items wrapped in hermetically sealed packaging (like candy bars) have a shelf life of about 12 months, except as follows:

Pastry items have a shelf life of only about 2 weeks.

2 months for chips and most bagged snacks.

3 months for cookies and crackers.

4 months for nuts.

Most anything that is canned (cold drinks, nuts, etc.) has a shelf life of several years.

If you refrigerate your stored product inventory, you can extend shelf life 50% to 100%, while excessive heat will reduce shelf life.

Product Storage Space

Usually, a spare closet or a space in the basement or garage is satisfactory. Be wary of insects, rodents, and temperature control when making this decision.

For longer shelf life try to keep the temperature STABLE, the colder the better, but in no event should you expose product to excessive heat.

Also, 'rotating' your products (first in - first out) is essential for freshness. Beware of freshness dates and avoid getting stuck with stale products.

You may want to buy some shelving to help you keep things organized and accessible. Some route operators will buy a used refrigerator for this purpose, which provides both shelving and temperature control (especially in hot climates).

Securing Suppliers

Discount Retail Stores

Believe it or not. . . and you may not, at first. . . your local DISCOUNT RETAIL stores will almost always be your best source for products to vend. These retailers are super-discounters and often sell well BELOW wholesale.

I'm referring to discount retailers like Sam's Warehouse, Price Club, Wal-Mart, K-Mart, Target, Longs Drugs, etc.

These huge warehouse or discount retail stores are conveniently located all over the country.

You will find it helpful to compare prices. Make a SHOPPING LIST of the primary products you will be buying for the type of machines that you will operate in your route. Then get prices from various sources. This will be well worth your time, since any money you save goes right into your pocket.

Buy Product Factory-Direct?

A few very large route operators buy direct from the factory, such as M&M Mars, Frito-Lay, etc. However, you generally must be in a position to buy at least 500 pounds at a time to do business with them. . . and even then, you will find that you will usually pay more than if you just bought from a local discount retailer, wholesale distributor, or route salesperson. In order to save any money buying direct, you would have to be able to buy a HUGE quantity.

Wholesale Distributors

You may want to look in your local Yellow Pages under 'candy', 'snack' or 'food' wholesalers and call them to get prices on the products you want. Sometimes they are a good source for CERTAIN items, like bagged snacks or canned juice drink products. You can usually get wholesale prices over the phone.

Route Sales

You may also want to check specific manufacturers since some products are available to you direct (at great prices) through their 'route sales department' See "Major Suppliers", below, for Frito Lay™, Dolly Madison™, and Hostess™.

Compare

After getting prices from the above sources, and comparing. . . you will be a believer.

Discount retailers are super-discounters and often sell well below wholesale. That may be hard to believe at first, but it's true. They will almost always be YOUR BEST SOURCE FOR PRODUCTS TO VEND.

These stores buy in huge quantities, and can offer very low prices on canned drinks, candy and snacks.

Many wholesale distributors tell me that THEY can't even buy from the manufacturer as low as these discount retailers SELL for. In fact, many of them are having a very hard time staying in business.

Discount retail stores can also supply any quantity, from 1 pound to 1 ton of a product, usually with a weeks notice.

I've had particularly good service from Wal-Mart for bulk vending, 'fun-size' vending, and various candy, snack, and drink items. They have a good selection. And their "Guaranteed Lowest Price Everyday" policy means that if I see a lower price anywhere else (which is not very often) they will match it. So I don't have to go to a lot of different places to shop.

Wal-Mart (and most retailers) would rather I contact one of their store buyers and order what I want, rather then come in and clean out all their shelves (which I've done!). Twice a week I can order any quantity of items I want and pick them up at the BACK of the store within 2 or 3 days.

Many discount retailers, besides Wal-Mart, will offer service like this. Many times, your decision regarding the store(s) you will buy from will depend upon the attitude and service mindfulness of the local management people. So try all these stores and make up your own mind.

Sales And Loss Leaders

Most retailers have major sales 3 or 4 times a year which allows you to stock up when prices are down. Watch for ads, or ask when their sales are and mark your calendar. The shelf life on most products you'll buy is long enough so you don't have to be too concerned about having stale inventory (see "A Word About Shelf Life" above).

Also, you'll want to keep an eye out for 'loss leaders'. These are items sold at a loss (less than their cost) in order to get people into the store to buy other items. This is routinely done by retailers, and can save you a lot of money.

If you happen to live in a small town it might be worth your time to make a trip to a city with one of these stores. If you only had to make the trip a few times a year it could be worth it for the money saved.

Major Suppliers

Most wholesale distributors will ship anywhere. Some have developed quite a large national business, and have very competitive prices. A partial list of some of the largest and best national wholesale suppliers, is listed below.

Also listed is major national manufacturers that you may want to contact for referral to their local distributor or route sales office.

Bulk Vending

Jerry's Nut House is a great source for any bulk products you may have difficulty finding locally. They sell it all. For example: Jelly Belly™ jelly beans can sometimes be difficult to find at a reasonable price locally, but they have them in a 10 pound box at a great price! They also carry assorted toy capsules for bulk vendors. . . and much more.

> Jerry's Nut House, Inc.
> 2101 Humboldt Street
> Denver, CO 80205
> 303-861-2262
> MO-FR, 8:00am-5:00pm, MST
> SA, 8:00am-1:00pm, MST

Packaged Candy, Snacks, Food, Canned Juice And NON-soda Drinks

V S A (Vendors Supply Of America) is probably the largest single wholesale distributor serving the vending industry. They have locations throughout the U.S., and will ship direct to you no matter where you are.

> NOTE: They have NO bulk vending or 'fun-size' vending products. They do sell juice and various other canned drinks but do NOT sell Coke™ or Pepsi™ products.

Contact the national office, below, and say: "Please refer me to your regional distribution center nearest me".

> V S A (Vendors Supply Of America)
> 370 17th Street, Suite 1400
> P. O. Box 17387
> Denver, CO 80217
> 800-288-8851, 303-634-1400
> MO-FR, 8:00am-5:00pm, MST

Frito-Lay™

Frito-Lay™ is a company that you may find yourself doing a lot of business with if you are operating full-size (not 'fun-size) packaged snack vendors. They handle a terrific line of bagged snacks, as well as the popular Grandma's Cookies™.

There are a couple of minor obstacles, however, in obtaining their products at a good price, and in the quantities you may want. Here's the problem, and the solution:

If you try to buy their products through the discount retailers, as you will buy most of your products, you will find that there is sometimes a packaging problem. At the discount retail stores, often small bags are sold only in VARIETY packs. You need to be able to buy what you need. . . not a variety pack.

Wholesale distributors will sell you what you want in case quantities. Some smaller ones may even split cases. But their prices are often too high.

You could buy direct from Frito-Lay™ through their direct sales or vending sales department. But they have a 65 case minimum order. . . and storage is a problem if you don't sell them quickly because the product shelf life is about 2 to 3 months. Besides, even if you bought 65 cases, you will find that you are paying more than if you buy through their route sales department.

The route sales department is the way to go! They operate trucks that deliver products direct to grocery (and other retail) stores. These people will sell Frito-Lay™ products to you at the lowest price you will find anywhere. And they will usually sell you any quantity you want. . . even splitting and mixing cases for you. This is the best way to buy for most all small to medium sized vending operations.

To find your local route sales person, contact the national office, below, and say: "Please refer me to the route sales office nearest me".

Frito-Lay™
P. O. Box 660634
Dallas, TX 75266
800-352-4477, 214-334-7000
MO-FR, 9:00am-4:30pm, CST

Dolly Madison™ And Hostess™

Dolly Madison™ and Hostess™ make the best lines of bakery products for you to vend. They are hot sellers! Both companies are now owned by a single corporation known as Interstate Brands.

As with Frito-Lay™ products, you will get the best prices and service if you deal with their route sales department.

To find your local route sales person, contact the national office, below, and say: "Please refer me to the route sales office nearest me, for both Dolly Madison™ AND Hostess™ products".

Interstate Brands Corp.
12 East Armour Blvd.
P.O. Box 419627
Kansas City, MO 64141
816-502-4000
MO-FR, 8:00am-4:45pm, CST

Coca-Cola™ And Pepsi™

It is not likely that you will be dealing with your local Coke™ or Pepsi™ bottler/distributor. With these product lines you will almost always get a much better price from the local discount retailers. Still, you may want to call them and check out their prices.

Also, you may need product labels for your vendors. These are the labels that are placed under the selection buttons, or in a display area on the vendor. They are color labels that display the product logo for items like Pepsi™, Diet Pepsi™, etc.

Product labels often come with the vendor, but if they do not, or if you need replacements, you can pick them up from your local bottler (or phone them and they'll usually mail them to you) at no charge.

To find your local Coke™ or Pepsi™ bottler, contact the national office, below, and say: "Please refer me to the bottler nearest me".

Coca-Cola™
P. O. Drawer 1734
Atlanta, GA 30301
800-GET-COKE (800-438-2653)
404-676-2121
MO-FR, 8:30am-7:00pm, EST

Pepsi-Cola™
1 Pepsi Way
Somers, NY 10589
800-433-2652, 914-767-6000
MO-FR, 9:00am-6:00pm, EST

Summary

You will do well, and stay out of trouble, if you start out using my "Vending Product List" above. It takes statistics into account, together with plain old experience with what sells best in what type of machine. While it is not all-inclusive nor perfect. . . it WILL help you get started on the right track.

Plan on having enough inventory available to fill all your machines at least 1/2 to 2/3 full initially. If your budget allows, have enough to handle the first service call as well. If not, at least have enough to service the first couple of machines. After you

collect your cash, you can go shopping and get stocked up better.

If you don't check anywhere else, check the DISCOUNT RETAIL stores as they will almost always be your best SINGLE source for products to vend. . . and if you're in bulk vending or 'fun-size' vending, they may well be the ONLY source you'll need.

If you're involved with full-size (not 'fun-size) packaged snacks, be sure to contact Frito-Lay™ and Interstate Brands (Dolly Madison™ and

Hostess™) right after you order your machines, because you're likely to need them just as soon as your new vending machines arrive. You should have no problem getting everything else you'll need from your local discount retail stores.

Regardless as to what type of machines you have ordered, you should start shopping for vendable products right after the machine order goes in.

That way, you'll be ready to get started just as soon as they arrive!

Have fun shopping!

Please see the chapters titled "Route Management", "Getting GREAT Locations", and "Getting Started" for more information relevant to topics covered in this chapter.

Notes

Chapter 10
Amusement Machines

Making money is fun and games!

It all started in 1971 when Atari first introduced 'Pong'. Now, coin-operated amusement is a $7 billion dollar industry! There's big money in all kinds of game machines, and many advantages not found in other types of vending machines.

There is usually:

- No product to buy!
- No sales tax to pay!
- No permits required!
- Very little servicing required!

Since these machines can generally hold at least $500.00 or more in quarters, you only have to service them about once every month or two. . . and that amounts to little more than just picking up your money!

Definition

When you're in the amusement machine business. . . you actually VEND FUN! An amusement machine is any device that offers, as it's primary product, some entertainment value.

Think about it. No products to hassle with. Drop by about once every month or two to pick up your money. It's a great business with lots of potential. But what's the catch? There are areas of tremendous opportunity, and also areas that are highly competitive:

Market Saturation

If you think amusement machines do best in arcades (or family entertainment centers) think again. According to the recent Vending Times Census Of The Industry, just 16% are in arcades, 45% are in tavern/bar locations, 14% in restaurants, 10% in malls, 8% in private clubs, and the rest in various types of locations. See the chapter titled "Getting Great Locations".

As with most all vending, there is little competition in some categories, and lots of competition in others. The best and lowest risk locations for someone new to the amusement industry is restaurants, malls, and other retail establishments. Here's why I say that:

Arcades

Setting up an arcade (or family entertainment center) is a huge undertaking for a novice. If you make a mistake regarding the location or the market potential you could be in big trouble. Also, it requires that you risk a very large amount of capital. It's not the place to 'get your feet wet'. They can be highly profitable, but get some experience before you even consider arcades.

Taverns And Bars

Taverns and bars are very competitive. Most of them contract with a SINGLE amusement operator who provides ALL their amusement equipment. . . video games, pinball, electronic darts, pool tables, etc. You will find that this 'exclusive contract' will keep you out of these locations unless and until you have the money, machines, and knowledge to provide for ALL of their needs. Then you will have an opportunity to 'bid', or compete for the location.

They will not let you in to place just 1 machine because that would usually violate their existing contract. Taverns and bars can also be very profitable, and the local competition is not always all that good, but it is not the place to start. And even if and when you do start, you will probably start off with the smaller locations that the big operators have less interest in.

Best Locations For Start-Up

With restaurants, malls, and other retail establishments you will find that amusement machines can do very well, and there is far less competition. The big operators just have too much overhead to concentrate on this type of location, and need the big arcade, bar, and tavern locations in order to make the kind of money they want.
Also, with this type of location, you can easily enter the business with only one TYPE of game. . .

and as few or as many of them as you want. This will simplify your life immensely!

Video Games

According to the recent Vending Times Census of the Industry: Video games account for about half of the entire amusement industry. They're also one of the highest producing amusement machines relative to their cost. . . averaging $52.00 per week, or about $200.00 per month gross. Of course, the hottest machines can do much better than the average.

Lets assume that if you get into the amusement business, you will start with restaurants, malls, and other retail establishments. That being the case, the following will be especially important:

Space: In most businesses space is a big consideration when deciding what entertainment equipment to offer.

Longevity: Many games tend to be trendy. Therefore, game 'longevity' is a crucial issue. Some types of machines have a relatively short life and can be very risky for that reason. If you invested in Pac-Man machines when they first came out you could have made a fortune, but they don't do AS well anymore

A good solution to these problems is one of the following:

MULTIPLE Game Concept: This is a machine that offers MORE than one

(perhaps several) games in just one cabinet. If NOT convertible (see below) the games tend to be of a 'time proven' nature, and which generally appeal to all ages.

CONVERTIBLE Game Concept: This may be a single OR multiple game cabinet (some offer several games). The convertible feature allows you to CONVERT the game to a DIFFERENT game. . . usually by inserting a software cartridge inside the cabinet, and by inserting new graphics under a glass display area. It's a quick and easy conversion.

Both of the above concepts keep you from getting stuck with a useless box. . . a trendy game that was hot for 6 months, didn't pay for itself, and now will hardly justify the space it takes up.

Since there is now the choice of multiple games, convertible, or both. . . they make perfect sense in locations where space is an issue. . . providing multiple game selections in just one cabinet.

Multiple and/or convertible game machines offer you MORE earning power, over time, than any other SINGLE game machine available in the industry! And can be popular with virtually ALL ages of players. These machines can NEVER become OBSOLETE.

Impulse Machines - A Hot Sleeper!

Impulse machines can offer a tremendous return and there is very little competition in most areas. For some reason, many route operators have a hard time conceiving how these little machines can make much money. . . so they don't try it out. That's just fine with you, right? You'll be laughing all the way to the bank!

Don't let the simplicity. . . or apparent silliness of these machines fool you! They are FUN. . . and can make BIG money with very little effort on your part. And there is VERY little competition. Good locations are plentiful.

Definition

In case you're not familiar with what an impulse machine is, let me describe it this way: It's a 'short-play' game machine, played on 'impulse' by customers who are typically 'passing through' (transient) rather than 'hanging around' (such as in an arcade or bar).

The most successful impulse operators learn to 'think impulse', which means thinking beyond the traditional video game location.

While every location that has a video game is usually suitable for impulse machines. . .

not every potential impulse location would be suitable for a video game. There's just a lot more profitable places to locate an impulse machine.

They do ESPECIALLY well in areas with a lot of transient customer traffic. . . like restaurant waiting areas, shopping malls, and various retail establishments. . . EXACTLY the type of locations I recommended for the new operator, as we discussed above.

Most of these locations would not be appropriate for a video game, yet impulse is perfect! Plus almost anywhere you see a video game is a good place for impulse.

It's fun and challenging to seek out new locations for impulse. They do well in such unusual places as shopping mall gift shops (which would not normally accept a video game), pretzel stores, and in a pet store by the puppy cage!   . . . Anywhere people tend to slow down a little.

Many locations are not familiar with impulse. Sincc they are small and lightweight, I've found it very helpful to bring one along when trying to place them. When the location sees how little space they take up. . . and how much fun they are. . . it makes your job easy! They are much more impressive in person, and a picture may not do them justice.

Examples of some impulse machines you may have seen are: The 'Heart Rate Meter', 'Stress Test', 'Physical Fitness', 'Talking Gypsy', 'Love Meter', 'Memory Quiz', 'Personality Analyzer', etc. Get the idea? Pretty silly, huh? But again I say, you'll laugh all the way to the bank.

Many, many machines which were placed on location over 10 to 15 years ago are still producing well for their owners.

This overlooked area of vending is a real sleeper. . . and could pay off big if you're willing to give it a try!

In my experience, impulse machines currently represent one of the very best opportunities in the amusement industry! Give it the consideration it deserves.

Other Amusement Machines

Unless and until you really know what you're doing, I strongly recommend that you stay away from the riskier amusement devices like:

'Trendy' video games, pinball, pool tables, electronic darts, electronic basketball, shuffleboards, air hockey, foosball tables, kiddie rides, prize dispensing games (like cranes), juke boxes, etc.

Unless and until you really know what you're doing, I strongly recommend that you stay away from this type of equipment.

Don't let anyone talk you into this if you're new to vending, unless you've got deep pockets and like to gamble. They can be difficult to locate and you can loose your "_____" if you're not very careful!

You can grow into some of this later, if your interested. . . and there's good profit potential. . . but it's just not the place to start.

It would be easy to fill an entire book on the subject of amusement alone. . . and yet we only have room for a single chapter. Nevertheless, if you follow the recommendations in this chapter you could enjoy a low risk, successful start in the business.

IF you are interested in learning how to get into other areas of amusement, my advise to you is to learn as you go. Get started with the type of equipment and locations I suggest. Then subscribe to amusement industry trade publications. . . join their associations. . . attend their conventions, ask a lot of questions, etc. Before long you'll be a pro, and you won't have risked your savings in the process.

Profit Potential

Since impulse machines are one of the easiest and most profitable amusement machines for the new operator to get started with. . . lets simplify our evaluation of the amusement business and look only at impulse machines for now.

You could do almost as well, maybe better in some cases, with other types of game machines. . . but you may have to invest more money, take more risk, and deal with more competition.

In my experience, a properly located quality impulse machine should gross at least $20.00 to $40.00 per week each. And it's not uncommon for these very inexpensive little machines to gross as much as $50.00 to $100.00 per month each, in some locations!

Since you will often have 2 or 3 machines on a single stand, in a single location. . .

you could double or triple the above. I'll refer to these as 2 or 3-headed machines.

For the sake of discussion, lets assume that in all your locations you have 2-headed impulse machines, and you average $20.00 per week, per head. That's $40.00 per week for each location (see middle column below).

You probably will be paying no more than 30% commission, so we'll deduct that from your $40.00 weekly gross revenue, giving you a weekly gross PROFIT of $28.00 per location (see middle column below) as follows:

Weekly Gross Revenue	$ 20.00	$ 40.00	$ 60.00
Weekly gross profit per location	$ 14.00	$ 28.00	$ 42.00
Monthly gross profit per location	$ 56.00	$ 112.00	$ 168.00
Monthly gross profit - 10 locations	$ 560.00	$ 1,120.00	$ 1,680.00

See chapters titled "Location Targeting And Analysis" and "Getting Great Locations"

NOTE: This is provided for illustrative purposes only. It does not include machine cost, freight, sales tax, locating, or other miscellaneous costs not specifically listed, if any. Figures may vary according to type of business, geographical location, fluctuations in customer traffic, and many other factors which can not be predicted. Therefore, the actual results achieved may vary and can not be guaranteed.

As you can see from the above illustration, the bottom line is that with 2-headed machines and $40.00 average weekly gross revenue, you could expect to enjoy a monthly gross PROFIT of $112.00 per location after paying commission to the location!

Commission

Commissions paid are typically 20% to 50% of the gross depending upon sales volume, the type and cost of the equipment, and/or what the location will accept.

Amusement operators generally negotiate a commission of 20% to 40%. . . up to 50% for a super hot location In locations where there is a lot of competition for the location, it's customary to pay 40% to 50% commission. But don't be too quick to accept that for ALL locations. Commission is negotiable, and you can obtain

great locations for as little as 20% to 30%, particularly for impulse machines.

Many operators find it best to simply offer locations a sliding scale commission such as this one:

20% of gross receipts up to $200.00 monthly.

30% of gross receipts if gross monthly receipts equals or exceeds $200.00.

40% of gross receipts if gross monthly receipts equals or exceeds $300.00.

50% of gross receipts if gross monthly receipts equals or exceeds $400.00.

You can adjust this scale to meet your own needs, and to whatever your local market will bare. If you print it directly on your 'Placement Agreement' it will look 'standard' and few locations will even question it. See the chapter titled "Route Management".

Profit Summary

As I've said, in my experience a properly located impulse machine should gross at least $20.00 to $40.00 per week for EACH head. If you operate only 2-headed impulse machines in all your locations (which is a good idea) you could gross at least $40.00 to $80.00 per week, per location.

If we take the lower figure and assume a $40.00 weekly average gross you could enjoy a monthly gross PROFIT of about $112.00 after paying 30% commission.

Since the machines only take about 15 to 20 minutes to service. . . and servicing is only required about once each month. . . you could be earning about $300.00 gross profit per hour.

A 2-headed impulse machine of the type we are talking about can be purchased for around $1,500.00, so your gross return on investment could be about 100% per year.

Overall, I believe it's reasonable to expect a pay-back of as quickly as 6 months, to as long as 18 months on impulse machines. . . depending entirely upon the quality of your locations. This equates to about 60% to 200% gross return per year!

Similarly, you could expect your gross profit per hour to run from a low of about $150.00 to a high of as much as $450.00!

Based upon the above illustration, after properly located. Of course you'll also have to plan on spending some time counting money (too bad), keeping simple records, etc. (this could run at least 15 minutes to 1 hour for every hour of actual route servicing time, depending upon various factors).

It is arguable that bulk vending has a faster pay-back than amusement, but as you can see, amusement potentially enjoys much higher gross profit per hour for your time. If you have substantial capital to invest, but very little time, amusement may be ideal for you.

Service Requirements

You need to be very careful about what type of equipment you buy. Some of it can be very complex. . . particularly if it has a video screen. With the help of the manufacturers customer service department, you can learn these skills or have a local technician handle it for you. Just be careful that you don't take on more than you expect in the beginning.

Regular servicing consists of simply wiping off the machine, confirming that it's still working properly, counting your money, filing out your Route Report, and paying a commission (about 15 to 20 minutes per machine, per month).

The machines typically have a large enough coin box (hold $500.00 or more) that you could service them every 2 or 3 months. . . if that were the only consideration. I recommend MONTHLY servicing. They represent such a large investment that I'd want to check up on them if for no other reason than to make sure they are still working okay.

There's been times I've gone in to service my game machines and found that something very simple was wrong (like the

machine was unplugged, and nobody had bothered to plug it back in). Had I waited 2 to 3 months to go in, I may have lost a substantial amount of income. Bulk vendors are about the only machine that can go that long (2 to 5 months) but then they cost a lot less money. . . don't require electricity. . . and are much less complex.

Technical Repair

Typically, amusement machines are extremely well made and very reliable. In the rare event of a malfunction you can generally get help diagnosing the problem from the manufacturers customer service department. Usually, it will be something you can fix yourself with simple instructions from the manufacturer. . . a couple of simple hand tools. . . and perhaps a soldering iron.

If the above is not an option for some reason, 'next day' factory repair service is usually available by either sending in a defective COMPONENT (usually not the whole machine) for repair, or by them sending you an exchange component. In this fashion, before long you will know a lot about the maintenance and repair of your amusement machines.

If you're not up to dealing with this type of technical work, you can take it to a local general electronics repair shop (television, computer, etc.) and they can do it for you. They could also make a service call. Most any competent local TV or computer repair technician can easily handle the kind of relatively simple maintenance and repair requirements you will have. And as I've said, you can easily learn them yourself if you are willing.

Suggested Amusement Start-Up Checklist

✓ Purchase 2 or more of the 2-headed impulse machines

✓ See chapter titled "Getting Started"

Machine Set-Up

One of the beautiful things about amusement machines is that there is virtually no set-up requirements. Just take it out of the box and plug it in.

Some types of machines MAY have some very simple programing requirements which will be fully explained in the owners manual.

SECURITY may be an issue with some SMALL amusement machines, such as a single impulse machine on a counter-top. I wouldn't concern myself with any machines on floor stands or floor cabinets. If you have a situation where security is an issue, I have a solution that will usually do the trick, and will look nice too. Attach the machine to something secure with plastic coated cable:

I recommend using 1/8" plastic coated cable (about 1/4" with coating) since it's very strong yet flexible, and won't scratch anything. About 6' to 7' in length is usually about right. Attach one end to an eyelet (which is bolted on the machine) and the other to a fixture (or screwed in eyelet) behind the counter or on a wall.

You should attach the cable as follows:

Strip off about 2" of the plastic coating and run the end of the cable through the eyelet on the machine, making a loop. Then clamp it together with a cable clamp. Or for a much cleaner and neater appearance. . . plus more security. . . clamp it using an oval sleeve (sometimes called a "ferrale"). To do this you will need a special tool called a "#2 Swage-It tool" which costs around $20.00.

Make a similar loop on the other end and attach using a small padlock or combination lock.

All the above materials and tools listed for securing your machines are available from many hardware stores, or direct from the following manufacturer:

S & F Tool Company
18437 Mount Langley St., Bldg P
Fountain Valley, CA 92708
714-968-7378
MO-FR, 8:00am-4:00pm, PST

Machine Recommendations

By now you know that I favor impulse machines. They are relatively inexpensive, quite trouble free (requiring little or no technical ability on your part) and have proven the test of time. . . always popular. Also, since locations are plentiful and competition is sparse. . . getting locations is relatively easy.

I recommend getting started with impulse machines. If after you've been in the business awhile, you find something that look better than impulse. . . give it a try later. But most impulse operators never find anything better. I know I haven't.

My 2nd best recommendation would be multiple and/or convertible games.

I like 2-headed impulse machines because I've found that they play off each other. One may attract a player, but after they play it they'll play the other one too. . . or visa versa. 2-headed machines can do much better than 1. On the other hand, 3-headed is not necessarily better. There is a diminishing return after 2 except for the very hottest locations.

Summary

Conservatively speaking. . . when you properly locate 10 of the 2-headed impulse machines mentioned above, you could expect a monthly gross profit of AT LEAST $560.00 to as much as 1,680.00 working only about 3 to 4 hours only ONCE a month! Imagine your profits when you build up to 50 or 100 locations!

● 6 to 18 month pay-back on your initial investment!

● 50% to 200% gross return on investment per year!

● $150.00 to $450.00 gross profit per hour!

● Service only once each month!

● No product to buy, load, or clean up!

● Usually no sales tax or permits required!

● Locations are plentiful, but proper locating takes effort.

Based upon the above illustration, after properly located. Of course you'll also have to plan on spending some time counting money (too bad), keeping simple records, etc. (this could run at least 15 minutes to 1 hour for every hour of actual route servicing time, depending upon various factors).

Your best bet is with impulse machines. My 2nd best recommendation would be multiple and/or convertible games.

Locating amusement machines takes more skill and effort to locate initially than vendors, but locations ARE plentiful. Vendors pay for themselves faster, and offer you an excellent return for your time as well. While impulse machines WILL pay you more money for the TIME invested. . . they do take longer to pay for.

Impulse machines are one of my personal favorites. But you'll just have to decide what's best for you based upon what you like, and how much time and money you have available. There's a lot of potential in ALL areas of vending and amusement.

For machine sources, costs, and ordering information, please refer to the Appendix.

Also see the last page of this book for FREE resources (reports, videos, etc.) including the "HOTTEST Vending Money-Makers" report!

Notes

Chapter 11
Other Opportunities - And Mistakes!

Space limitations require that I focus on what I feel are the 'best bets' in the vending industry. I'm exposed to a lot of different machines and opportunities in this industry, and you can bet that if something is HOT and it works, I'm involved... it's on my price list... and it's covered in this book OR in my FREE supplemental report titled "HOTTEST Vending Money-Makers!" (This report is an essential and integral part of the book, which I highly recommend you obtain.)

See the last page of this book for FREE resources (reports, videos, etc.) including the "HOTTEST Vending Money-Makers" report!

To illustrate my point, let me just say that in my vending machine distributing company, FREEDOM TECHNOLOGY, I offer a reasonably full line of vending equipment. My product line is limited only by my policy, which is to promote ONLY what I feel you can operate at the lowest personal risk, and for the highest potential profit.

These are opportunities you can build a business and a career on. If it's HOT, I probably sell it. You really don't need anything else.

If you're interested in something that is not covered in Vending Success Secrets or my HOTTEST Vending Money-Makers report, there may be a very good reason. Please contact FREEDOM TECHNOLOGY and we'll either explain our position to you, get you a special report, find a good source of supply for you. . . or if there are problems with what you're considering, we may try to talk you out of it!

There are so many options in this exciting, growing industry that it's easy to get bogged down and never make a decision to do anything... which would be a huge and terribly expensive mistake for you to make.

I've purposely left out discussing the following types of vending equipment. I've listed them here just to let you know they're not forgotten. Some of them are very poor choices for ANYONE. Others can be very profitable if you have a little experience and know what you're doing, but

they're not the place to start for most people. More discussion on this follows the list.

● Full food service and commissary operations equipment.

● Hot or canned food venders.

● French fry and pizza vendors.

● Cold and frozen foods.

● Hot popcorn, hot roasted peanuts.

● Mint patty vendors.

● Lolly-pop honor boxes.

● Coffee and hot drink vendors.

● Cup drop cold drinks.

● Bottled drinks.

● Personal products: Fragrance vendors, toilet seat covers, condoms, toiletries.

● Cigarettes and lighters.

● Stickers, stamps, cards, balloons and toys.

● Scales.

● 'Trendy' video games, pin ball, electronic darts, electronic basketball.

● Pool tables, air hockey, shuffleboards, foosball.

● Prize dispensing games (like cranes), etc.

● 'Coin drop' (gambling) devices with prize pay-outs.

● Music (jukeboxes).

● Breath alcohol analyzers.

- Kiddie rides.

- Pay phones.

- Long distance phone card vendors.

- Laundry mats.

- Car washes.

WARNING: Unless and until you really know what you're doing, I strongly recommend that you stay away from this type of equipment. Don't let anyone talk you into this if you're new to vending, unless you've got deep pockets and like to gamble. You can loose your "_____" if you're not very careful!

This list is not meant to be all-inclusive, however, it should give you some sense for the size and scope of the possible options.

Let me give you some brief examples as to why things on this list could get you in trouble:

Full Food Service

Some people think it would be a good goal to offer "full service". Maybe so. But you need a bare minimum of AT LEAST 100 employees (or compensating customer traffic) to make money in full service. AND THEN you will have some pretty stiff competition. It CAN be very profitable. And this may be a good goal. . . it's just not something to start out with. See chapter titled "Location Targeting And Analysis".

Cold Food Vendors

I don't know of anyone who ever paid for a cold food vendor (sandwiches, fruit, etc.). Sales are only about .30 per person, per day for a machine that must be totally dedicated to ONLY cold food. And food spoilage can be up to 50% or more. They don't make money. Vendors only put them in because they have to in order to get the profitable snack and drink business in large locations. See chapter titled "Location Targeting And Analysis".

Hot Food Vendors

There is usually no spoilage problem with hot food vendors, however, sales are only about .20 per person, per day for a machine that must be dedicated to ONLY hot food. Many general merchandise vendors will vend microwavable foods, which is much better since you have more options with this machine. A dedicated hot food vendor can make money, but only in very high use locations. See chapter titled "Location Targeting And Analysis".

Mint Patty Vendors

In my opinion, this is just a total fraud. There is not enough demand for mint patties to justify a machine dedicated to them. And most machines I'm aware of do not even work. I don't know of ANYONE doing well with these machines. Forget it.

Hot Popcorn Vendors

There are several companies promoting hot popcorn as a 'hot' opportunity because popcorn has a very high markup, and it's generally well liked. Some even offer special flavored toppings, and machines with exciting graphics. Since it is often popped after it is vended, they say the smell will attract other customers.

The truth is that when it is offered in a full line snack vendor, popcorn is not even one of the best sellers. Bagged snacks like Doritos™ and Cheetos™ will outsell popcorn. So why would you want a machine dedicated to nothing else? You wouldn't.

See specialty machines, below. Also see the chapters titled "Products And Inventory" and "Location Targeting And Analysis".

Specialty Machines

Many people have been lured by the attraction of new concepts like hot french fry or pizza vendors. It's possible to make good money with machines like this, but only in very high use locations.

The type of location they will do well in is the SAME location that the full service vendors are in. You will have to be prepared to offer a full line of vendors, and compete with the big guys.

You can NOT build a business around just one 'type' of machine of THIS nature.

Stickers And Cards

I know people who are doing very well with stickers, sports (and other) collectors cards, temporary tattoos, etc. They seem to do best in large retail store foyers, busy restaurants, and similar retail environments. As a result, locating can be tedious and slow because you are often making proposals to corporate headquarters. It's not a bad opportunity, but I prefer bulk vending and impulse machines in these types of locations.

Bar Games

I routinely come across companies promoting various bar or tavern games. Typically a counter-top poker game, some combination of many games offered in a single cabinet, electronic darts, etc. These games are often very well made and actually big money-makers.

The problem is that it's almost impossible to locate them in the bar locations where they do best, because of exclusive contracts with other game operators who provide the bar with ALL their amusement devices. See chapter titled "Amusement Machines"

Prize Dispensing Games

The example you'll probably be most familiar with is the 'cranes' that are in many grocery stores, arcades, etc. These can make good money, but they only do well in a few types of locations, and they take up a lot of room. The best locations were snapped up long ago, and there is much competition for them. There are better opportunities.

Also, it's very important to make sure there is a clear element of 'skill' involved. . . and not chance. Otherwise, law enforcement may declare them to be gambling devices. I've seen this happen on prize dispensing games of all kinds. See "Coin Drop Devices" below for more on this.

Coin Drop Devices

These are one of the biggest money-makers I've ever seen! They are often known by names such as Aqua Skill™, Skill Shot™, Water Bloop™, etc. A common feature is that you drop a coin in and (using various methods of operation and levels of skill) you try to make the coin end up in a certain place to win a prize.

There is almost always a charity sponsorship tie-in of some sort. The money (or part of it) that you deposit goes to charity, but if you win, the business donates a prize. Often the money, less a

royalty to the charity, is split between the business and the route operator.

You will see them in many Burger Kings™ and McDonalds™ around the country, and many other locations as well.

I've made a lot of money with these, and so have many other people. I've even sold quite a few of them through my company, FREEDOM TECHNOLOGY.

The problem with them is that more and more you will find a county District Attorney or State Attorney General who will 'declare war' on them. They want to classify them as "gambling devices" because they think the key element of 'skill' is lacking. . . and that they are actually a game of chance.

With many of these devices I think they are clearly wrong. . . because if skill is a significant factor, they are not gambling devices. Nevertheless, they will often seize the machines and destroy them. . . keep the money. . . and charge the operator with the criminal charge of operating illegal gambling devices!

The reason Burger King™ and McDonalds™ can get away with it is because ALL of the money they collect goes to charity (no one takes a cut). . . and perhaps also because they are large and well respected companies, authorities look the other way. If you operate them for profit, you MAY have a serious problem to contend with.

Most people just aren't up for dealing with this possibility, once they are aware of it. In some areas, authorities consider these games a trivial matter and will not bother you. But even if you ask in advance, there is no guarantee that they will leave you alone in the future.

While I am not one to shy away from controversy, I do believe that people should be fully informed as to what they're getting into. I no longer promote these devices because of the risks involved, but I do have a good supplier and sell them on a special order basis to those who are willing to deal with those risks. They are also promoted and sold through various trade publications. See chapter titled "Trade Publications, Organizations, And Shows".

Pay Phones

Ever since the big phone company breakup, pay phones have been promoted as a great opportunity. I do know that success is possible, but competition is very stiff. I'm not aware of many people who are doing very well with them. Yet I routinely run across people who are not. It's definitely no 'cake walk'. I've found nothing that makes me want to get further involved, as there are better opportunities out there.

Long Distance Phone Card Vendors

Prepaid long distance phone cards have become increasingly popular. There are many people who don't have (or can't get) a long distance credit card, or who have long distance call restrictions placed on their phone at home. For many, these cards are much less expensive and more convenient than putting money in pay phones.

Nevertheless, these cards are readily available at convenience and discount stores. . . and sales are not high enough to justify dedicating a machine to this purpose except in extremely high traffic locations.

A vendor of this nature will only do well in a large bus station, airport, or similar location. There is already much competition for the best locations. And the long term success of the concept can not be predicted.

Summary

There are many fine opportunities in this industry, and many scams as well. There is always someone looking for a way to 're-package' and OLD concept. . . or promote a NEW concept as the best thing since sliced bread. In general, if something looks 'marketable' as a business opportunity, it will be sold regardless as to its merits.

After reading this book (if I've done my job) you really shouldn't have a hard time telling the good from the bad. . . or at least identifying the questionable. If you don't already, you will soon understand why most any concept works, and why another one won't.

You will find it helpful if you learn to question both the obvious and hidden motives of ANYONE who tries to sell you on the merits of ANYTHING. . . and don't exclude me. For example:

If a company sells only one product. . . do you think they'll have much of anything but GOOD to say about it? Don't be naive. It's not because they honestly believe it's the only good (or best) opportunity out there.

If a company emphasizes the importance of establishing a long-term relationship, and down-plays the importance of the first order. . . yet they have a minimum order of $5,000.00 or more. . . something is wrong. If a company, product, or concept is so good. . . they won't mind you starting out small and proving it to yourself. You'll reorder. All their excuses to the contrary are just that. . . excuses!

I've built my company around giving people what really works, and what they want. I could, and would sell about anything that I knew to be a quality product and opportunity. I don't sell just 1 item, but many. And because I know that what I sell is fair priced and will do what I say it will do. . . I don't hesitate to sell just 1 at a time, and offer a money back guarantee.

I'm not saying I operate the ONLY good company who offers the ONLY good opportunities. There are others. But they can be difficult to find. I hope that the above, and this book, will help you as you begin to unravel all the options and take action to begin your new venture.

See chapters titled "Pitfalls, Risks, and Rip-offs!", "Products And Inventory" and "Location Targeting And Analysis".

Also see the last page of this book for FREE resources (reports, videos, etc.) including the "HOTTEST Vending Money-Makers" report!

Chapter 12
Coin Mechanisms And Bill Acceptors

You may think that this would be a dry topic to read, but I think you'll find that it's actually VERY interesting. Coin changers and BAs (bill acceptors) actually make money themselves! The type of coin-mech (coin mechanism) and possibly BA that you choose can have a HUGE impact on your profitability!

Many vending novices make big mistakes in evaluating (or NOT evaluating) coin-mechs and BAs. This is a very important chapter.

Definition

Coin mechs and BAs are devices that are designed to accept coin or currency. . . validate it's authenticity. . . and determine it's denomination. Using various technology, it then 'authorizes' the machine to dispense the product being purchased, or activate the machine in some other way (start amusement device, washing machine, etc.).

Mechanical, Electric, Electronic. . .

When I refer to a MECHANICAL coin mech, I mean that it does not require electricity to operate the COIN MECH. Most of the time, a MACHINE with a mechanical coin mech will not require electricity to operate at all, but there are exceptions: Such as a cold drink machine with a mechanical coin-mech (electricity required for refrigeration), or a mechanical snack machine with a light kit.

The ELECTRIC coin mech performs a similar function as the mechanical coin mech but, of course, does require electricity.

The ELECTRONIC coin mech not only requires electricity, but it's most distinguishing feature is that it operates from some sort of a 'controller board' or electronic brain, similar to a very small computer. All BAs are electronic, and will only work with an electronic (not electric) coin mech.

In machines where electronic coin mechs and BAs MAY be used, the computer controller board is generally included with the machine and is not something that comes with the coin mech or BA. In other words, it is usually not something that you

must purchase separately, or that you would or could add-on later.

Plastic VS Metal

Many mechanical coin-mechs are made ENTIRELY of plastic (and most electric and electronic coin-mechs and bill acceptors have plastic components).

Most people assume that metal is better, but this is not always the case. For example, some types of all plastic coin-mechs will outlast some types of all metal coin mechs.

Regarding ALL plastic coin mechs: My advise to you is to stay away from any coin-mech made of polycarbonate (they don't hold up well). Celcon or delrin are very high quality plastics most commonly used, and is recommended. Exercise caution if considering any other type of all plastic coin-mech.

Lower grade plastics are often used as components in coin-mechs and bill acceptors, and in the machines themselves. . . without consequence. This is fine. It's the ALL plastic coin-mechs I want you to be wary of. Just make sure you know what TYPE of plastic is used and you won't have a problem.

With FREEDOM TECH, don't bother even asking. I wouldn't offer a machine with inappropriate plastic components.

Single Price VS Multi-Price

Regardless as to weather the machine is mechanical, electric, or electronic. . . plastic or metal. . . some will operate using a SINGLE price system. This means that each item sold in the machine MUST be sold at the exact same price.

Sometimes it doesn't matter very much. If you're selling only sodas out of your canned cold drink vendor, you may not mind being stuck with a single price option, since all your products are priced the same anyway, at about .55¢. But what if you want to add some juice selections at .75¢? You'd be out of luck.

With multi-pricing, you can price each individual product selection at whatever price you want. This is an important advantage in snack and drink vending.

I don't recommend single pricing. All the machines I sell through my machine distributorship, FREEDOM TECH, are multi-price.

Coin-Mechs

Fixed Price Mechanical Coin-Mech

These coin-mechs are made to vend at one price only, such as .25¢ (and will typically accept 1 or 2 coins of the same denomination only, no other coin combinations). You often can not change the price at all, or if you can, you must buy additional parts.

They're typical for bulk vendors. With bulk vendors, as vended product costs go up or down you can simply adjust the AMOUNT of product dispensed. So it is not important to be able to adjust the coin-mech on this type of machine. In other types of machines, when vending other types of PACKAGED products, I think you can see that this could be a big problem when product costs go up (as they always do).

Fixed Price Electric
Or Electronic Coin-Mech

In concept, this is virtually identical to the fixed price MECHANICAL coin-mech, except for the ELECTRIC or ELECTRONIC operation.

This coin mech is most commonly seen in amusement equipment, or other electric machines in which the vend price is not likely to change.

Adjustable Price
Mechanical Coin-Mech

Some mechanical coin-mechs are made to be easily adjustable without buying additional parts. They could have from 1 to 5 coin slots, but most of the ones you're likely to see will probably have 4 coin slots. The 4 coin slot adjustable coin mech will generally accept MULTIPLE coins in any combination of 1 to 4 coins (nickels, dimes and quarters only) from .05¢ (a nickel) to $1.00 (4 quarters).

For a .25¢ vend you would use 1 slot, for 1 quarter (the other 3 slots would be made inaccessible). A .30¢ vend would take 2 slots; for a quarter and a nickel. A .45¢ vend would take 3

slots, for 1 quarter and 2 dimes. A $1.00 vend would take 4 slots, for 4 quarters. . . and so on. The only combination you can not make would be .90¢ and .95¢ because that would take more than a 4 coin combination (using nickels, dimes and quarters only).

This type of coin mech is usually seen in various low cost food and drink vendors. It's quick and easy to adjust, but in SOME situations MAY present problems you need to be aware of, which I'll mention below.

Coin Accumulator

A coin 'accumulator' does just what it says. . . it 'accumulates' any combination of coins (nickels, dimes, and quarters only) to equal the vend price. They do not make change, so if you exceed the vend price you lose the excess money. They are typically electric or electronic.

The best example of a coin accumulator type coin-mech that you are sure to be familiar with would be a standard pay phone. If you make a local call for a .25¢ charge you may deposit 1 quarter; 2 dimes and 1 nickel; 1 dime and 3 nickels; or 5 nickels to equal .25¢. But if all you had was 3 dimes, you COULD deposit them and make your call but you would pay .30¢, because the pay phone will not return the nickel change due you.

They're not really very desirable for any situation, in my opinion. They tend to 'tick-off' your customers!

Coin Changer

A coin changer is the best type of coin-mech to have, when practical. Like the coin accumulator, it also accumulates coins to equal the vend price, but it will MAKE CHANGE. A very important feature. These, too, may be electric or electronic.

Since they have to be able to make change, the coins can not ALL simply drop into a coin box as with other coin-mechs. SOME of them are sorted and 'escrowed' into columns of nickels, dimes, and quarters. Once each escrow column is full, any additional coins deposited simply overflow into the coin box. In come situations, the escrow can be empty of a certain coin (say nickels) in which case a light would come on to indicate "exact change only". Obviously, this does not mean the coin box is empty, only the escrow column.

It is important to remember this concept, and the term 'escrow' when you read about BAs, below.

Bill Acceptors

A BA (bill acceptor) is an electronic device which can read currency and validate the authenticity (to a reasonable degree) as well as the denomination ($1.00, $5.00, $10.00, or $20.00).

A DBA (dollar bill acceptor) is essentially the same device but accepts $1.00 bills only.

Most have 'bill stackers' which will hold around 350 bills or more.

It is important to 'match-up' the right coin-mech with the right BA. Since a BA is an ELECTRONIC device, it can not 'talk to' standard electric coin changers. It needs an ELECTRONIC coin changer.

> Since many people buy machines WITHOUT a BA and want to add them later, you may want to make sure you order it with an appropriate electronic coin changer 'up front', or you may have to dump it and buy another later (which will set you back at least a couple hundred dollars unnecessarily).

Also, if the BA will accept $5.00 bills (or higher) you better make sure you have a very large coin 'escrow' (see coin changers for definition) in your electronic coin changer, unless you're selling something that is priced very close to $5.00. Obviously, if you're selling .60¢ products and taking $5.00 bills, your coin escrow will almost always be empty because of the amount of change you are making. And your customers will be very frustrated that the "exact change only" light will be on too much.

Generally, BAs that accept larger denominations of currency have the capability of being set to accept what you want it to (like dollar bills only) and you can change it later if your needs change.

In my vending equipment distributorship, FREEDOM TECHNOLOGY, I make sure that all machines I sell have a BA compatible coin changer IF a BA is an option. . . so that they can always be added later without having to buy another coin changer. Also, the coin changer is matched up to the optional BA so that the coin escrow will be reasonably adequate. This only makes sense, and yet you would be surprised how many people make this mistake!

Bill Changer

A bill changer is a device that includes a BA as it's primary component. It performs a function similar to the bill acceptor, except that it is not tied into the operation of any particular vending or amusement machine. It stands alone. It's sole function is to make change. If you put in a bill, it will give you the same denomination back in coins. You can then insert these coins into vending or amusement machines.

Bill changers are very common in laundry mats, car washes, game arcades, large employee lunch rooms, etc. A slight variation on this is the token dispenser which is common in game arcades (accepts bills and dispenses tokens instead of coins).

In locations where a bill changer is available, there is much less value in having a BA on any individual machine at that location. . . and it is much less expensive to have 1 bill changer than several BAs.

Debit Card Acceptors

With DCAs (debit card acceptors) a pre-paid 'debit card' can be purchased in varying denominations, which is inserted into the DCA (instead of using coins or bills). The DCA notes the requested purchase amount, reads the magnetic strip on the card and notes the available balance, then if the balance is high enough to make the purchase it will authorize the sale and note the debit (or charge) on the card. When the card is spent, it is thrown away.

DCA's are becoming very popular in large businesses, college campuses, etc., where you have a large group of 'in-house' users. The machines will usually accept coins and bills also, but the in-house user may have the additional

convenience of the card, plus they often get a substantial discount that outsiders don't have access to (such as a $10.00 card for only $9.00).

You are not likely to be dealing with this type of location unless and until you have built up a very large operation and can compete for this type of location. Nevertheless, I thought I should mention them.

Slave Machines

I highly recommend using electronic SLAVE machines whenever possible. They can save you a lot of money.

A electronic slave machine has no coin mechanism, bill acceptor, or computer controller board of any kind. It is a SECONDARY machine that plugs into another machine that it sits next to, under, or on top of.

The MASTER is the PRIMARY machine and has a coin mechanism, (maybe a bill acceptor) and computer controller board which serves BOTH machines. Hence, the 'slave' has no brain or

money accepting ability of it's own, and does what it is told to do by its master.

The obvious advantages is that you save the cost of a coin mechanism, bill acceptor, and computer controller board for one of the two machines.

The only disadvantages are that you can't operate the slave machine alone. . . so you can't ever separate the pair. And if there is a problem with the master machine, BOTH machines are out of service. In my opinion, these are not big issues and the advantages far outweigh the disadvantages.

Coin Changers And Bill Acceptors Make Money Too!

Surveys show that the average person has LESS than .60¢ in change in their pocket! What are the odds that they will have the correct COMBINATION of coins for an 'exact change' vending machine? Not very good if the sale price is over .25¢ or so. And what if they have few coins, but adequate currency?

When catering to outside customer traffic (the general public) CONVENIENCE is particularly important since much of the buying is done on impulse and they may have nowhere to go for change.

You won't be surprised to learn that:

Surveys indicate that a machine with a COIN CHANGER may INCREASE SALES as much as 15% to 30% over an 'exact change' type coin-mech.

Similarly, surveys indicate that a DOLLAR BILL ACCEPTOR may INCREASE SALES as much as 15% to 30% more still.

Both have EVEN MORE impact on sales in locations where there is a lot of OUTSIDE customer traffic (general public access).

EMPLOYEES will often plan ahead and bring change to work, or get it from co-workers, the secretary, petty cash, etc., making a coin changer and BA A LITTLE less important in this situation. . . particularly in small businesses. STILL, the lack of a coin changer and BA WILL cost you money! If people were so good at planning ways to have correct change available for vending machines, they would just bring their own snacks and drinks instead!

However in locations relying on OUTSIDE customer traffic, or with large numbers of employees, a coin changer and BA are really mandatory. . . and lack of it will cost you plenty in lost machine performance and profits.

Summary

In light of the above, you can certainly see the value of coin changers and bill acceptors. . . and the impact they can have on sales. However, they are only practical in appropriate locations where the sales will justify the extra cost.

In machines that vend a low priced item (like bulk vendors, fun-size vendors, and most amusement machines) they are usually unavailable AND of little importance.

Many route operators have built up successful snack and cold drink routes using machines with no coin changer or BA. These machines are less expensive and can be very profitable. . . but they should be confined to locations catering primarily to no more than 10 to 30 employees. . . and NO OUTSIDE CUSTOMER TRAFFIC.

In amusement machines, coin changers and BAs are becoming more and more common, however, they are not really required. Of course, it is even less of a consideration if there is a dedicated bill changer on site.

Coin CHANGERS and BA's are of most value:

● When vend price is based upon more than 1 (or sometimes 2) coins.

● In high use locations of all kinds.

Don't underestimate the importance of understanding all types of COIN MECHS, COIN CHANGERS, and BAs. Make sure you are getting the right type for the machines you are buying. . . and for the type of locations you are going after. It can have a huge affect on your profitability!

Notes

Chapter 13
Getting GREAT Locations!

As you might guess, getting GREAT locations is one of the primary objectives for a successful vending business. Even with the very best vending or amusement concept. . . the highest quality machine. . . and the hottest selling merchandise. . . you will not make any money if the machines just sit in your garage (the world's worst location)! In such case, your machines would have little value to you or to anyone else.

By the same token, if you have all your machines located in the very best, highest producing locations. . . you'd feel like you had gooses laying golden eggs! Each time you serviced your machines, you'd feel like you just hit the jackpot in Las Vegas! The route would be so valuable to you that you'd probably never consider selling it. . . but if you did, you could get top dollar.

> In fact, a really good location can actually be worth much more than the vending machine itself!

While I can't over emphasize the importance of 'doing locating right'. . .

> I must loudly proclaim that 'locating right' is not at all difficult! It just takes a little knowledge and effort. And ANYONE can do it!

You'll find that there IS a way that's right for YOU. Just choose a method and follow the simple instructions outlined in this chapter.

You can quickly and easily obtain very profitable locations yourself. . . but if you'd rather not. . . I can help you hire it done in a number of very effective and inexpensive ways. In fact, there are various levels of personal involvement. . . from not at all. . . to doing some of the leg work. . . to completing the whole job.

There are literally hundreds of excellent locations that need and want your machine! There's never a shortage of good locations if you know what you're doing. Here are just a few suggestions:

Locations From A To Z

Airports	Dry Cleaners	Malls	Retirement Homes
Amusement Parks	Factories	Manufacturers	School Staff Rooms
Apartment Clubhouses	Fast Food Chains	Marinas	Service Stations
Auto Dealerships	Garages	Medical Buildings	Shopping Centers
Auto Service Centers	Golf Courses	Meeting Halls	Stock Brokerages
Banks	Government Offices	Military Bases	Taverns
Barber Shops	Grocery Stores	Motels	Teachers Lounges
Bars	Health Clubs	Movie Theaters	Tire Stores
Beauty Salons	Hospital Waiting Rooms	Night Clubs	Tourist Attractions
Billiard Parlors	Hotels	Nursing Homes	Travel Agencies
Bowling Alleys	Industrial Parks	Offices	Truck Stops
Bus Terminals	Insurance Agencies	Pizza Parlors	Tune-Up Centers
Car Washes	Laundromats	Police & Fire Stations	Universities
Coffee Shops	Legal Offices	Private Clubs	Video Arcades
College Campuses	Lodges	Real Estate Offices	Video Stores
Community Centers	Lounges	Recreation Centers	Waiting Rooms
Doctors Offices	Lube Centers	Restaurants	Warehouses
Drug Stores	Lunch Rooms	Retail Stores	Zoos

Locating and Relocating

No matter how good a job you do locating your machines INITIALLY, you'll probably find that you'll love about 20% of them. . . hate about 20% of them. . . and the rest will fall somewhere in the middle (but keepers). You'll probably have to relocate the bottom 20% or so.

In addition, locating is usually an ongoing process to some degree. You should probably plan on relocating about 5% of your locations every month.

This is partly because you will lose some locations due to businesses closing down, changing ownership, or changing their mind about your machine. But mostly because you'll want to continually upgrade the quality of your route. . . relocating the lowest producers to better locations.

Your Options

There are several options to choose from regarding how you will obtain your locations. Regardless as to the method you choose, this chapter will help you accomplish your goal of "Getting GREAT Locations"!

There are three primary methods of obtaining locations, which are:

- On-site (in person)

- Telemarketing (by telephone)

- Direct Mail (mail brochures)

And there are several ways you can get it done, such as:

- Professional locating company

- Local telemarketing service

- Local mailing service

- Local individual

- Do it Yourself

And before you can do anything, you'll have to make a decision regarding:

- Charity sponsorship?

- Or not?

Chapter Objectives

First lets discuss the pros and cons of a charity sponsorship. Then we'll go over how to do locating yourself using the 3 primary methods of obtaining locations (helpful to read even if you're not doing your own locating). Finally, we'll cover how to contract (hire) out the locating work, in case you should decide that you don't want to do it yourself.

The Charity Sponsor Concept

No commission is generally paid to the locations on bulk or fun-size vendors. In many situations, the 10% to 30% (10% typical) commission you might offer a location is often not enough money for them to get enthused about, and often won't motivate them to let you install a machine.

What WILL motivate locations is the ATTRACTIVE CONVENIENCE of the snack machine for customers and employees. . . and/or HELPING OUT A WORTHWHILE CHARITY.

Of course, you always have the option of offering a commission for a terrific location if it makes sense to do so. This could be instead of, or in addition to the charity sponsorship.

Obtaining top locations for bulk and fun-size vendors is especially easy using the CHARITY CONCEPT.

This locating concept can also be used for honor systems, packaged snack and cold drink vendors, and maybe even amusement

machines in some situations. . . although it is most commonly used for bulk and fun-size vendors.

It would be nice to say that most vending operators use this concept to help out worthwhile charities, but the truth is that there are 2 other reasons why the charity locating concept is so popular with operators:

- It makes locations EASIER to get.

- It COSTS LESS than paying commission.

Before you start feeling like the route operators are uncaring and self-serving, keep in mind that most charities absolutely LOVE the program, and here's why:

- They NEED the money.

- They don't have to do ANYTHING to get it.

● They like the FREE ADVERTISING they get from their name being on the machines.

These are essentially 'licensing' agreements. The charity gives you permission to use their name and/or trademark(s) in your vending operations in return for a royalty payment. . . usually a flat rate, but sometimes a commission, or a combination of the two. This is completely legal and ethical in every way.

Your monthly donation to the Charity Sponsor is usually about $1.00 to $2.00 for each honor system, bulk or fun-size vendor, and about $2.00 to $5.00 for other types of machines (depending on the policy of the particular charity). This is generally much less expensive to you than if you paid the location a commission.

I have found that there are many worthwhile charities that will work out just fine, but the ones that work the BEST from a vending operators point of view are one of the following:

● A CHILDREN'S charity of some sort.

● ANY well known LOCAL charity.

The best overall would be a LOCAL charity that serves CHILDREN, if one exists in your area.

There are several major national charities that actively seek out licensing arrangements with the vending industry. They are usually very helpful and supportive. You will find them advertising in the various trade magazines (see chapter titled "Trade Publications, Organizations, And Shows"). Some of the major ones I suggest are:

Child Quest International
1625 The Alameda, Suite 400
San Jose, CA 95126
408-287-4673
MO-FR, 8:00am-5:00pm, PT

'Hugs Not Drugs™'
Family Life International, Inc.
1013 Lucerne Avenue, 1st Floor
Lake Worth, FL 33460
800-700-6697, 561-585-7771
MO-FR, 9:00am-5:30pm, ET

Missing Children Awareness Foundation
13094 95th Street North
Largo, FL 34643
800-741-7233, 813-584-4698
MO-TH, 9:00am-4:30pm, ET
FR, 9:00am-2:00pm, ET

Vanished Children's Alliance
2095 Park Avenue
San Jose, CA 95126
408-296-1113
MO-FR, 8:00am-4:00pm, PT

Contact them and ask for their "vending operators licensing information". If you ask by phone, they may ask you what type of machines you have, so if you don't have them yet just tell them what you plan on having.

If you contract with one of the above charities, they will provide you with their stickers to place on your machines. But if you approach a local charity you will probably have to arrange and pay for the stickers.

Many of them offer a lot of other support materials like a 'Certificate Of Appreciation' that you can give to your locations (which many will frame and hang on the wall) promotional clothing, handouts and premium items, etc.

LOCAL Charities

I suggest you start with one of the above-mentioned national charities. In the beginning, you don't yet have much to offer a LOCAL charity, and you probably won't come across very knowledgeable either. Also, you won't have the benefit of as much support materials. After your route is fully set-up and established (and at least 50 to 100 machines in size) then you may want to consider making a proposal to a local charity.

When doing so, just remember their primary motivations, mentioned above. They need the money. . . they don't have to do anything to get it. . . and they get free advertising from their name being on the machines. Point this out to them.

The agreement can be as simple as an authorization letter, written by them, that says they are allowing you to use their name in your vending operations in exchange for a monthly royalty. If you want, you could copy one of the more formal agreements used by the above mentioned charities and retype it, leaving a blank line to fill in the name of the charity.

NOTE: The publisher and author are not engaged in rendering legal, accounting, tax or other advice or services for which a professional license may be required. The author is simply sharing his personal experience, beliefs and opinions. If required, the services of a competent licensed professional should be sought.

If you start out with a charity that is already skilled in working with vending operators, you will learn a lot that you can use later in setting up a similar deal with a local charity. As I've said, LOCAL charities make it a little easier to get locations. . . but I wouldn't recommend starting out that way.

Handouts

It's good public relations. . . and ultimately good for business. . . to help promote the charity you are working with. Show the locations that you care about the cause, and not just the almighty dollar!

A good way to do this is with handouts. Most charities have some sort of descriptive brochure that you can give away. You would certainly want to distribute them during the locating process. But you may also want to distribute them on your machine with a little plastic "Take One" brochure dispenser. They are inexpensive and stick right on the machine. It won't cost you a lot to give brochures away, because not that many are taken anyway. . . but it IS a community service and it DOES look good to the location (and will also impress the charity you are working with).

You'll purchase the brochures directly from the charity you are working with. Some of them also sell the plastic dispensers (such as Hugs Not Drugs) or you can order them from:

Beemak Plastics, Inc.
16639 South Gramercy
Gardena, CA 90247
800-421-4393, 310-768-0750
MO-FR, 8:00am-4:30pm, PST

Following you will find an example of the procedure suggested for use with 'Hugs Not Drugs™'. They are one of my favorite charities for vendors because they are very supportive of vending operators, and locations are very receptive to accepting machines with the 'Hugs Not Drugs™' name. Also, they are dealing with America's #1 problem (alcohol and drug abuse) which touches all of us in one way or another.

A similar procedure is appropriate for other charities as well.

Locating Machines Yourself

If you decide to start doing your own locating, you'll likely find it to be quite EASY and rather ENJOYABLE, for the most part (more so than you thought). Of course, you NEVER HAVE to do any locating yourself unless you want to. There are many effective and low cost ways to contract it out.

You certainly COULD do your own locating right from the beginning. It's easy. There is one primary reason why many people don't even try. That's because they THINK it's a SALES job. . . and they THINK they won't be any good at it, or that they'll hate it. Some people shouldn't think so much!

Is It Sales?

About 80% of the people don't like selling. . . think they can't sell. . . or think they hate selling.

Many people will even tell you they hate salespeople. The truth is:

IT'S ALL A MATTER OF DEGREE!

On one extreme: We've all been hounded by a pushy, obnoxious 'salesperson' that wouldn't take "no" for an answer. We don't like this treatment, and we often don't like this person. This is not a professional salesperson. . . this is an idiot!

On the other extreme: We're all salespeople. When you were younger, you 'sold' your parents on giving you what you wanted (getting a toy, going to the movies, staying at a friends house). If you're married, you 'sold' your spouse on marrying you. If you have a job, you convinced (sold) someone that you'd be a good person to hire, etc.

An actual 'professional' career salesperson is someone who has learned to respond to a potential buyers inquiries in a polite and interesting way. . . answering all questions and explaining the features and benefits of what he or she sells in an enthusiastic and knowledgeable manner. Naturally, they try to present their product or service in the best possible light. But the pros do not lie or embellish, manipulate or push. If they do their job right and still get a "no", they know that the Buyer either wasn't ready to buy yet, or is not really a Buyer for what they offer. They don't take "no" personally, and don't feel rejected (it is often this fear of 'perceived' rejection that keeps many from trying ANY level of sales activity).

What's involved?

You can match the METHOD of locating with the LEVEL of 'salesmanship' you're comfortable with. Many methods put you in a position of being little more than an ORDER TAKER. For example:

If you get a phone call or a post card from a local business asking you if you could stop by and place a snack and drink vending machine in their business. . . could you say: "Sure, would Tuesday morning be okay, or would afternoon be better"? And then could you go? Of course you could. . . ANYONE could. This can happen as a result of direct mail, a phone book yellow page listing, or in other ways.

Now suppose you have a telemarketer make cold calls (phone calls to people they don't know, and who have not requested information). That's a tough sales job that few people are well suited for. They'll call maybe 10 to 20 people in order to find 1 that is interested (and all those "no's" can be hard to take). But when they find that person, they will give you a note saying

something like: "Bob Jones at E-Z Copies would like to see your bulk vendor, and thinks it'd be okay to put it by the front door". This is not a SURE thing. . . but if you'll just stop by and show Bob a picture of your machine (or better yet, just bring in the actual machine) he will almost always say okay. You didn't have to sell. . . all you did was show up. . . and MAYBE answer a simple question or two. Could you do that? Of course you could. . . ANYONE could.

ANYONE can follow up on inquiries that come from yellow page listings, direct mail or telemarketing.

Could you make cold calls (contact people you don't know, and who have not requested information) either by telemarketing or on-site (in person)? If you're comfortable with that, then you'll have even more options as to how you could locate. If not. . . then don't locate that way. . . or have someone else do that part for you.

Some people are not comfortable using the "on-site" or "telemarketing" techniques themselves. Do whatever feels right for you. You might start out using a professional locator or direct mail. . . try "on-site" locating later. . . and then evolve into some form of telemarketing at some future date. Or hire a telemarketer to do the hard part for you, and just follow up on the leads (requests for more information) they give you.

Any one method can be very effective, so you won't ever have to do anything you're not comfortable with. But you'll probably find that as you gain experience and confidence, you won't mind doing more and more of the locating work. . . in fact you may even find it to be enjoyable and fun!

On-Site Locating

On-site (in person) locating is one of the most common and most effective methods of obtaining quality locations. You simply call upon the types of businesses you interested in serving, and briefly tell them what you can do for them.

When on-site locating, don't be disappointed that you can't get every one you go after. Some people will say "no" just because they're having a bad day (or some other unjustified reason). If you call on

them again in 2 or 3 months, they will often say "yes".

You'll be doing very well if you get 10% - 25% of the businesses you call on. Depending upon your skill level, the type of equipment, and the area, you should be able to secure AT LEAST 1 out of 10 locations contacted. Just remember that locating is a numbers game. Be persistent. Keep calling on those businesses and you'll be a successful locator.

Your Appearance

Dress neat and clean, but relatively casual. Men should not wear a suit or tie, nor should women wear 'dressy' clothes or jewelry. Many people are offended by heavy perfume or cologne, so use sparingly if at all.

If you're working with a charity sponsorship:

Always wear your charity (authorization) name badge, pin or button, and/or promotional clothing (shirts, sweaters, jackets, caps, etc.). Most charities have these items available, especially if they work with vending operators.

If you own a late model BMW, Cadillac, or Mercedes, leave it at home at take a less pretentious car. Or don't park it in view of the location. An affluent look will not be an asset when charity locating.

Locating Portfolio

It's a good idea to put together a 'locating portfolio'. This is a place to keep any visual aids you may use in your machine placement activities. This will not only make your brief presentation more interesting and professional looking, but it may also help you feel more comfortable having something to show.

Get a clear 'overlay' 3-ring binder (the kind that has a clear pocket, front and rear, to insert a sheet of paper). A color photo or brochure of your machine is inserted into the front cover pocket of your binder. If you're working with a charity, in the rear cover pocket insert something identifying the charity (such as a bumper sticker, brochure, etc.). This alone will give you a nice visual aid, if all you did was exhibit the front and rear cover of your portfolio

Use as many references and visual aids as you find helpful, and insert each of them in a plastic sheet protector which you'll put in the portfolio. Try photos of your machines in various locations, machine brochure and specifications, laminated candy labels to capitalize on brand name recognition, charity authorization letter and certificate of appreciation, etc.). You can use the front and rear inside pockets to keep charity brochures and 'Placement Agreements' (should you decide to use a written agreement).

Some operators summarize their presentation with a couple of brief headlines which they print on a sheet (or sheets) of paper in their portfolio. This will help you remember what you want to say, and also emphasizes what you're saying to the location manager. It make look something like this:

Attractive Convenience (or Amusement)

We Service

Costs You Nothing

New Profit Center (if applicable)

If charity sponsorship involved:

Benefits Hug Not Drugs

Sign Indicates Support

Good Public Relations

You should make the above headlines in large type (at least 1/4" high). This can be easily produced with a computer and printer if you have access to one. If not, go to any office supply store and buy some 'press apply' transfer letters. These look like they were professionally typeset and are easily applied by simply placing on a sheet of paper and rubbing the back side with a pen.

I advise you to keep your locating portfolio with you at all times, particularly when you are servicing your route. You never know when you will be asked about your machines, or when you'll have an opportunity to ask for a location. Many of my best locations have been obtained in the normal course of my day (without even trying). When I go out for lunch, I may end up with a new restaurant location before I'm through eating!

Many route operators keep their route records in the back of their locating portfolio, rather than have 2 different folders. That way it's always with you when your out servicing your machines.

Wear A Name Badge

A name badge gives you a professional image, and tells everyone who you are and what company (or charity) you're with. It also makes it easy to remember your name. Name recognition improves business relations. And if someone forgets your name, they won't have to be embarrassed about it because they can just look again.

By the way, it pays to go the extra mile and make an effort to remember the names of the primary people you deal with while locating (and route servicing). Consider setting up an index file on 3" x 5" cards, or making a note in your locating portfolio or route records.

If you're working with a charity, some of them will have name badges of various types available for purchase (sometimes free). Just ask.

You can also order a very attractive plastic or metal one from most trophy suppliers. Be sure to include the charity trademark or logo (if working with a charity) or your own (if you have one). They can copy it off of ANY printed matter, and reproduce it in ANY size (provide them with the LARGEST copy you have available because it will look better reduced, rather than enlarged). Otherwise, you may want to use some sort of stock graphics that are available, to dress it up a little.

Check your yellow pages under "Name Badges", "Name Plates" or "Trophies". These name badges look very permanent and professional and give you a look of substance. You'll find they help a lot when locating.

You can also use the above mentioned 'press apply' transfer letters to produce a quick, good looking yet inexpensive name badge. Just take a piece of card-stock 2-1/4" high X 3-1/2" wide. Apply your name on the card. Then cut out the charity trademark or logo from one of their brochures, or your logo from your business card or letterhead, and glue it on next to (or above) your name. Finally, insert the card into a plastic name badge and you're done (you can find them in any office supply store, either pin-on or clip-on type).

What To Do and Say

Call on all types of businesses during normal business hours, but avoid rush periods. Choose businesses that you estimate will have enough employees or customer traffic to be profitable (see the chapter titled "Location Targeting And Analysis").

You'll find it relatively easy to get good locations. There really isn't much of a 'pitch' involved. . . and there are seemingly unlimited quality locations to call on.

Below you'll find some suggested 'scripts' you may want to learn to use in approaching businesses. Obviously, you would put this in your own words which you are comfortable with. . . but it is helpful to plan and write down what you intend to say in advance.

You probably should not try to memorize your script word-for-word (although you could if you feel more comfortable having a definite 'track' to run on). Use it as a guideline. Change whatever is necessary to make yourself feel more comfortable with it. Above all. . . make the words your own, or it will not sound natural.

Many people find it very helpful to practice what they're going to say, in front of a mirror and/or tape recorder. . . or better yet, try role-playing with a friend.

Obviously, the person you're talking with doesn't have a script to follow. You don't know exactly how they will respond, and when. So you'll have to 'ad-lib' a little. Just stay loose and go with the flow! And get back to your script when you can.

Above all, show enthusiasm. Be friendly and cheerful. You'll do much better, and have more fun in the process. If you're not feeling well, or you're in a bad mood, stay home!

Bulk Vendors And Fun-Size Vendors

"Hi, I'm John Smith (associated) with Hugs Not Drugs. Are you the owner or manager? (Talk with the right person). It's nice to meet you. I'm working on a local fund-raising project, but I'm NOT asking you for any money today. Are you familiar with Hugs Not Drugs? Great!"

(If not, a brief description): "Hugs Not Drugs is the nation's most respected charity dedicated to empowering the family to end the demand for drugs through early education of children." (Hand them a charity brochure).

"We're asking businesses like yours in the area to donate just a SINGLE square foot of space for a SMALL, candy vending machine. These machines provide an attractive convenience (show picture of machine) for you and your people. We service regularly with FRESH, NAME

BRAND candy. The BEST part is that the revenue from these little machines benefits Hugs Not Drugs and the children in THIS community (show sticker sample)."

"Is there any particular item you'd like to have in your machine? Would here by the door (pick a good place) be a good place to put it, or would over there be better? Could I please have your address for our records (start filling out the Placement Agreement or Route Report). Please OK this form (if you're using a written agreement). We'll have your new machine installed by tomorrow. THANK YOU."

That's all there is to it! Pretty simple, right?

In addition to. . . or instead of paying your charity sponsor, you may want to consider paying 10% of the gross sales to the business establishment. . . 15% to 20% if you have to (for a great location). . . and in some cases, up to a maximum of 30% (for extremely outstanding locations only).

These commission rates apply only to bulk-vending. I wouldn't pay over 10% to 15% commission on a fun-size vendor.

Furthermore, I know operators with hundreds of these machines that neither pay commission nor use the charity approach. If you offer quality, attractive, late model equipment many locations will accept it as a convenience to them with no compensation at all. No Kidding!

Blockbuster Approach!

For Bulk Vendors, Fun-size Vendors, And Honor Systems

This method takes a little guts, but it is by far the FASTEST and MOST EFFECTIVE way to locate bulk vendors and fun-size vendors. . . and get them EXACTLY where you want them. It also works best for honor systems. It's completely legal and ethical, but not everyone is comfortable with this. So if that's you, just use the standard locating method covered above.

The most outstanding feature of the blockbuster approach (also called the "assumptive approach") is the 'assumptive attitude' required for this to work. And it does work great! Here's the basics:

Lets assume you are locating HOT bulk vendors, and that you're working with Hugs Not Drugs as your charity sponsor.

You ASSUME that EVERYONE wants a HOT bulk vendor because of its very unique appearance, features, and benefits (as covered in the chapter titled "Bulk Vending").

And you also ASSUME that EVERYONE wants to support a major charity such as Hugs Not Drugs, who is fighting America's #1 problem (drug and alcohol abuse).

So you simply show up at any location you want, WITH the machine in hand (or on a dolly) all ready to place, and say (with a smile on your face):

"Hi, I'm John Smith with Hugs Not Drugs. I've brought your new candy vendor! Is here by the counter okay, or would over there by the door be better."

Often, their only response will be simply "oh great. . . over there is fine". Does this always work? No. But you would be absolutely amazed how often it does!

If someone starts questioning you, you simply revert back to the standard locating method covered above. No big deal.

Much of the time they'll agree to try it out, just because IT'S ALREADY THERE, and they like it anyway.

Even if the owner or manager isn't there, the employees will often let you leave the machine on a 'free trial' basis. For one thing, they often ASSUME that the owner or manager ALREADY knows about this and has approved it (due to your assumptive attitude). Besides, if it's a free trial anyway, the worst that could happen is they'd call you and you'd pick it up. . . right?

On whatever basis you leave a HOT bulk vendor or fun-size vendor. . . once it's there it will most likely be staying. Just getting them to see it in person is 90% of the job (pictures may not do justice). And if they live with it awhile, they won't want to part with it.

Snacks And Cold Drinks

"Hi! I'm John with Smith VENDING Systems. Are you the owner or manager? (Talk with the right person). It's nice to meet you. We'd like to offer you this brand NEW (or late model) space-saving snack and drink vendor (show picture of machine) complete with a coin changer and dollar bill acceptor. We service regularly with FRESH, NAME BRAND snacks and cold drinks. And there's NO COST or obligation to you except for the items purchased *."

> * If you're in a location with very high profit potential you might consider adding: "In fact, we're going to pay you a 10% commission on all sales".

"Is there any particular item you'd like to have in your machine? Would the copy machine area (mention a good place) be a good place to put it, or would over there be better? Could I please have your address for our records (start filling out the Placement Agreement or Route Report). Please OK this form (if you're using a written agreement). We'll have your new machine(s) installed by tomorrow. THANK YOU."

Don't be too quick to offer a commission, however. You'll find that you'll rarely have to pay it unless you're approaching a very high volume location. Nevertheless, if you have an opportunity for a high volume location, your profit will be so attractive that you will not mind paying a commission. Commissions on this type of product sales typically range from 5% to 15% (typically averaging 10%) and is very negotiable.

If you're locating in places with over 20 employees or high sales volume, you will often find that they already have vending equipment. Don't worry. The world is packed full of poorly managed vending operations and old, obsolete equipment. If you're told "we already have vending machines", just emphasize:

> "If you're not 100% satisfied with your present vendors, please consider that we're in a position to offer you a brand NEW (or late model) space-saving vendor complete with a coin changer and dollar bill acceptor.

And our routes are very CAREFULLY managed to make sure you're always fully stocked with only FRESH, NAME BRAND products. Would you like any health oriented products in your vendor? (Then start writing up the order)."

Does this work all the time? No. But you'll probably be amazed how often it will! A new or late model machine with a coin changer and bill acceptor is usually highly prized by locations, and they probably won't have one. And even if they do, your promise of "careful management" and "fully stocked" machine with "only fresh name brand products" is VERY POWERFUL. And the odds are in your favor that they are not happy with their current vending service.

Amusement Machines

"Hi! I'm John with Smith VENDING Systems. Are you the owner or manager?" (Talk with the right person). "It's nice to meet you. We'd like to install this space-saving entertainment profit center (show picture of machine) for you and your customers. We service regularly, and there's NO COST or obligation to you. . . in fact, we're going to PAY YOU up to 50% CASH commission on all sales (show commission schedule). Would the counter area (mention a good place) be a good place to put it, or would over there be better? Could I please have your address for our records (start filling out the Placement Agreement or Route Report). Please OK this form (if you're using a written agreement). We'll have your new system installed by tomorrow. THANK YOU."

Many locations are not familiar with impulse machines. Since they are small and lightweight, I've found it very helpful to bring one along when trying to place them. When the location sees how little space they take up. . . and how much fun they are. . . it makes your job easy! They are much more impressive in person, and a picture may not do them justice.

Also, when locating impulse machines in a retail store or mall environment, be sure to point out that they are 'traffic stoppers'.

> "People will stop to look (if not play) and at the same time, they can't help but notice your window displays"

Don't Worry. . . Be Happy!

If you don't have any experience in sales or public relations work you may be reluctant to try locating yourself. But don't cheat yourself out of a chance to have ultimate control over your business (and save money) by doing your own locating. It's easy.

Just go out and try it. . . and do it with this attitude: It doesn't matter if you do a poor job and blow EVERY location. Just go out and approach 10 or 20 locations tomorrow, and don't plan on getting ANY of them. After leaving each location, just ask yourself "what could I have done better". . . and LEARN from your experience.

> Just have fun and don't worry about results at first.

And don't worry that you may have blown some locations. I can assure you that there are PLENTY more. . . AND if you come back in 2 or 3 months, they won't even remember you anyway!

Besides, you'll 'stumble' upon many good locations even if you don't do the most professional job. . . just by being there. Many locations want what you offer and will say "yes" just as soon as you show it to them!

It's A Numbers Game

Every locator has figured out their average number of calls required to get a location. For example, you may have to approach 5 locations in order to locate 1 bulk vendor. For a snack machine, maybe you'd approach 8. If approached by telemarketing, it may take double or triple that amount.

You'll figure out your locating rate soon enough. The key is to remember that this is just a numbers game. If on average you have to approach 10 locations to secure 1. . . then every "no" puts you a little closer to "yes". . . and represents 10% completion!

If you remember this, watch your attitude, don't worry, and be happy. . . you'll do fine locating. It may take a little guts at first. . . you may have to get out of your 'comfort zone' a little. . . but you CAN do it. And if you will, you'll most likely find that it's fun, easy, and very profitable!

Handling Questions/Objections

You may want to learn to deal with a certain amount of questions and objections. You can answer them to the extent that you're comfortable with it. I don't even encourage you to deal with them unless you are totally comfortable in doing so. Many route operators just make their little pitch, and if they hear anything other than a simple "yes" they just say "thanks anyway" and go on to another place to ask again.

As I've said, locating machines is just a simple numbers game. Keep walking and talking. If you walk into enough of the right places and ask for a location, you'll soon have a very profitable route put together. You'll hear "yes" enough even if you don't learn to handle questions and objections well.

But always remember this. . . an objection is usually JUST a request for MORE information. It is NOT a rejection or "no". Often, they are not even a real concern. Don't let them bother you or unnerve you. In time, you'll learn to expect them. . . even welcome them. And you'll learn how to respond appropriately.

If you decide you'd like to learn how to handle questions, objections and delays well. . . just follow these simple guidelines:

What To Do And Say

First of all, a common and easily avoided delay is simply erring to talk with the right person. Make sure that you're talking with the owner, manager, or decision maker.

VALIDATE their question or concern, sometimes making general references to others. . . then play down it's importance and/or answer it directly. For example: "Good point, Good question, Most businesses that participate in our program showed concerns like yours, BUT found that they COULD (enjoy the benefits, or ???), and here's why (how). . . ." ANSWER the objection/question, and immediately PROCEED with your presentation.

If appropriate, NOTE the concern on the Placement Agreement or Route Records (i.e: Put machine next to coffee table. No peanuts. Business establishment not responsible for machine. Service

TWICE-a-month, etc.). Show your concern to eliminate or minimize their concern.

In some cases it may be helpful to ISOLATE the question(s) or objection(s). ("Mr. Smith, except for your lack of space, is there any OTHER concern you have about accepting one of our machines?") Then resolve the matter(s) and you've got the location.

After you get a little experience, you'll know what kinds of objections to expect. They'll be the same ones (just a couple of them) and you'll hear them over and over. Once you find a good response that works for you, you'll have no problem dealing with them most of the time.

Commissions and Placement Agreements

Suggested and customary commission payments vary according to the type of equipment, and have been covered elsewhere in this and other chapters. Remember, however, that commission is always negotiable.

> Furthermore, I know operators with hundreds of machines that neither pay commission nor use the charity approach. If you offer quality, attractive, late model equipment many locations will accept it as a convenience to them with no compensation at all. No Kidding!

If you're using a WRITTEN Placement Agreement. . . and if you're paying commission to the location. . . you would write in the commission in the section of the agreement titled "Miscellaneous Provisions".

Many route operators disagree on the use of 'written' Placement Agreements. I think it's good business to have a written agreement, but the argument against them is that they slow down the locating process. Some business owners are reluctant to sign anything (and if they do at all, they study it very carefully). You'd probably be amazed at the number of operators who do

business on a simple handshake. . . even when placing very expensive equipment!

My suggestion to you is this. Use a written agreement. . . at least in the beginning. If, after you have some experience under your belt, you feel okay with verbal agreements. . . fine. But consider that a written agreement establishes you as the rightful owner of the machine, and gives you certain valuable rights in adverse circumstances. And of course, they help avoid misunderstandings.

A sample of a typical Placement Agreement (one that I use) may be found in the Appendix under "Forms And Miscellaneous". However, Placement Agreements used for charity sponsorship are shorter, simpler, and vary somewhat depending upon the charity. The charity will provide you with a copy of their recommended locating agreement.

> NOTE: The publisher and author are not engaged in rendering legal, accounting, tax or other advice or services for which a professional license may be required. The author is simply sharing his personal experience, beliefs and opinions. If required, the services of a competent licensed professional should be sought.

Telemarketing

Telemarketing (phone calling) is another good way to obtain good locations while saving wear and tear on your car (and your feet). You will not obtain as many locations per number of businesses called on (compared to a personal visit) but you will probably find that you obtain more locations per day worked because of the increased efficiency.

Many route operators use telemarketing simply as a way to determine if the business has any need or interest in their vending services, the name of the person to talk with, and the time of day they are in.

Then they call on them in person (with or without an appointment). This combination of telemarketing and on-site locating is usually more effective than telemarketing alone would be.

The telephone approach is similar to how you would handle on on-site approach (see above) with some slight modifications.

When telemarketing, the objective is OFTEN not to get them to "OK" machine placement on the phone. Instead, you're 'prospecting' (or 'looking' for interest in what you offer). You want to get them to say "OK" to you stopping by and showing them your machine (or a picture of it) and explain your service to them.

The primary exception to this would be in locating honor systems, bulk vendors, or fun-size vendors. . . particularly if you're using a charity sponsorship. You can easily get the "OK" on this over the phone. Then all you need to do is drop by and set it up. Telemarketing is as great way to locate this type of equipment.

You can use a script similar to the ones mentioned above.

If you're locating bulk vendors and going for the "OK" over the phone, for example, you could use the script 'as is'. Just delete the portion regarding asking for their signature on a Placement Agreement. Do that when you stop by.

If you're locating snack/drink or amusement machines and are just screening for interest level, contact person, and maybe appointment setting, at the end of the above mentioned script just add something to the effect of:

"I'd like to stop by and briefly show you what we can offer you. Are mornings OK, or would afternoons be better?"

Telemarketing is one of the most cost effective ways to locate vending and amusement machines. I highly encourage you to consider it in your vending operations.

Direct Mail

Direct mail can be a very easy, inexpensive, and effective way to obtain good locations. This involves mailing a flyer (brochure) and/or letter to the types of businesses you're interested in. A VERY good response to such a mailing would be 3% to 5%. . . meaning that for every 100 brochures you send out, you may expect 3 to 5 replies. . . and probably about 1 to 3 or those will result in a quality location being obtained.

Your objective with direct mail is usually not to get an "OK" directly from the mailing, but rather to 'prospect' (or look) for interest. After you receive your response you will stop by and handle it pretty much the same as the on-site approach. The difference is that they want to see you. . . they asked to see you. . . they expect to see you. . . and you already know they are interested in what you offer! It certainly makes it easy.

I have found that direct mail is VERY effective for snack and drink machines. But I can't honestly say I'd recommend it for anything else.

I have included a sample of a typical flyer that may be used, for your reference (look in the Appendix under "Forms And Miscellaneous"). Most any copy shop or quick printer can take a look at this sample and make up something similar for you that will get the job done. It can be very effective without being fancy or expensive.

You probably won't be doing enough mailing over a long enough time period to justify buying a bulk mailing permit from the Post Office. There's a one-time application fee, plus an annual fee. You would receive a lower postage rate, but you have to do a lot of mailing to recover these initial costs, and more time is spent sorting the mail and filling out forms. I'd start out using first class mail, and if you like the results and start doing more volume, then contact the Post Office for bulk rate information.

Another option would be to use the bulk rate permit of a mailing service. The postage you save may pay for their service, and you won't have to buy the permit! More on that to follow.

Contracting Out Your Locating

There are several options available to you regarding how you may 'hire out' your machine locating. . . some are excellent, and some not so good. Other than doing it yourself, these are your primary options:

● Professional locating company

● Local telemarketing service

● Local mailing service

● Local individual

Each one merits some discussion and consideration.

Professional Locating Company

These companies are in the business of specializing in locating vending machines only. The majority of them do on-site locating, but many do telemarketing, and some do direct mail.

Virtually ALL biz-op (business opportunity) promoters use these companies, although many of them are not very 'up front' about it. Many who sell you equipment promise you that "OUR locators will get you your locations" but they simply sub-contract to these companies.

I use the word "professional" loosely when referring to these locating companies because, with shamefully few exceptions, very few are professional at all. In my opinion, there are so few that are worthy of your time and money that my advice to you is to assume that they are ALL absolutely worthless! I am hesitant to make gross generalizations about anything, but this is a situation that warrants such a strong statement.

> Having said that, you should know that there ARE a couple of companies that are OK. If you contact my company, FREEDOM TECHNOLOGY, we will give you their names but I will not print them in this book.

I will not print the name of any locating company in this book because I want more control when it comes to having the option of withdrawing a referral if I see signs of trouble. In my business I may see it coming long before you would, and I would not want these names circulating in thousands of books with no way to withdraw them quickly.

Why is this necessary? I have given you dozens of referrals to other companies throughout this book. This type of business is problematic (see "What's The Problem" below) and most of these companies are unstable. Even though there may be some that I feel good enough about to refer to you, because of my past experience with locating companies in general, I am not comfortable making a blanket recommendation with no quick method of retraction.

By the way. . . no, I do not receive any commissions or kick-backs from locating companies, nor do I have any ownership interest in any locating company. Aside from the fact that I consider that to be unethical and would not do it, the Federal Trade Commission frowns on it as well.

I've thought about setting up a locating company so I could control the job to assure that it's done right, but the above makes that impossible unless I quit selling machines (which I am not interested in doing).

So What's The Problem?

On-site Locating Companies

The biggest (but not only) problem is with the ON-SITE locating companies. It's just a flawed concept that can almost never work. Here's why:

First of all, let's assume you pay an on-site locating company $2,000.00 to get a certain amount of locations for you. Usually only about half, or $1,000.00 goes to the person that is actually going to do the work. The rest goes to the company to pay their overhead and a LARGE profit.

Now, the locator who will do the work is almost always from out of town. So he (or she) will have travel expenses to your town, PLUS daily living expenses of at least $50.00 to $75.00 for hotel, eating out, etc. Obviously, they are VERY motivated to get the job done and get out of town.

In order to find people willing AND able to do this kind of work, put up with the travel, etc, you generally have to pay them at least $1,000.00 gross per week (their expenses come out of that). Since this is contract work, the only way they can make this kind of money is to do the job very quickly. Even the ones that seem sincere and have good intentions just can't really afford to take the time to do the job right. . . or if they can, they generally don't.

In the above example, you have paid $2,000.00 for the locating job. Only $1,000.00 goes to the person doing the actual work. And he is going to move heaven and earth to limit you to no more than 5 days of his time for all that money you paid!

The same principle applies, regardless as to the size of the job or the amount of money you paid. They just CAN not. . . or at least most WILL not do a good job for you.

It is easier to sell vending and amusement machines if you refer people to these companies and just tell them that "they will get good locations for you". People want to believe that this is true, and are quick to accept it. But I can not and will not do that in my business.

There are good solutions to this problem. And I'll be covering what does (or can) work.

Telemarketing And Direct-Mail Locators

Here, I am NOT referring to a GENERIC telemarketing or direct-mail company, but rather, to a company that SPECIALIZES in locating vending and amusement machines.

Most of these TELEMARKETING specialty companies have no minimum order, which is an obvious advantage to you. If you're starting out with just a couple of machines, it may be difficult to find anyone else to do the job for you (besides yourself, of course). And if you have a big locating job, you can try them out on just a couple of locations before you commit to the whole job.

It's more common for a direct-mail company to have a minimum order, but the minimum is usually not very big.

These are concepts that at least have the POTENTIAL to work. They are relatively inexpensive, and there are no travel costs, etc.

Still, there are many such companies that are simply unscrupulous. They often will charge too much money for their services, take a month or two to do the job, and even then you'll get crummy or inappropriate locations.

> Again, we at FREEDOM TECHNOLOGY can refer you to a couple of locating companies that are OK. If you contact us we will give their names to you.

If you are working with an honest and ethical locating telemarketer or direct-mailer, who charges fair prices, then you CAN get good locations for your money. The key is THE CONTACT LIST.

Some of them will put together a good list for you, and some will not. Just to be sure, I advise you to buy or make up YOUR OWN LIST.

If they only contact the names on YOUR list, it is much less likely they will ever get any location that you do not want. Therefore, you can pick out your own great locations by simply putting only great locations on the list! You know your area. . . in some situations, it may be as simple as you going through the phone book yellow pages, or driving around busy sections of town, and writing down what you know to be busy businesses.

> See the chapter titled "Location Targeting And Analysis" for information about how to buy or put together such a list.

For more information, please refer to the "Telemarketing" and "Direct-Mail" sections that appeared earlier in this chapter.

Location GUARANTEES

Don't be fooled just because some locating companies may guarantee their locations. Look for the loopholes in their offer.

Most of them offer a 'placement' guarantee, which is fine. This usually says that if the location will not accept your machine when you show up, they will replace it for you. Some companies extend this to 7 or 14 days after placement.

The guarantees you have to watch out for are the 'performance' guarantees. There are many variations, but basically, they offer to replace any locations (free, or half price) that don't do well, or that you don't like after a certain period of time (like 3 to 6 months). You must leave the machine in the location during this time period or the guarantee is void. They'll agree to relocate maybe one or two times (sometimes unlimited).

The problem with this is that it's usually not designed to assure you of good locations. It's designed to help them market their services, and ultimately wear you out. If they get you a poor and/or inappropriate location you will know within the first month. By making you tolerate the location for 3 to 6 months, they hope you will just get another one on your own, or pull the machine out (in either case they would not owe you another location). If you do comply, the odds are that your next location will not be any better.

As I said, there are many variations on this. Just be careful and look for the loopholes.

Local Telemarketing Service

Any generic local telemarketing company can locate vending machines. They're skilled in selling most anything by telephone, and represent all sorts of companies, products, and services. Not only is it unimportant that they be a vending machine (specialty) locating company. . . in fact, they may be less expensive if they are not, due to more competitive pricing policies and lack of long distance phone charges (if in your calling area).

They may not always be lower priced on small jobs, because there is often a set-up charge or minimum order (usually not so with the specialty companies).

As a rule, they will do a better job for you than the locating specialty companies. . . but not always. As I've said, there are a couple of good locating companies that we can refer you to if you contact us here at FREEDOM TECHNOLOGY.

You can find a local telemarketing service by looking in the phone book yellow pages under "Telemarketing Service" or "Telephone Marketing Service".

Just copy one of the scripts out of this chapter. . . make your own. . . or give the whole book to the telemarketer. They will take what you give them, read the relevant parts, and make up a their own script that they are comfortable with.

Charges for this type of service varies widely. Some charge by the hour, regardless of results. I prefer a results-oriented payment plan that pays them a fixed amount for a location obtained (or an appointment).

Whether you do it yourself, hire a local individual or company, or a locating specialty company. . . telemarketing is one of the most inexpensive and effective ways to locate almost any type of vending or amusement equipment. For more information, please refer to the "Telemarketing" section that appeared earlier in this chapter.

Local Mailing Service

Here I'm referring to the local direct mail services that operate in your community. They do contract mailings for all sorts of different businesses. They have their own postal bulk rate permit and high speed mail handling equipment.

Most of these companies are mailing list brokers, and some will even help you with the preparation and printing of your direct-mail piece.

Check your phone book yellow pages under "Mailing Services".

Direct mail is a low cost and effective way to locate snack and drink vendors, but I would not recommend it for any other type of vending or amusement machines. For more information, please refer to the "Direct Mail" section that appeared earlier in this chapter.

Local Individual

Whether you want to do on-site locating, telemarketing, or even direct mail. . . one of your best options is to hire a local individual (not a company).

It will cost less, even though you can afford to pay that person more than he (or she) would receive if they worked for a locating company. Also, that person will not have travel expenses. The net result is that being qualified, being local, knowing

the area, and being well paid. . . they can potentially do a much better job!

But how do you find someone like this? Forget trying to hire someone with vending locating experience. This is so specialized that you will not likely find anyone. All you really need is someone with sales, telemarketing, or public relations experience (or ability).

Unless you are starting out very big, this is probably going to be a part time job for someone. Keep that in mind. After the initial locating job, you will (hopefully) be growing steadily. And you can expect to relocate about 5% of your (lower producing) machines each month. So there will be ongoing work, but still, you need someone who is not going to complain when there is little or no work to do.

Start with people you know. Who do you know that has sales or public relations experience (or ability) that would like to make a few extra bucks on the side?

Another EXCELLENT source is retirees! There are lots of retirees who need extra money and want part-time work. Even through they are eager to work, they often find it difficult to find any, and are very appreciative of any opportunity. Generally, they are a very high quality, honest, and reliable labor pool. And they're usually flexible on work hours. The only drawback: If you have a full-time job, you may have to divide it up between 2 or more retirees. . . big deal.

Since they come from all walks of life, you can find a retired salesperson or telemarketer who would be well suited for this job. The best and most effective locators I've ever had have been senior citizens. Due to their respected status, locations give them extra attention, and show them extra courtesy.

You could find one that could not only do your locating, but run a route and even run your whole business (if you want). See chapter titled "Route Management".

> Check with your local senior citizens centers or Department Of Labor (employment) office. They can almost always refer you to someone who coordinates jobs for senior citizens in your area. You'd be surprised how fast they can match you up with the right person.

Your local Department Of Labor (employment) office is also a good way to reach the general population of job seekers, however, it is not as effective for finding part-time workers. But it's usually free, so you may want to at least try it.

As a final option, I'd try a classified ad in the 'part-time jobs' section of your local newspaper. Something like this will be effective:

Find locations for vending machines. $200.00 month (or $?) commission only. Sales or public relations experience required. Call 123-4567.

Regardless as to whom you hire, just give them this book (or at least the relevant chapters) and let them take it from there. It will be your job to supervise them and make sure they are getting you appropriate locations. Do not accept any locations that do not fit your requests. See chapter titled "Location Targeting And Analysis"

What To Pay?

Locating fees are highly negotiable and prices may vary according to the market you are in. Below is a rough idea what you might expect to pay to get a quality job done by a local individual. Locating company fees are a little higher.

The telemarketing price listed assumes that you will do whatever minimal follow-up that is necessary (with bulk and fun-size vendors there should be very little or none). If you hire a locator who is going to do a combination of telemarketing and on-site locating, I would pay them the on-site price.

	On-Site	Tele
Bulk	$35.	$25.
Fun-size	35.	25.
Honor snack tray (deliver while locating)	15.	N/A
Snack (low volume)	100.	50.
Snack (high volume)	200.+	100.+
Cold drink (low volume)	100.	50.
Cold drink (high volume)	200.+	100.+
Impulse location (1-3 machs)	100.	50.
Video game	150.	75.

These prices do not include set up, except for honor snack trays which are generally carried in, shown, and placed while locating.

At these prices, don't expect your locator to guarantee the location either, except for placement. If you go to place the machine and they've changed their mind, the locator is not entitled to payment. In fact, it is customary to extend this for 7 to 14 days past placement for possible cancellations only.

Be fair and pay your locator well. Someone who does a good job is very valuable to you.

In general, a locating fee will be equal to the expected gross monthly profit on a given machine for about 1 to 3 months, depending upon the difficultly of the job.

You can get creative and do a lot of different things to provide a financial incentive for a locator to do a good job. And you'll both be a lot better off. These methods save you money on the locations that don't work out. On the other hand, you can afford to pay more for the ones that do work out. For example:

You may want to pay a little less up front (25% to 50% less) but offer a bonus if the machine is still on location after about 3 to 6 months. The total of the initial payment and the bonus should equal more than you would have paid otherwise (125% to 200% of the standard payment). This would apply whether the location asked that it be picked up. . . or even if you picked it up because it was a low performer.

A variation on this is a royalty payment. Pay less up front (as mentioned above) but instead of a bonus, pay on ongoing royalty (for as long as you have the location, or you could put a limit on it if you want, say 5 years). You could offer 5-10% of gross monthly profit, or whatever makes sense to you. In general, I'd set it up so that in an AVERAGE location the initial payment, together with the royalty payment, would equal my standard payment schedule (above) after about 12 months. This

method requires that the locator trust you to report your correct income to them. . . and that you open your records to him or her upon request.

I suggest you try to come up with some way to offer financial incentive to your locator. It's such an important job, and they don't get the benefit of ongoing income for a good location (like you do). You can afford to pay a lot for a really good location, but you don't want to pay much for a mediocre one. Think about it.

Also, I recommend avoiding 'employee' status due to additional complexity and cost. 'Independent contractor' status is preferable since you don't have to withhold for taxes, pay F.I.C.A., etc. You just pay them and those things are their responsibility.

Independent contractors usually are paid a fixed rate or percentage, provide their own car, supplies, etc. . . and work their own hours (a brief description).

NOTE: The publisher and author are not engaged in rendering legal, accounting, tax or other advice or services for which a professional license may be required. The author is simply sharing his personal experience, beliefs and opinions. If required, the services of a competent licensed professional should be sought.

For more information, please refer to the "On-site" and "Telemarketing" sections that appear earlier in this chapter.

Summary

I believe you'll find the following to be a good rule of thumb:

● On-site locating works well for ALL types of machines.

● Telemarketing works well for OBTAINING locations for honor systems, bulk vendors, and fun-size vendors. . . but is also very effective in PROSPECTING (looking and screening) for interest in most all other types of machines.

● Direct mail is very effective but only for snack and drink vendors.

Don't underestimate the importance of asking your current locations for referrals! They almost always know other businesses that would be interested in your machines, but if you forget to ask they probably won't remember to tell you.

Doing your own locating is preferable, but not required. If you're doing your own locating, I would recommend doing everything with the on-site approach at first. Use the blockbuster approach for honor systems, bulk vendors, and fun-size vendors if you're comfortable with that. And consider trying telemarketing or direct mail after you've got a little more experience.

If you are hiring out part or all of your locating my recommendations are different: I would recommend using local people and companies whenever possible. Use on-site or telemarketers for bulk vendors and fun-size vendors. Use on-site, telemarketing or direct-mail for snack and drink vendors. And use on-site for everything else.

If you're operating snack/drink vendors I would recommend that you place a phone book listing in the yellow pages under "Vending Machines (or Services)". You'd be surprised how many calls you'll get from locations that are unhappy with their current vendor. Also, having a name that appears towards the front of the list (alphabetically) won't hurt either.

Regardless as to how you locate, make sure you have an answering machine (or answering service) connected to your phone. When you get a call from a potential location (or existing location requesting service) it will hurt your business if they can't reach you or even leave a message.

If and when you're willing to try doing your own locating, you may find it helpful to seek out additional motivational support and training materials. Your local library and bookstore will be a good source for such materials. In addition, one of the best sources for sales, marketing, business, and motivational training I have found is Nightingale Conant. I suggest you call for their exceptional free catalog:

Nightingale Conant
800-323-3938
MO-FR, 8:00am-9:00pm, CST
SA, 9:00am-1:00pm, CST

See the chapter titled "Location Targeting And Analysis" for important information that will help you determine what type of locations to approach, how to find them, mailing lists, etc.

Good Luck. . .

Although you won't need it! This approach to placing your machines, coupled with the terrific design and appearance of those I've recommended in this book, assures you that there are many profitable locations willing to accept a machine placement. You should always have a waiting list of locations ready to accept a machine from you.

Chapter 14
Location Targeting And Analysis

This is a fun chapter that is intended to help you decide for yourself what are reasonable expectations regarding vending machine location performance and profitability. Also, it will help you choose a method of 'targeting' the locations you want to go after.

Don't allow yourself to get bogged down in this chapter. While it is helpful for you to understand the basics of the subject. . . it is not necessary for you to be able to do a COMPLEX analysis in order for you to be successful in this business. In fact, many operators do not do them at all!

This chapter goes hand-in-hand with the previous chapter titled "Getting Great Locations".

Please note that information from this chapter has been used to illustrate the profit potential of many of the various types of vending machines discussed in other chapters. The following 'disclaimer' followed each such illustration, and applies to this entire chapter as well:

NOTE: This is provided for illustrative purposes only. It does not include machine cost, freight, sales tax, locating, or other miscellaneous costs not specifically listed, if any. Figures may vary according to type of business, geographical location, fluctuations in customer traffic, and many other factors which can not be predicted. Therefore, the actual results achieved may vary and can not be guaranteed.

There really are many factors which can affect machine performance, and it is very hard to predict with any degree of certainty how any particular location will perform. You may find it helpful to consider national averages, vending surveys, etc. Then you can decide for yourself what is reasonable to expect.

Obviously, with experience in the vending business, you will become more proficient in anticipating machine performance. But when you're new to the business you have to do a little 'homework' to be sure you're making a prudent decision.

Even though not 'guaranteed' I believe my profit illustrations (shown in other chapters) to be reasonable and conservative. They're based upon experience. . . not simply multiplication tables. Besides, I have a personal stake in making sure you have reasonable profit expectations:

Through my company, FREEDOM TECHNOLOGY, I sell a variety of vending and amusement machines with NO MINIMUM ORDER. I could not stay in business selling as little as 1 machine at a time if people were not happy with the results from those machines. . . they simply would not reorder. Companies with $5,000.00 minimums can stay in business regardless, because many of them have so much profit built into their prices that they really don't care if you reorder or not. . . no matter what they say. It's not good business, and sometimes its downright fraudulent, yet these outfits are very numerous.

Some people think that they are being even more conservative by reducing ALL profit illustrations by 25%, 50%, or some other figure that they're comfortable with. They figure that's the "worst case" scenario.

If you do that with my illustrations, you will probably distort the true picture of things. Because I have already taken that into account, and I believe my figures are reasonable.

On the other hand: I've seen many unethical vending promoters who will mislead you with figures so ridiculous and inaccurate that even if you cut them in half. . . and in half again. . . you will still be way off.

DO YOU WANT TO BUY FROM THE BIGGEST LIAR. . . BECAUSE YOU WANT TO BELIEVE WHAT THEY SAY. . . or do you want to KNOW the truth for yourself?

No, the answer lies in educating yourself on the subject so you will know REAL numbers when you see them. In fact, you'll know how to do your own profit illustrations and projections. . . and

they'll be reasonably accurate.

How To Pick 'Em

There are 3 major elements to consider when you analyze the probability that a particular location will be profitable. They are:

● TRAFFIC: Number of employees (inside traffic) - and/or amount of outside customer traffic.

● LOCATION: Location of machine within the business.

● COMPETITION: Competition within or outside (near) the business.

If you have this information you can often reasonably predict how well a particular location will do. Also, by specifying certain elements of the above, you can 'zero right in' on the best locations. . . whether you retain the services of a professional locator, or do it yourself.

The number of employees is usually easy to determine, either by simply asking, observing, or by checking various business directories available in the reference section of your library. This is very valuable. . . and FREE. Many of these directories also offer other valuable information such as names of contact persons, sales volume, type of business, etc.

Some of the excellent directories available in libraries are: Contacts Influential, Dun and Bradstreet, Cole Directory, Johnson Publishing, etc. The American Business Information services are among the best, though not available in libraries (see details below).

Outside customer traffic information is harder to come by. . . unless you have the cooperation of the business location. This can be determined by estimates made from business records (sign in sheets at health clubs, number of checks (transactions) per day, or by survey). Sometimes this information can be estimated fairly accurately (see "Vending Industry Survey" below).

The location within the business is also important and is not always something you can control. Obviously, if you are installing a bulk-vending machine in a dry-cleaning (retail) establishment

you'd rather have it by the door or the cash register. . . not off in some obscure corner.

Sometimes you have to just take what you can get for starters, and try to UPGRADE LATER. If the location within the business is not working out well, try talking to the owner or manager about it. They will often be quite accommodating!

Competition in or near the business is also a factor. If there is another vending machine in the same office, floor, or building as your snack machine. . . you will lose some sales to the other machine. Also, if the business is right next door to a fast food restaurant or convenience store, they may cut into your sales somewhat.

Don't eliminate a potentially good location due to possible competition. . . just be aware of it. You machines can compete quite well with others due to added convenience, better products, top notch service, and a number of other factors.

This should give you some idea of the variables you will experience in your vending locations.

Don't let the above complicate your thinking. This is really quite a simple business.

You can't always plan for all of the above. But if you do a good job managing your vending route, everything will 'average out' and you'll do well. After all, the worst that can happen is you get a bad location. . . just move it, right?

American Business Information

One of the best and least expensive sources of business location information I've found is the American Business Information services (not available in libraries). They provide the name of each business, the contact person (owner or manager), employee size, SIC code (TYPE of business - U.S. Standard Industrial Classification), address, and phone number.

This amazing computer database includes over 11 million business listings. It was compiled from the national phone book business listings and then telephone verified with additional information added.

All information is available on computer printed lists, 3" X 5" cards, and/or mailing labels!

American Business Information does a computer search according to YOUR instructions, and can search by SIC codes (TYPE of businesses), number of employees, geographical area (zip codes or telephone area codes), or by a number of other criteria.

They can provide you with EXACTLY the list you want, which you can then use in your direct mail, telemarketing, or on-site LOCATING efforts. The contact person and phone number is available for follow-up. For example, you could request:

All businesses with 20 to 49 employees, who are close to you (by zip codes). An excellent prospect list for snack or drink vending machines. Or. . .

All copying and duplicating services (SIC code #7334-03), with over $500,000. in annual sales, who are close to you (by zip code or phone prefix). An excellent prospect list for bulk vendors.

The lists are inexpensive, costing as little as .05¢ a name! The minimum order is small, and they offer

a good money back guarantee! You can obtain a free catalog and ordering information by contacting them as follows:

American Business Information, Inc.
5711 South 86th Circle
P. O. Box 27347
Omaha, Nebraska 68127
800-555-5335, 402-592-9000
MO-FR, 8:00am-6:00pm, CST
SA, 9:00am-12:00pm, CST

Their free catalog is loaded with reference material that is so helpful, I'd order their catalog even if I wasn't sure I was going to do business with them or not. It's very helpful. And you may want to do business with them sooner than you think.

And that's not all! Say you need some information on a particular prospective location you think may be great. . . and you want it NOW! Anytime you need ANY of the business information available in the computer database listed above, you can GET IT NOW by calling the 'Info Access' number listed below. The charge is VERY reasonable.

Info Access, A Service Of:
American Business Information, Inc.
800-808-4636, 402-593-4650
MO-FR, 7:00am-6:00pm, CST

Vending Industry Surveys

The following information was compiled by me from current vending industry surveys. Figures may vary according to type of business, geographical location, fluctuations in customer traffic, and many other factors which can not be predicted. Therefore, the actual results achieved may vary and can not be guaranteed.

It takes OUTSIDE customer traffic of AT LEAST 6 people (depending upon type of business and how long they linger) to replace the purchases of a single employee. For a simplified method of computing anticipated sales from outside customer traffic (if the amount of traffic is known) divide the traffic by 6 (or more) then compute their anticipated purchases AS IF they were employees, using the simple 'Employee Use' chart (below).

EXAMPLE: If a location has 4 employees and the known outside customer traffic is 100 people per day passing through, divide 100 by 6 = 16. Add 16 employees to the ACTUAL employee list of 4, totaling 20 employees, and compute anticipated sales using the 'Employee Use' chart (below).

The "Reference Table For Weekly Product Sales" (which follows) makes it possible to approximately extrapolate (or figure out) other product sales from a known sales figure. For example: If you know, or can estimate what soda sales will be, you can calculate the approximate sales for juice, snack items, pastries, etc. You may find it interesting and helpful.

Below is the results of the Vending Industry Survey.

Employee Use

Number of items sold per employee, per day:

Snacks	Pastry	Sands.	Hot food	Soda	Juice	Hot Drinks	Milk	Cigarettes
.75	.20	.30	.20	1.	.25	2.	.20	.20

Typical break times, or purchase times:
  7:30 a.m., 10:00 a.m., 12:00 p.m., 3:00 p.m., (maybe 5:00)

Customer Traffic

Determine traffic
  Estimate or obtain from business records
    Sign in sheets (health clubs, etc.)
    Survey
    # Checks (transactions) per day
    Gas stations: # gallons sold per day divided by 10 (gallons) = # cars

15 to 21% of customer traffic will buy a cold soda drink (up to 47% in health clubs).
  15% Below average
  18% Average
  21% Above average

3% of customer traffic will buy cigarettes.
  Up to 12% in some locations (bars, etc.)
  1 in 4 adults smoke. Addictive. Habit forming. Decreasing, but not going away.

People per day X days open = weekly customer count X traffic % for item = vends for item.

NOTE #1: Extrapolate other product sales from "Reference Table For Weekly Product Sales" which follows.

NOTE #2: It takes OUTSIDE customer traffic of AT LEAST 6 people (depending upon type of business and how long they linger) to replace the purchases of a single employee. For a simplified method of computing anticipated sales from customer traffic (if the amount of traffic is known) divide the traffic by 6 (or more) then compute their anticipated purchases AS IF they were employees, using the simple 'Employee Use' chart (above).

Miscellaneous Business Surveys

Motels and Hotels
  Items vended per rented room, per day:

Snacks	Pastry	Soda	Juice	Hot Drinks	Cigarettes
.85	.50	1	.25	1.50	.20

Sundries
  $6.00 gross sales per rented room (occupancy rate), per month

Apartment Buildings
  Items vended per rented apartment, per day:

Snacks	Pastry	Soda	Juice	Hot Drinks	Cigarettes
.85	.20	1	.25	.75	.20

Laundromats
Washers + # dryers = Cold drink vends per day

NOTE: Extrapolate other product sales from "Reference Table For Weekly Product Sales" which follows.

Reference Table For Weekly Product Sales

Weekly unit sales volume for various products based upon each other, or a known sales figure:

Snacks	Pastry	Sands.	Hot food	Soda	Juice	Hot Drinks	Milk	Cigarettes
18.	5.	7.	5.	25.	6.	50.	5.	5.
37.	10.	15.	10.	50.	12.	100.	10.	10.
75.	20.	30.	20.	100.	25.	200.	20.	20.
112.	30.	45.	30.	150.	37.	300.	30.	30.
150.	40.	60.	40.	200.	50.	400.	40.	40.
187.	50.	75.	50.	250.	62.	500.	50.	50.
225.	60.	90.	60.	300.	75.	600.	60.	60.
262.	70.	105.	70.	350.	87.	700.	70.	70.
300.	80.	120.	80.	400.	100.	800.	80.	80.
337.	90.	135.	90.	450.	112.	900.	90.	90.
375.	100.	150.	100.	500.	125.	1000.	100.	100.

You can use this table in 2 ways:

● When you have any KNOWN sales figure, you can extrapolate all the other product sales. For example:

If you are going to replace someone else's cold drink vendor with your new 'state-of-the-art' combo snack and cold drink vendor, you should ask how many cold sodas per week they have been selling (they will be able to tell you). Lets assume this is a 20 employee business, plus they have substantial vending sales from outside customer traffic, so they've been selling about 200 cans of soda per week. Look in the soda column, above, and follow it down to 200 (cans per week). Now, if you follow this line from left to right, you will find what your approximate sales could be for the other products you are going to offer (150 snacks per week, 40 pastries, etc.)

● You can also use the table to simplify your estimates and projections. For example:

If you want to estimate product sales for a business with 30 employees, and the general manager can tell you (based upon sales tickets) that they have at least 150 customers walk through the door every day, CONVERT EVERYTHING TO NUMBER OF EMPLOYEES AND SODA SALES:

Since it takes OUTSIDE customer traffic of AT LEAST 6 people (see "Customer

Traffic", above) to replace the purchases of a single employee, first CONVERT outside customer traffic to employees. Do this by taking 150 and dividing by 6, which equals 25. In this example, this means that outside customer traffic of 150 people would buy about the same amount of products as 25 employees.

Now add this figure (25) to the 30 people that are actually employees, and the total is 55. To analyze this location, just simply treat it as if there were 55 employees there!

If you refer to the "Employee Use" chart, above, you will see that it lists 1 soda, per day, per employee. So to convert this to weekly sales for this particular location, simply multiply 55 employees X 1 soda per day = 55 sodas per day X 5 days (work week) = 275 sodas per week.

Now you can either calculate the remaining products you expect to sell using the "Employee Use" chart, above. . . or you can simply go to the "Reference Table For Weekly Product Sales" and look up soda sales (round down to 250) and it will give you all the other sales figures.

This table, together with the "Employee Use Chart", is a very valuable and simple tool to use in analyzing locations. In my experience, it is both conservative and reasonably accurate. After you've be in vending for awhile, you will be able to put together information like this based upon your own actual experience.

Census And State Of The Industry

The "Census Of The Industry" is compiled by Vending Times magazine, and the "State Of The Industry" is compiled by American Automatic Merchandiser magazine. Both are made available each fall for the prior year. See chapter titled "Trade Publications, Organizations, And Shows".

Both are very good reports. . . and each offers helpful information that the other does not. In addition, the Census covers amusement.

They provide valuable information regarding national sales figures and trends. . . average sales per machine or weekly unit volume (# of vends). . . plus other important facts like the 'Vended Prices/Sales Share' (i.e. % of candy bars selling at .45¢, .50¢, etc.).

In prior printings of this book I included many pages from the Census, which I reprinted by special permission from Vending Times Magazine. I have since omitted this for a couple of reasons:

While good information, much of the information in both the Census and the State Of The Industry reports are not very relevant to a new, or small, vending operator.

Most people, being not that analytical, are not willing to study it.

But mostly: I have to live with space limitations, and its just beyond the scope of this book. Besides, throughout this book I have made references to these reports. So the most relevant information is already included herein.

If are the analytical type and think you would benefit from having these reports, ordering information is included in the chapter titled "Trade Publications, Organizations, And Shows".

Summary

Locations analysis and targeting is both a fun and challenging aspect of your new business venture. . . but don't let it get you bogged down. While it is helpful for you to understand the basics of the subject. . . it is not necessary for you to be able to do a COMPLEX analysis in order for you to be successful in this business.

You will find that the various directories of business information can be very helpful in targeting locations for most types of machines. With many types of machines it beats the phone book "Yellow Pages", or wandering around just 'looking'.

The survey information should be particularly helpful to you if you're getting into packaged snack and drink vendors.

Census and State Of The Industry data is referenced throughout the book and is also helpful in determining what level of machine performance is a reasonable expectation. Complete copies are available for those interested in a very detailed analysis. See chapter titled "Trade Publications, Organizations, And Shows".

Bulk vendors, fun-size vendors, and amusement machines are less predictable than packaged snack and drink vendors. While it may be helpful to put together a profile of the best type of locations, there is more trial and error in the locating process. See the chapters covering those machines.

An interesting note from the recent Census: There are over 9700 vending route operators in the U.S. The majority of them (69%) are very small, employing 3 or fewer people. And 26% comprise the owner only. So as you can see, you don't need a big operation or a huge financial investment to be successful!

See chapters titled "Getting GREAT Locations" and "Trade Publications, Organizations, And Shows".

Notes

Chapter 15
Route Management

Setting up and servicing your route is easy and takes only a few minutes per machine.

Upon obtaining each location it is important to set-up the machine as soon as humanly possible, but in no event more than 1 week. 1 to 3 days is best. Make sure everything is ready to go before you start locating so you can meet this objective.

If you don't place your machines promptly, you risk losing the location: Because they are more likely to either forget about it or change their mind. And equally as important, you're sending a message to the location about your service (or lack thereof). It's not professional, and it's not good business either.

Regular servicing consists simply of driving around to each location and completing the following:

● Restock products, if applicable.

● Collect cash.

● Fill out Route Report.

● Check machine for proper operation.

● Wipe off machine.

● Pay commission, if applicable.

● Check for pay-outs (pay back any refunds the location may have made)

That's the basics. Some of the above is self-explanatory and does not all warrant further discussion here, is covered elsewhere in this book, or is in your machine owners manual. See individual machine chapters under the section titled "Service Requirements".

Now let's go over the most important elements to fun and successful route management.

Vending is a relatively SIMPLE business. There's only about 3 major pitfalls to be concerned with, and they're EASY to handle:

Concern	Solution
Poor servicing: Dirty machine, out of product, etc.	Keep it CLEAN, filled, and working properly.
Selling the wrong candy/snack product.	Offer NAME BRANDS. Try other selections.
Poor location	Simply RELOCATE if/when necessary.

There's little question that you'll be able to handle these simple management requirements. There's just NO EXCUSE for not succeeding in vending. It's not easy. . . but it's not hard either. It is a business, and should be treated as such. It works if you do.

Attitude Is Everything!

Be sure to watch your ATTITUDE when servicing your route. Take time to say "hi" to people, ask "how's the service" or "what would you like to see in the machine", hand out a sample or two, and be friendly. In short: Be noticed and be liked. You'll never have to worry about keeping the location.

Special Tips

It's okay to load your machines 1/2 to 2/3rds full until you know what your sales volume for each location will be, and determine what sells best in each location. This will also help keep your initial start-up costs down.

This will not affect sales and, in fact, may even offer a psychological advantage (a machine that is kept too full, too often, looks unused to regular customers and could actually decrease sales).

Ask your customers what they'd like in the machine (or post a product 'Want List' on the machine). Even though you're stocking your machine with quality, name brand products, you will sell more if you 'custom pack' the machine according to the individual likes and dislikes of each location.

Along this same line of thinking, it's advisable to rotate at least 10% to 30% of your products to new products each time you service the machine (full size packaged snack vendors only). That way, you keep your customers interested and always looking for 'what's new in the machine'. This works especially well if you've posted a 'want list'.

Here's a couple of great little tips that have proven successful for building good will and promoting your machines:

> Whenever you service your snack or drink machine always try to find some regular customer and ask them what they like the best. . . then give them one. . . or better yet, put the money in the machine and let them pick one. Don't do this in front of a large group or you'll get stuck giving free product to everyone.

> Also, try taping a $1.00 or $5.00 bill to the back of a product in the machine. Let them know you've done this both verbally, and with a note on the machine that says something like: "Win A Cash Surprise Inside". Whoever get's that money will be probably be promoting your machine all day long.

> Sometimes you can make a special buy on something, or even get free samples, or free pastries that are close to the expiration date. Offer a 'sale' selection for some ridiculously low price, or even free. The selection will run out fast, which is okay, but you'll make some friends.

Try to think of more ideas like this. Be friendly. Make it fun to do business with you. Your customers will use your machine more, talk to others about it, and help you protect it. . . it's a cheap investment that pays and pays.

If you not only do a good job, but you're well liked and fun to do business with, your locations will be so loyal to you they'll never even consider proposals from competing vendors who may stop by.

Pay-outs Happen

Most of your locations will have a cashier, receptionist, or manager that will make refunds if one of your machines should malfunction. Keep them on your side by stopping by and paying back any refunds.

I wouldn't draw attention to the potential problem by asking "did you have to make any refunds since I saw you last"? I'd just make a quick and friendly stop at the desk of the right person to ask "is everything OK with the vendors"?

I should point out that few locations will tolerate excessive pay-outs, and this can really ruin your business. With any man-made device an occasional malfunction is inevitable, but it's important to minimize them. The only way to do this is to buy QUALITY machines and keep them properly MAINTAINED.

"For Service Call 123-4567"

It's very important that you remember to place a service phone number on each machine (a sticker, or a business card is fine). The number must be one in which a party may reach either you, your representative, your answering service, or your answering machine during (at least) normal business hours.

You need to be reachable if a machine malfunctions, runs out of product, business location is closing down, etc. Remember, YOU are in business. . . this is YOUR business. . . and if you want to stay in business and prosper, you MUST offer good service. Good service starts with being ACCESSIBLE.

> This is also a very effective form of advertising (in addition to word of mouth referrals)! Other business people will see your machine, get your phone number off of it, then call and ask you if you'd install a machine in their business.

Some vending operators I know insist that they leave their phone number off their machines because they want maximum privacy. Even so, it's not good for business. If you don't want to put your personal phone number on your machines for privacy reasons, here's the solution:

You can get a private voice mail box, complete with a phone number, for only about $15.00 per month. This works just like an answering machine. You just call in regularly and pick up your messages. Most will even activate a pager (which you can buy or rent) to let you know when you have a message in your box. Check the phone book yellow pages under "Voice Mail" or "Telephone Voice Mail".

Time Required

It takes close to the SAME amount of TIME to service ANY location. While it's true that some machines may take more or less time to service, the bulk of your time will be spent handling duties that have similar time requirements.

For this reason, it makes sense to have as many machines as possible in a single location, building, or part of town, whenever possible.

For virtually every type of machine, you will spend about the same amount of time driving to and from, wiping off the equipment, bagging and counting the money, and keeping records.

This is the biggest reason why the large operators want locations with 100 to 150 employees or very high traffic. Their overhead is high, and it costs them just as much to service the smaller locations. As a small, low overhead business, you have an advantage that makes it very profitable to service these locations.

Refer to the individual chapters covering specific machines for route servicing time estimates (typically discussed in the "Profit Analysis" and "Profit Summary" area). And remember that these are only estimates. It is difficult to predict exactly how long it will take an individual in any given situation because people work at different speeds, and the distance between your locations (driving time) is unknown right now, etc.

Also, keep in mind that these time estimates are for actual route servicing time only. You'll also have to plan on spending some time buying product (except amusement) counting money (too bad), keeping simple records, etc., and other items mentioned in this chapter. This could run at least 15 minutes to 1 hour for every hour of actual route servicing time, depending upon the type of machines you have and various other factors.

Servicing Made Easy

Naturally, you'll want to service your route as quickly and easily as possible. Not only because time is money, but to make the job more pleasant. Here's the basics, together with a few special tips:

To minimize the time it takes for servicing, make sure you always have everything with you that you'll be likely to need. Extra trips out to your vehicle are very time consuming. As a minimum, you'll need the following (where applicable):

● Products for restocking (if applicable)

● Large picnic cooler(s) (in hot climate)

● Cash bag

● Route record book

● Spray cleaner

● Paper towels

● Misc. small tools required, if any, for normal servicing or simple repairs.

● Misc. parts required for simple, common repairs, if any. Don't concern yourself with this right now. You'll learn this from your owners manual and experience.

Repair parts are usually not worth trying to anticipate and keep around. You don't need them very often, and can get them quickly if and when you need them. If there are exceptions to this, you'll learn about it from your owners manual and experience.

Service Tray Or Cart

You'll need something to put your servicing supplies in. A 'service tray' is one good option. Pick up a plastic housekeeping tray or tool tote tray at a discount store (like Wal-Mart). For some types of machines (bulk vendors, amusement, etc.) one or two of these will be large enough to hold everything.

If you have too much to haul around in service trays, a good solution is plastic crates or boxes. You'll find them at most discount stores (like Wal-Mart). They're small, lightweight, and stackible.

A small dolly (hand truck) is handy too. You can stack the plastic crates on the dolly to make servicing a lot easier.

Service Vehicle

You'll want to consider what type of service vehicle you need for the type of equipment you intend to operate. Often, the family car is adequate. For larger equipment, however, you may need a station wagon, van, or truck.

Often, an inexpensive trailer is a good alternative for moving large machines, which makes it possible to get by with a smaller vehicle for service calls.

If you build up a large route, you may find it more convenient to dedicate a vehicle just for route servicing. That way you can leave most of your supplies in the vehicle (instead of always taking everything in and out) and keep things a little more organized.

Product Handling

Temperature control can be an issue when servicing your route, particularly if you live in a hot climate. You may need to store your product in a refrigerator at home, and when in your vehicle, keep it in a large picnic cooler. If you're going to be out for a long time on a super hot day, you may even need to add blue ice (reusable frozen cubes that are not wet, available at discount stores).

Small electric or propane coolers are also available from sporting goods, camping, and recreational vehicle stores. . . and specialty coolers for vendors are advertised in the trade magazines. See chapter titled "Trade Publications, Organizations, And Shows".

You'll also need to provide for storage of your product inventory (if applicable). See chapter titled "Products And Inventory" for more on this.

Handling Cash

Some route operators like to count and roll the coins on the spot, paying commission due (if applicable) in cash. Others prefer to count and roll at home while watching TV, paying the commission due (if any) either at the next visit, or by mail. It's up to you.

In large vending operations, sorting, counting, and packing coin and currency can be a big job. This is a problem you'll love to have! When you do, just be aware that there are machines available to handle this for you (they make your life a lot easier). In the meanwhile, there are also inexpensive appliances that can simplify and speed up the job.

Initially, I'd recommend that you purchase a coin sorting, counting and rolling appliance. They are very inexpensive and are sometimes available in local office supply stores. If not, I have listed 2 sources below where you can purchase this appliance, as well as high speed machines, plus coin and currency wrapping and packing supplies. Contact them for their free catalog.

A B C Coin
8524 Fifth Street
Frisco, TX 75034
800-752-7277, 214-377-7100
MO-FR, 8:30am-4:30pm, CST

M M F Industries
370 Alice Street
Wheeling, IL 60090
800-323-8181, 847-537-7890
MO-FR, 8:00am-5:00pm, CST

Coin wrappers come in boxes of 1000 wrappers for pennies, nickels, dimes and quarters. Many office supply stores also carry coin wrapping and packing supplies, but I do not recommend buying them there due to their high prices. The above sources are much less costly.

If you have dollar bill acceptors on your machines, you may have a lot of currency as well. Most operators just wrap them in $100.00 bundles with a rubber band. Or if you prefer, there are paper wrappers available which indicate the dollar value of the bundle.

Another good source for coin and currency wrapping and packing supplies is a bank. If you have an account there, they will often give you all you need for free. Otherwise, most banks will still sell to you very inexpensively, even if you don't have an account with them.

If you DEPOSIT your coin and currency in a bank, they will sort, count, wrap and pack it for you. Some banks charge a small service fee for doing this, while others don't. In most cases, you'll still have to at least count your money in order to complete your a route report for each location. However, some machines do have counters that keep track of sales and tell you how much money is (or should be) in the cash box. They're usually very accurate.

Being an all cash business, MANY route operators do not deposit their money in banks and handle most or all their financial transactions in cash or money orders. This is often for financial privacy reasons. You'll have to decide if that's an issue for you. See chapter titled "Why Vending?" and read the section titled "All Cash Business!".

I know route operators who actually pay their mortgage payment in $10.00 rolls of quarters! If you like the idea of handling your financial transactions in cash, but this seems a little inconvenient to you, consider this:

> You can 'cash in' your coins and small denomination currency for large bills at any bank without having to deposit it in a bank account. . . you don't even have to have a bank account at that bank. Sometimes they will charge you a small service fee.

> Another way to do this is to use your coins and small denomination currency to purchase money orders, cashiers checks, or travelers checks. These checks can be made out to yourself or others. And can be used to pay your bills or get cash later in other locations.

> One of the least expensive ways to do this is through the Post Office. Any U.S. Post Office will sell you a postal money order for a very small fee, and you can pay for it any way you want.

> Excess cash can be CONFIDENTIALLY invested in more vending machines. . . or in most anything else for that matter

(through the use of domestic or offshore trusts).

Many other interesting and affordable options will be disclosed as well when you learn more about "freedom technology - the PRACTICAL means to live free and prosper in an increasingly unfree world".

If the concept of freedom technology interests you, and you want to learn more (which I highly recommend to everyone) please see the chapter titled "Why Vending?" and read the section titled "Freedom Technology". For more advanced information, contact my company (Bill Way's FREEDOM TECHNOLOGY) and ask for a complimentary copy of the 'Freedom Technology Report.'

Doing business in cash is NOT inconvenient. . . it's just different. After you adjust, you'll find it's no big deal at all. And of course, you could just deposit all that cash in a bank if financial privacy is not important to you.

Security

Good security starts with proper locating and common sense. Obviously, you don't want your machines in areas of high crime, or in obscure (unsupervised) places. Theft and vandalism can be kept to an almost nonexistent level if you just follow this simple advice above.

Also, PHYSICAL security may be an issue in ALL locations with some SMALL, relatively expensive amusement machines, such as a single impulse machine on a counter-top. I wouldn't concern myself with any machines on floor stands or floor cabinets, but in any situation where you're concerned you can physically secure them as well.

In such a situation where physical security is an issue, I have a solution that will usually do the trick, and will look nice too. Attach the machine to something secure with plastic coated cable:

> I recommend using 1/8" plastic coated cable (about 1/4" with coating) since it's very strong yet flexible, and won't scratch anything. About 6' to 7' in length is usually about right. Attach one end to an eyelet (which is bolted on the machine) and the other to a fixture (or screwed in eyelet) behind the counter or on a wall.

You should attach the cable as follows:

Strip off about 2" of the plastic coating and run the end of the cable through the eyelet on the machine, making a loop. Then clamp it together with a cable clamp. Or for a much cleaner and neater appearance. . . plus more security. . . clamp it using an oval sleeve (sometimes called a "ferrale"). To do this you will need a special tool called a "#2 Swage-It tool" which costs around $20.00.

Make a similar loop on the other end and attach using a small padlock or combination lock.

All the above materials and tools listed for securing your machines are available from many hardware stores, or direct from the following manufacturer:

S & F Tool Company
18437 Mount Langley St., Bldg P
Fountain Valley, CA 92708
714-968-7378
MO-FR, 8:00am-4:00pm, PST

Equipment Maintenance And Repair

Most route operators learn routine maintenance and repair from their owners manual, factory customer service department assistance, and experience.

Quality vending and amusement machines typically have a useful life of at least 20 years and are very reliable.

If your vendors are mechanical, there is little to wear out, and it is not unusual to go 10 to 20 years without a single repair.

With electric or electronic vendors or amusement machines, there is more complexity, and a higher possibility of repairs, however, they are typically very reliable.

Regardless of the brand of snack or drink vendors, they typically will all use the same major components. There are only a few major companies that manufacturer coin changers and bill acceptors, such as Coinco and Mars, for example. These major manufacturers all produce high quality components.

Most repairs you can do yourself very economically. If the problem is not obvious, usually a call to the manufacturers customer service department will result in a quick diagnosis. And the repair will usually amount to replacement of a relatively low cost component, such as a coil motor (these motors have a typical life of about 10,000 vends per motor, so you won't have to replace them very often.

In cases where it is necessary to send the component to the factory for repair, you can typically get a 2 or 3 day turn around by using Federal Express.

Repair parts are usually not worth trying to anticipate and keep around. You don't need them very often, and can get them quickly if and when you need them. If there are exceptions to this, you'll learn about it from your owners manual and experience.

Don't concern yourself with this too much right now. You'll learn all you need to know from your owners manual and experience in due time.

Record-Keeping

As in any business, record-keeping is very important in your vending business. It can also be very simple. And there are many benefits in knowing 'where you are' financially at any given time.

Some people get bogged down in numbers, and/or don't like to do their own book-keeping. DON'T LET THAT STOP YOU. Since there are many low cost book-keeping services around, you may want to consider having this done for you.

You need this information. It can help you be more aware of a need to move a particular vending machine, for example, by spotting a poor performing location. It is invaluable when applying for expansion financing for you business. And of course a certain amount of record-keeping is required for tax purposes. Obviously, there are many other benefits as well.

There are 2 primary elements to your vending business record-keeping system:

● A route report system

● A General Ledger system

Route Report

For a sample of a Route Report form that I designed (and use myself) look in the Appendix under "Forms And Miscellaneous". Just copy it and use it as is. It works great for all types of vending and amusement machines.

A Route Report is a record of the activity of a single machine, so you'll use a separate form for each machine. It provides you with interesting and important DETAILS about each and every machine. The information from ALL your route reports is TOTALED on a summary sheet and transferred to your General Ledger, which is your main book-keeping system (see below).

Most of the Route Report form is self explanatory, but there are a couple of things I like to point out:

"SERVICE" section: Note the space to list "number of days between service". This makes it easy to convert your gross sales and number of vends to a MONTHLY figure in the "sales" section. I find that it's much easier to summarize and compare how everything is going if I convert everything to MONTHLY.

"PRODUCT" section: Product position # simply indicates which slot, section, or canister the product is in (start from the top and go left to right). You will note that vended products are each assigned a number for simplicity (For example: A Snickers™ bar could be assigned #1 instead of writing out the word, etc.).

Many route operators SHORTEN their Route Report by listing just the TOTAL sales and not listing the sales for each product. This is up to you. It just depends upon how much detail you feel you need or want.

General Ledger

Your general ledger is your main book-keeping system where you will keep track of all income and expenses. The detailed information from ALL your route reports is TOTALED on a summary sheet and transferred to your General Ledger.

If you have access to a computer system, you will find that there is software available that will make keeping a General Ledger a breeze. If you know a little about accounting, you can even set it up using a simple spreadsheet program.

If you don't have a computer system and want to do your own record-keeping, I recommend you go to an office supply store and pick up a 'Dome Simplified MONTHLY Book-Keeping Record'. They have put together a quality system complete with instructions that anyone can follow.

As I've said, some very successful route operators just don't like keeping records. . . and frankly, some of them don't keep ANY records, yet still do very well. I recommend you AT LEAST keep your simple Route Reports. If you do that and save all your receipts for expenses, you can turn it all over to a book-keeping service at any time during the year and they can complete your books for you.

NOTE: The publisher and author are not engaged in rendering legal, accounting, tax or other advice or services for which a professional license may be required. The author is simply sharing his personal experience, beliefs and opinions. If required, the services of a competent licensed professional should be sought.

Run Your Profits Through The Roof!

In addition to running your route right, as described above, there is more you can do to make sure you're making the most from your vending or amusement route.

● Upgrade your locations!

● E X P A N D and add more machines!

● Hire help!

Upgrade

You should probably plan on relocating about 5% of your locations every month. This is partly because you will lose some locations due to businesses closing down, changing ownership, or changing their mind about your machine. But mostly because you'll want to continually upgrade the quality of your route. . . relocating the lowest producers to better locations.

E X P A N D

If you're smart (and you are, since you're reading this book!) you'll CONSISTENTLY expand your route, adding more machines on an ongoing basis. Consistency is the key. To some, it may seem like a mind-boggling task to set up a 100 machine route (for example). But if you start with just a few machines and add to it consistently, before you know it you'll be surpassing your own expectations!

Hire Help

Short on time? Want to make better use of your time? Want to expand beyond what you can handle on your own? Hiring some help may be the answer. Truthfully, it can also be a big headache in this day and age. Getting the right person(s) is the key, and while there are many ways to go about this, I'll share with you my own success secret. . . the best kept secret about the best and most reliable labor force in America. . . retirees!

There are lots of retirees who need extra money and want part-time work. Even through they're eager to work, they often find it difficult to find any, and are very appreciative of any opportunity. Generally, they are a very high quality, honest, and reliable labor pool. And they're usually flexible on work hours. The only drawback: If you have a full-time job, you may have to divide it up between 2 or more retirees. . . big deal.

Since they come from all walks of life, you can find a retired service person, handyman, salesperson, business manager, or whatever you need. You could find one that could not only run a route, but do your locating and even run your whole business (if you want). See chapter titled "Getting Great Locations".

You could pay a retiree $5.00 to $10.00 per hour (or a small percentage of the gross receipts, say 5

or 10%) to do all the route servicing work for you, and you keep the difference!

> Check with your local senior citizens centers or Department Of Labor office. They can almost always refer you to someone who coordinates jobs for senior citizens.

There are other sources for help as well. Naturally, you'd want to consider people you know. Who do you know that might be available for what you have in mind?

Your local Department Of Labor (employment) office is also a good way to reach the general population of job seekers, however, it is not as effective for finding part-time workers. But it's usually free, so you may want to at least try it.

As a final option, I'd try a classified ad in the 'part-time jobs' or 'full-time jobs' section of your local newspaper. Something like this will be effective:

> Service vending machines. $1,500.00 month (or $?, or commission only). Public relations experience required. Must be bondable, pass background check and drug screening. Call 123-4567.

Honesty is a big issue when you have someone handling your finances in an all cash business. So you'll have to be careful who you hire. Tell all applicants up front that they must be bondable and pass a background check and drug screening. Whether you actually do it or not, you will screen out a lot of people who know they won't pass. And while, bonds, background checks and drug screenings do not guarantee you honesty, it certainly increases the odds, and it's relatively inexpensive.

The best way to keep your hired help honest is for you to stay on your toes, and let them KNOW you are. If you've been running the route up until now, you know about what it should do. Regardless, compare with past performance. Also, keep careful records of product inventory purchased and compare that with your actual sales (it should be very close). Occasional spot checking of your route is helpful too (check certain locations the day before servicing and make a note of what SHOULD be in the cash box).

Also, I recommend avoiding 'employee' status due to additional complexity and cost. 'Independent contractor' status is preferable since you don't have to withhold for taxes, pay F.I.C.A., etc. You just pay them and those things are their responsibility.

Independent contractors usually are paid a fixed rate or percentage, provide their own car, supplies, etc. . . and work their own hours (a brief description).

Regardless as to whom you hire, just give them this book as their training manual (or at least the relevant chapters) and let them take it from there. It

will be your job to supervise them and make sure they are doing their job right.

NOTE: The publisher and author are not engaged in rendering legal, accounting, tax or other advice or services for which a professional license may be required. The author is simply sharing his personal experience, beliefs and opinions. If required, the services of a competent licensed professional should be sought.

In Conclusion

Please don't try to re-invent the wheel. If you follow the advice offered in this chapter, you will likely be amazed at how well you will do!

After everything is set-up and running well, go ahead and experiment with your own ideas. And when you discover a new management or

promotion technique that works well for you, I'd appreciate it if you'd share it with me. I'd like to hear from you. Best wishes to you!

See individual machine chapters under the section titled "Service Requirements".

Notes

Chapter 16
Financing: Start-Up And Expansion

If you do not possess sufficient funds to start-up or expand your vending business, I think you'd agree that it makes sense to borrow money when possible.

Any time you can invest money with the potential of making as much as 100% to 500% return. . . it certainly makes sense to borrow and pay the 12%, 15%, 18% (or even higher) interest rate you may have to pay.

The interest rate isn't too important if you have the potential to make this kind of money. . . AVAILABILITY of funds is what really matters, right?

Financing for a new start-up business CAN be difficult but there ARE some very effective ways to get it done.

The problem is that (since your business is new) you can't PROVE to a lender how much money you are (or will be) making. For this reason, most new route operators who need financing obtain it as either an 'unsecured' loan (no collateral), or secured by something OTHER than their vending machines.

When you have 6 to 12 months (or more) of experience with your route, you will find it much easier to obtain expansion financing because you will have 'proven yourself' a successful vending route operator. Keeping good records is important, so that you can show lenders how well you've been doing.

Lenders like to lend money. . . in fact they MUST lend money to stay in business. You just have to structure it in a way that works for them. Sometimes, it makes a very big difference what TYPE of lender you apply to:

Friends And Relatives

Of course, the very best source for financing is from your friends, relatives, or prior business associates. They know, like, and trust you. . . know your character. . . and usually want to help you. This is the first choice to consider IF it is an option to you.   See "The 'Elephant' Technique" below.

Credit Cards

I'll bet you'd be amazed to know how many substantial businesses have been capitalized with credit cards. I know many route operators who've started and expanded with this as their ONLY source of financing. I've done this myself. It not only works, it works great!

Many route operators have MasterCard and Visa credit lines of $100,000.00 or more. Yes, it's difficult to get a single card with a credit limit that high. But it's not at all difficult to get one card with a $2,000.00 to $5,000.00 limit (or more). There is NO LIMIT to how many cards you can have, so many people eventually have 10, 20, or 30 cards!

You can start with the ones you have, if any. Often, a quick and easy way to get financing (if your cards are near their limit) is to apply to have your credit line increased. Then every month apply for 2 or 3 more cards from any sources you can find.   As a result you will soon be receiving unsolicited applications in the mail. . . possibility even pre-approved cards (if your credit is very good).

Don't do more than 3 credit applications of ANY kind in a given month, because too many credit inquiries can hurt your credit report and cause you to be declined for new applications.

Some route operators are actually adding 2 or more credit cards every single month, with credit lines of $2,000.00 or more each! They do this until they have all the financing available that they want.

You should know that few machine distributors will accept credit cards for machine purchases, so typically you will simply get a CASH ADVANCE on your card, then send in a check for payment.

Also, keep in mind that SOME cards (not all) have a lower limit for cash advances. For example, a card may have a $5,000.00 credit limit for purchases, but limit cash advances to half of that ($2,500.00).

It may seem strange, but credit cards is one of the best ways for the average person to finance a new vending business. Don't think of it as consumer borrowing. You're investing in a 'money machine'!

Finance Companies And Credit Unions

A credit union (if you are a member) can be one of the best sources for a loan since they often have less demanding loan guidelines. Finance companies are also very good places to apply. Both will typically loan you 100% of your needs (no down payment).

First you should try any sources where you've already had some loan experience, if any. Otherwise, just apply at any finance company.

I believe you will find that (in most states) FINANCE COMPANIES and CREDIT UNIONS are prohibited (either by law or by their own charter) from accepting commercial property (like vending machines) for loan security (this is not true of banks).

> They will make you a loan all right, but it often must be secured by something else (car, home, furniture, etc.). Often they will do them 'unsecured', but the loan amount is usually smaller (i.e. $1,000.00 to $5,000.00, maybe more).

Banks

You may want to try applying to the commercial loan department of the bank where you have your checking account and/or some loan experience.

> When applying, be sure to list the cost of the equipment and initial start-up expenses, as well as your own personal profit projection (or 'Income and Expense Projection'). Your FREEDOM

TECHNOLOGY Vending Consultant can help you with this if you like.

The bank WILL accept your machines as security (collateral) but MAY not loan you a very high percentage of value (around 50%) until after you're established as a vending operator. This is not always the case, however. If you've had very good prior credit experience with the bank, and/or have a high net worth (assets) they may loan you as much as 100%!

Leasing

Leasing is usually an option only for established vending operators, or individuals with exceptionally good credit ratings and/or high net worth (assets). for those who can qualify, it can be very attractive, and has gained popularity during the past several years. The reason is simple. . . it makes sense!

A commercial equipment leasing company could, for example, lease you your vending machines for 12 to 60 months (1 to 5 years) with a purchase option at the end. When you compare leasing to conventional financing you will find that the cost is often similar, and there are even some advantages:

● Payments are usually 100% tax deductible when actually paid (i.e. over 36 months). When financing, equipment is usually depreciated over about 7 years.

● No down payment. (Sometimes a small deposit is required).

● Application approval is often faster and easier when used for expansion of your successful route.

You can find a local leasing company by looking in the yellow pages of your phone book under "Leasing". Also, most commercial bankers can refer you to the best local leasing companies.

Creative Financing

If you're having a hard time borrowing the money you need, here's a technique that can work great. It has for me, and others.

The 'Elephant' Technique

You're not an elephant (yet) so you need to find one. An elephant is someone who has excellent

credit and/or a hefty financial statement, and has enough business sense to want to make some money in a low risk and intelligent manner.

Who do you know that fits this description? It doesn't have to be a friend or relative because you're not asking for a favor. This is a business proposal. There are limitless variations on how this can work, but here's a couple of ideas:

A Paid Guarantor

You pay your elephant a fee for guaranteeing (co-signing) your loan (a loan which you could not have received otherwise). The payment can come right out of the loan proceeds. It can be a flat fee, a small percentage of your profits, or whatever you can agree on.

Once I needed a $50,000.00 real estate loan to buy a piece of property I wanted. I bought it for about 20% under value with no money down. My elephant co-signed the loan for me in exchange for a 1% fee ($500.00). The fee was very low, but then again, the risk to him was very small.

Assigned Collateral

Here, your elephant does not guarantee your loan, nor does he/she loan you any money. They just loan you some of their property for 'collateral'. In can be most any type of property. . . house, car, stock and bonds. . . even cash. For example:

Not too long ago I needed an additional $20,000.00 credit line for a business purpose and was unable to get it on my own at the time. I made a deal with a very nice lady who had a lot of money in bank CDs (certificates of deposits). I applied for a loan at the same bank where she had the CDs. My $20,000.00 credit line was secured by $20,000.00 worth of her CDs. The lady kept her CDs and received her interest income as always. In addition she received an additional 2% A.P.R. (annual percentage rate) from me in exchange for her loaning me the collateral I needed.

Private Lease

Your elephant buys your vending machines for you. He/she owns them and leases them to you for a monthly payment which includes a nice return on his/her investment. You could agree that after a certain number of months you would own the machines for a $1.00 purchase price (whatever works). This works great too, and is much easier to put together than through a commercial leasing company.

Partners

Partnerships are like marriage in a sense, except that they can be MORE difficult to make work. Nevertheless, sometimes a partnership can make sense if you can't get the money you need in any other way. Your elephant (or partner) would get a percentage of the business ownership in exchange for putting up the money. You'd manage the route in exchange for your ownership.

Consider a 'Limited Partnership' in which your investor is a silent partner with business liability limited only to his/her investment, and you are the General Partner with total management control.

Better yet, consider a U.B.O. (Unincorporated Business Organization or pure contract trust). The trust certificates (like stock certificates) can be divided up any way you want, and you can be appointed the trust manager. See the chapter titled "Getting Started!" under the section titled "Your Business Organizational Structure" for more on this.

In Conclusion

These are just a few of the creative ways you can get the money you need to start your business. There are many others, and many books have been written on the subject of creative financing. The above mentioned techniques are among my favorites, and are very practical for the situation that you may be in. I hope they get you to thinking.

Do not doubt for a minute that these, and other, creative financing techniques can work. As you can see from the above, they can and do. And these are TIMELESS techniques. People have used them for years, and they're still using them today. Another example:

Back when I was a small home building contractor I was 'on fire' with passion and enthusiasm for what I was doing at the time (much as I am now for the vending business and freedom technology). Needless to say, I was anxious to grow. I managed to obtain a $500,000.00 line of credit secured by someone else's real estate. At the time, I had excellent credit but my personal net worth was less than $10,000.00! The property owner benefited by helping me, and I used this borrowed money to quickly build a million dollar construction and land development business. Within about a year my production shot up to about 1 new home a week (50 per year).

If I can do it. . . if so many others can do it. . . YOU CAN DO IT TOO, if you will!

Scam Financing

I regularly come across people who regret having been duped into paying 3 to 4 times too much for vending machines when some slick promoter convinced them that their special financing added value to the equipment offer.

The way this works is: The promoter offers financing that sounds extremely attractive. It's almost never available at the initial purchase, however. . . only for later expansion, or after buying a minimum number of machines first. Usually it involves no interest (or very low interest) and very low or no down payment. Sometimes the down payment is on a sliding scale (i.e. so many machines at 50% down, so many at 25%, and a certain number thereafter at NO down payment).

While this may sound great on the surface, there are many pitfalls.

These companies are usually 'fast buck artists' who go for the quick 'one-time' sale. They don't expect you to ever buy from them again, although they will make glowing statements about how "this is the start of a long and prosperous association". They make their living by preying upon ignorant buyers. . . making one quick, profitable sale. . . and then going on to the next poor sucker.

Consider this outrageous example:

Option #1: Buy a machine at guaranteed lowest factory-direct wholesale price of $1,000.00 from a discount distributor like FREEDOM TECHNOLOGY. Obtain 100% (no down payment) financing for 36

months at high finance company rate of 20% A.P.R. (much lower rate is often available). Monthly payment is $37.16 for 36 months. Total of payments is $1,337.76.

Option #2: Buy the same machine from a slick promoter for $2,000.00 to $4,000.00. Whether bought now, or using their proposed financing later, your total of payments is at least $2,000.00 to $4,000.00 (more if they charge you interest)!

Obviously, this is a very bad deal. But some people take part anyway because they are ignorant as to the true cost of equipment, financing, and vending profit potential. . . and they're very enthusiastic about expanding and don't believe they can obtain expansion financing elsewhere.

What they fail to realize is that they would be doomed to failure if they paid these kind of prices just to get the promise of some future 'lousy' financing. If they do make such a deal they will not BE expanding. . . in fact they may well fail altogether.

Surely you'd agree that it's better to SAVE up to 75% on price, and then get your own 'legitimate' financing without suffering through one of these rip-off financing scams. You can't really expect to make a good profit if you pay 3 to 4 times the fair price of your machines.

See the chapter titled "Pitfalls, Risks, And Rip-offs!" for related information.

In Conclusion

As successful as I've been in other businesses, nothing I've ever seen or done has been better than the vending and amusement business. As a result, I believe that nothing is more worthy of your vigilant and persistent efforts to begin, and to finance if necessary. If you can find some way to get the money you need to get started, you may

well find yourself skyrocketing to a level of wealth you never imagined possible just a short time ago!

As I've said before, just don't start too big, too quick. If you start at a level you've comfortable with and PROVE to yourself that there's big money involved here. . . you'll be very comfortable borrowing all the money you can get your hands on to expand. . . and you won't much care what the interest rate is either!

If you need to borrow some to get started, why not do it? What have you got to lose? How big is the risk, really?

If you're short on funds, financing can be a great way to get your new business off to a fast start. As you can see, there are many good sources for financing, and the longer you're in business, the more options you will probably have.

As an alternate viewpoint, I'd like to point out that many route operators decline financing altogether. They start their business with whatever funds they have and grow from profit alone. A business with this much profit potential can grow fast with or without financing. And there IS something to be said for being and staying debt free. . . an option you may want to consider as well.

If you need help with financing, I invite you to contact us at FREEDOM TECHNOLOGY. We can often help more than you may think. We'll take a loan application over the phone (or by mail or FAX). After analyzing your application, we will package and present it in the best possible way, to our lending source that we feel is most likely to approve your loan at the best rates (most of which probably have an office in your area). We do this promptly by FAX and often get loan approvals in a day or two.

If this interests you, please complete the loan application that you will find in the Appendix under "Forms And Miscellaneous", and mail or FAX it to us.

You may find it helpful to refer to the "Computing Loan Payments" table, also found in the Appendix under "Forms And Miscellaneous". This will give the monthly payment for most loans you may be considering. Compare the small monthly loan payment you will have with the profit you expect.

Please don't hesitate to call your personal FREEDOM TECH Vending Consultant regarding your financing questions. Your Consultant is here to serve you, and all information you provide is kept strictly confidential.

NOTE: The publisher and author are not engaged in rendering legal, accounting, tax or other advice or services for which a professional license may be required. The author is simply sharing his personal experience, beliefs and opinions. If required, the services of a competent licensed professional should be sought.

Notes

Chapter 17
Trade Publications, Organizations, And Shows

One of the best ways to learn about the vending industry (or any industry) is from trade publications, magazines, organizations (or associations) and their regular trade shows (and/or conventions).

I highly recommend that you subscribe to one or more trade MAGAZINES. This is one of the quickest, easiest, and lowest cost methods of increasing your knowledge of the industry, much of which you can apply in the successful start-up and ongoing management of your business. These magazines are usually not directly connected with any trade organization, but are typically independent publishers.

Many trade organizations put out helpful publications of their own, offer various products and services of value, and sponsor one of more shows (and/or conventions) each year. You don't even necessarily have to join. You may be able to save your money and get what you need without joining. Most of them will sell your their reports, booklets, etc. and let you attend their shows as a non-member. It may cost a little more, but depending upon what you need, you can often save a lot of money by NOT joining.

Contact the organizations that interest you and ask them to mail you membership information. While you're at it, ask them to send you show information and registration details, plus a list of any publications they may have available for purchase (ask. . . they don't always include this with membership information).

You'll find trade shows to be both interesting and educational. Plus they are usually held in great locations at the best time of year for the local climate. . . a great way to get a tax deductible vacation (check with your tax advisor)! These shows are sponsored by trade organizations and often include educational seminars (although usually not geared towards the beginner). Also, various machines, products, and services are displayed. If you can spare the time and money to attend at least once, you will find it helpful and you'll be in a good position to decide if it's worth it to attend others in the future.

The approximate date of each organization's show is listed below. Contact them in advance for the exact date and location, and ask them to send you show information and registration details (together with membership information and list of publications available). Show seminar information will be included with show details.

A Note Of Caution

Having highly recommend trade publications, organizations, and shows as a valuable source of information, I must now point out a glaring deficiency that you should really be aware of.

These trade associations are typically run and managed by large, well-established vending and amusement operators. They are the 'primary' members and they sit on the board of directors of the organization. Manufacturers are usually 'associate' members and have less status and control (they have their own manufacturers associations).

In my personal experience I've found that these organizations are almost never INTENTIONALLY helpful to a new vending operator. In fact, they often go out of their way to DISCOURAGE anyone from entering the business.

Often they cite the "blue sky biz-op" (business opportunity) promoters which I covered well in the chapter titled "Pitfalls, Risks, And Rip-offs". And in my opinion they unfairly compare and degrade ANY company that PROMOTES the vending and amusement industry.

It's obvious to me that they know they have a good thing going, and they really don't want to see increased competition in "their" industry. Well, the industry does not BELONG to them!

Because the trade magazines primarily serve these large well-established vending and amusement operators, they're motivated not to offend them. Therefore, many of their articles are anti-promotional as well.

Anyway, I've seen some very one-sided articles and publications that they continue to put out which is designed to discourage you from entering into the business.

It's similar to me publishing this book and only including the chapter titled "Pitfalls, Risks, And Rip-Offs". Everything I'd write would be true, but you'd miss out on all the good stuff. . . and may be too discouraged to give it a try.

I could give you many examples of this, but one of the easiest for you to pick up is the brochure distributed by the Better Business Bureau. It's called "Tips On Automatic Vending Machines" and is actually put out by N.A.M.A. (National Automatic Merchandisers Association). If you read it, you'll see what I mean.

I've talked to various manufacturers about this, who agree with my point of view. Obviously, they have different incentives since they sell machines. Regardless, the industry should be fairly presented to the public without the one-sided bias, and it very often is not.

I believe you'll find that you'll get more help out of these organizations if you do not go out of your way to tell them that you're "considering" or "new to the business". If you just take what you can use from them, they can help you a lot (whether they really want to or not)!

I've seen no evidence that new operators have been treated poorly at conventions, shows, or elsewhere. So don't let this discourage you from participating. I just want you to understand my opinion and position on their motivations in case you come across an attitude, or a article or publication that seems negative.

V A N A

The exception to the above is V A N A (Vendors Association Of North America). They do actively promote the vending industry, however there are a couple of points I must make that I believe to be very important:

I believe you will find that virtually all trade associations are non-profit organizations. However, V A N A is a 'for profit' business.

They work with biz-op promoters: Offering references for prospective buyers, support for their customers, etc.

They also publish a booklet (about 60 pages) called "Developing A Successful Vending Business". My personal review: Extremely superficial. Not recommended.

I am not going to refer you to V A N A. I'm of the opinion that their primary purpose is to support biz-op promoters, and not to offer any service of real value to route operators.

There may be other associations similar to V A N A. If you join an association of any kind try to make sure they are what they appear to be, and what you think they are.

I regret that I had to take this position on these trade publications and organizations, but I really had no choice. To do otherwise would have been a disservice to you.

Trade Publications

The following magazines, guides, and reports are excellent publications and they will also inform you of upcoming trade shows which you might want to attend.

You will note that Vending Times is the ONLY magazine that covers vending, OCS (office coffee service) AND amusement, and while they're all very good, this one is my personal favorite.

If you don't subscribe to anything else. . . subscribe to Vending Times. If you're unsure what to do, order a sample issue (details below).

'American Automatic Merchandiser Magazine' is published monthly. Covers vending and OCS only - no amusement. $6.00 sample. $40.00 year.

> PTN Publishing Co., Johnson Hill Press
> 1233 Janesville Ave.
> Fort Atkinson, WI 53538
> 800-547-7377, 414-563-6388
> MO-FR, 8:00am-4:00pm, CST
>
> Also publish the 'Blue Book' (buyers guide) each June. Comes free in June with subscription or available for $25.00 anytime.
>
> Also publish the 'State Of The Industry' each August. Comes free in August with subscription or available for $6.00 anytime.

'RePlay Magazine' is published monthly. Covers amusement only - no vending. $6.00 sample. $65.00 year.

> RePlay Magazine
> 22157 Clarendon Street
> P. O. Box 2550
> Woodland Hills, CA 91365
> (818) 347-3820
> MO-FR, 9:00am-5:00pm, PST

'Vending Times Magazine' is published monthly. Covers vending, OCS AND amusement. $5.00 sample. $35.00 year.

> Vending Times Magazine
> 1375 Broadway, 6th Floor
> New York, NY 10018
> 212-302-4700
> MO-FR, 9:00am-5:00pm, EST
>
> Also publish the 'International Buyers Guide' each June. Comes free in June with subscription or available for $25.00 anytime.
>
> Also publish the 'Census Of The Industry' each August. Comes free in August with subscription or available for $25.00 anytime.

Trade Organizations And Shows

These are the major national trade organizations (or associations) you should be aware of. The approximate date of their shows (and/or conventions) are listed as well.

Contact the organizations that interest you and ask them to mail you membership information. While you're at it, ask them to send you show information and registration details, plus a list of any publications they may have available for purchase (ask. . . they don't always include this with membership information).

A M O A (Amusement And Music Operators Association) covers amusement only - no vending.

> A M O A
> 401 North Michigan Avenue
> Chicago, IL 60611
> (312) 245-1021
> MO-FR, 9:00am-5:00pm, CST
> $200.00 Annual membership fee
> National convention and show in September or October.

N A M A (National Automatic Merchandisers Association) covers vending only - no amusement.
> N A M A
> 20 North Wacker Drive, Suite 3500
> Chicago, IL 60606
> (312) 346-0370
> MO-FR, 8:45am-4:45pm, CST
> $200.00 Annual membership fee
> Western convention and show in April.
> Eastern convention and show in October.

N B V A (National Bulk Vendors Association) covers bulk-vending only.

> N B V A
> 200 North LaSalle Street, Suite 2100
> Chicago, IL 60601
> 312-621-1400
> MO-FR, 8:30am-4:30pm, CST
> $100.00 Annual membership fee
> National convention and show in April.

N C S A (National Coffee Service Association) covers OCS only.

> N C S A
> 4000 Williamsburg Square
> Fairfax, VA 22032
> 800-683-6272, 703-273-9008
> MO-FR, 9:00am-5:00pm, EST
> $350.00 Annual membership fee
> National convention and show in July.

Finding Trade Information

Above I have listed the major trade publications and organizations you should be aware of. There are also various specialty publications which may be of interest to some (for example, "The Journal Of The Automatic Laundry Industry" which covers laundry mats). And in some areas there are also small REGIONAL trade organizations. Sometimes these publications and organizations can be helpful as well. If you're interested in researching these, follow the instructions listed below.

Go to your public library reference section and ask for help with the directories. There are directories for everything. Look up trade associations and trade publications for the business you are interested in. Try these two directories:

National   Trade   And   Professional Associations Of The United States and Canada, and;

Ulrich's International Periodicals Directory.

Chapter 18
Getting Started!

Now were at the point where it's appropriate to make some decisions and begin planning. This is the best part! Lets get started making some serious money!

I believe you'll find that this chapter will do a pretty good job of answering your questions regarding the start-up phase of your new venture! Also, it will help inform you as to what to expect after you place your order. . . and (along with the rest of this book) will aid you in a quick, positive, and profitable start in the vending or amusement business!

Some of the specific information provided in this chapter relates to doing business with my company, FREEDOM TECHNOLOGY. I hope we will have an opportunity to serve you, but regardless as to where you buy your machines, you will find this book to be very valuable. . . and you still receive my best wishes for your new venture!

If doing business with someone else, do not assume that the shipping and delivery schedule will be as quoted here. . . ask. And make sure that if your order is not shipped within a reasonable time that you have the option of requesting a refund (sometimes you can wait for a very long time).

By now, you know what to check for when looking for machine suppliers. When dealing with reputable companies. . . when all else is equal. . .

FREEDOM TECHNOLOGY stands out primarily due to our written Satisfaction Guarantee and much lower prices. Remember, we guarantee the lowest price or DOUBLE the difference refunded! (See "Satisfaction Guarantee" in the Appendix under "Forms And Miscellaneous" for details). Also, we do more than anyone to help you get started on the right track (such as this book, consulting, etc.).

See the section titled "What Makes FREEDOM TECHNOLOGY Different?" in the chapter titled "A Better Way".

What's The Best Opportunity?

By now, you may have decided what type of machines you're most interested in. If you follow the advice given in this book, and order the type of machines I recommend, you really can't go wrong... ESPECIALLY if you follow the recommendations I make in the "HOTTEST Vending Money-Makers!" report (see below).

If you're having a hard time making up your mind, maybe I can help a little bit. I'm always getting asked what I think is the best way to go.

I sell a lot of different types of machines, and I can certainly sell anything I want. I have little or no incentive to promote one thing over another, except that I promote what I feel is the best opportunity overall. My reorder sales depend on it.

My recommendations and suggestions are based upon my own personal experiences with various machines, as well as feedback I receive from my customers. And there are other considerations as well. For example:

If a machine sells well, but reorders are low, I'd want to investigate why that is so. Many vending and amusement CONCEPTS look good and are easy to sell to a novice who does not know any better. . . but they don't necessarily do well. As you know by now, I won't sell that way.

On the other hand, some machines are hard to promote (like impulse machines) because the PERCEPTION is that they would not do well, but REORDERS are high because those who actually give them a try discover how great they really are and a very high percentage reorder.

Bulk vendors (for example) can work out well for most anyone. However, I wouldn't recommend you get involved in any type of snack and drink vendors if you have a job that requires you to work normal business hours, because this is when you'll need to service these machines.

There are many good choices and you can be successful with any one of them. Much depends upon your own needs and personal preferences.

You may find it helpful to review the chapter titled "What's Best For You?"

4 Month Pay-Back! ● Little Time!

My personal goal (which I am achieving) is to identify the newest and best vending and/or amusement machines with the potential to pay for themselves within NO MORE than 4 to 6 months, earn AT LEAST 200% annual return or $200.00 monthly per $1,000.00 invested (gross profit) and to do this with the SMALLEST time investment possible! These are the...

HOTTEST Vending Money-Makers!

Before you make a decision I highly recommend that you obtain a copy of my FREE supplemental report titled "HOTTEST Vending Money-Makers!" This report is an essential and integral part of the book. It is updated frequently and covers information that is not practical to print here.

See the last page of this book for FREE resources (reports, videos, etc.) including the "HOTTEST Vending Money-Makers" report!

FREE Vending Consultation!

I invite you to call us at FREEDOM TECHNOLOGY for a FREE consultation to review the options that might best fit your needs, wants, and available funds. . . and to discuss other matters, plans and questions you may have regarding your new venture (like initial product inventory and machine locating options for the machine of your choice, etc.).

There is no charge for the initial consultation, nor for brief future consultations. Those who have read this book generally require very little or no consultation and often just send in an order and get started. We do charge in situations where consultation is substantial, because my machine prices are just so low that we must charge separately for this. See "Consulting Services Available" in the Appendix.

Your First Order

I'd suggest you start out with at least 5 or 10 machines if you can (2 minimum). Some people want to try only 1, but that's really not a very good test. Whether the experience is good or bad, 1 is not a good representative sample.

Also, if you're thinking about getting your locations before you place your machine order, my advice is to forget it. Order however many machines you're comfortable with, but don't concern yourself with the locations prematurely. Getting them will be no problem, and if you go after them too early (for whatever reason) you will probably loose them anyway. See "Route Set-Up" below for further details on this.

Start-Up Checklist

In the following order, I'd suggest you...

✓ Contact FREEDOM TECH for a FREE copy of the 'HOTTEST Vending Money-Makers' report!

✓ Contact FREEDOM TECH for a FREE consultation.

✓ Place a machine order.

✓ If your machines vend a product, after reviewing the sections on product inventory and machine placement you may want to go ahead and purchase your initial product inventory (except for highly perishable items).

✓ Also, you'll need to make plans regarding machine placement. If you're going to do it yourself, review the chapter titled "Getting GREAT Locations". If you're going to contract it out, now is the time to begin making plans as to who you will work with. Call us for referrals to locating companies, if that interests you.

✓ Make a decision regarding insurance, if any (see below).

✓ Make a decision regarding permits, licenses, and charity sponsor, if any (see below).

✓ Make a decision regarding business organizational structure (see below).

Insurance

You may want to check with your insurance agent for information regarding insurance protection against fire, theft, vandalism, and liability. Most route operators do NOT carry fire, theft or vandalism insurance, but most DO carry business liability insurance (which is not expensive).

Vandalism And Theft

It's difficult or impossible to obtain fire, theft, and vandalism insurance on vending and amusement machines at an affordable price. Here's why:

If you owned a retail store and wanted to buy your own soda vendor, you would have no problem insuring the machine because it's on YOUR OWN premises.

The problem with vending route operators being insurable is that their machines are on OTHER peoples premises. The insurance companies don't like to underwrite policies like this because they have a hard time keeping up with WHERE the machines are. . . and they don't know if any particular location is low risk, high risk, or what. If they will write a policy at all, the premium is generally so expensive that it's much cheaper to self-insure (save your money, take your chances and pay any losses out of your own pocket).

New vending operators are sometimes nervous about the risks of fire, theft and/or vandalism,

however in the real world losses are NOT very frequent. And when they do occur, they are usually NOT very significant. If insurance companies understood this, rates would probably be much lower.

Large and well-established vending and amusement operators CAN get this type of insurance at reasonable rates do to their history in the business which makes them more attractive to insure.

If you want to explore insurance for fire, theft and vandalism, check with your insurance agent. If they can't help you, try an 'independent' insurance agent (one that represents all sorts of companies, not just one).

Business Liability

Vending is a relatively low liability business. BECAUSE of that. . . business liability insurance for vending operators is low cost.

A general business liability policy covers you for risks that any business could potentially be sued for (like accidents, etc.). Often, you can simply add a rider to your renters or homeowners insurance policy.

Many vending operators do not bother with ANY type of insurance, and although I'm not aware of any serious problems as a result, it may be prudent to consider having business liability insurance, at least.

Permits, Licenses and Charity Sponsor

Be sure to check with your local city, county, and/or state government to determine what, if any, business permits and/or licenses are required of you. The vending and amusement business is NOT very heavily regulated and usually there are very few or no requirements in this regard. But you should check to be sure.

In regard to sales tax, check with your local and state Department of Revenue. Some areas require an inexpensive permit sticker be purchased and applied to each machine. Many areas do not charge sales tax on small sales under .25¢ to .30¢. In addition, some states offer special exemptions to bulk vending operators in particular. Usually you are not required to pay sales tax on games or

impulse machines since you are not selling a tangible product.

If you are required to pay sales tax, you would usually report your sales and pay the tax on a monthly or quarterly basis. Since this is a cash business, this is accomplished using THE HONOR SYSTEM.

I have received legal counsel and done personal research that indicates that there may be no legal requirement to comply with the ALLEGED sales tax requirements mentioned above.

This would apply on the sale of personal property that you own (candy/snacks included) if you pay cash for it (no checks, because checks bring the transaction under the Uniform Commercial Code). . . if you own it outright (no loan against it, U.C.C. again). . . and particularly if you paid sales tax on it when you purchased it (although this item may not always be relevant).

Obviously, you'd rather pay sales tax on the lower cost of the products BEFORE you sell them. . . rather than on the higher SALES cost. The government would prefer just the opposite. There are also privacy (and other) issues involved.

I would certainly never advise anyone to break any valid law, but you may as well know that many, many vending operators simply pay sales tax on their product when they buy it (if requested) and do not get involved with sales tax permits, etc. It simplifies the business. And as a practical matter, legal or not, it's not very enforceable. You decide what to do.

If this issue is important for you to fully understand, and if your Department of Revenue asks you to pay sales tax or purchase permits, you may want to consult with your attorney (By the way, it's not unusual for a governmental body to provide incorrect information, so double-check).

Unfortunately, I've found that most attorneys are not very knowledgeable on this issue and are likely to tell you to get a permit and pay the tax. If you want the truth, you may have to be diligent to find it.

Also check with you local department of health. They usually won't require a permit, but may have a requirement to check your food storage area (which could be in a closet in your home) but there is usually no inspection fee or other charges.

If you're planning on working with a Charity Sponsor to obtain vending locations you should make arrangements with them right away. See chapter titled "Getting Great Locations".

> NOTE: The publisher and author are not engaged in rendering legal, accounting, tax or other advice or services for which a professional license may be required. The author is simply sharing his personal experience, beliefs and opinions. If required, the services of a competent licensed professional should be sought.

Your Business Organizational Structure

In most business books of this nature, this is where the author makes the usual summary of each of the known business organizational structures. Well, I'm not going to do that because I believe it's a waste of your time to even consider most of these options. Here's why:

For most people, the best way to get started is as a sole proprietor. If you and a relative or good friend are going to be doing this together, you may want to consider a partnership (at least for a little while). There IS a better organizational structure that you can switch into later after you get your vending business under way and have time to study the matter (see below).

> This usually involves little more than filing a 'Trade Name Affidavit' (which you can buy at office supply stores) with your local county clerk. The total cost probably won't be more than $10.00.

> If you have a partner, in some states you may need to file a similar form with the Secretary Of States office. And you may want to put together a simple partnership agreement (all available at office supply stores or libraries).

> Of course, you can do business under common law without doing any of the above, if you want to.

I have personally set-up sole proprietorships, general partnerships, limited partnerships, and have filed charters for several different corporations I have owned over the years.

Corporations don't provide the advantages they used to, and the corporate 'vail' of perceived protection is easy to pierce.

The Looting Of America

In America today, government has become larger and more invasive, controlling our people and their property through LAWS designed to embezzle all rights, security, and assets (worth).

In addition, our government allows CONDITIONS to exist which aggravate the situation further. The facts are apparent and made available through the media and other sources. For example:

● Every year, billions of dollars are illegally seized through government lies and deception at ALL levels. Just one quick example: Civil asset forfeiture defines a new standard of justice in America. . . or more precisely, a new standard of INjustice. Through over 200 laws, the government can (and does) seize property from average citizens when an 'alleged' crime has been committed. Forget due process and conviction. . . they'll keep your property, even when NO CHARGES ARE FILED! Think you can get it back? Just try! (See examples in my 'Freedom Technology Report,' contact FREEDOM TECH for your complimentary copy).

● A lawsuit is filed every 1.75 seconds in this country, according to the American Bar Association! Not only that, 94% of the worlds lawsuits are filed in the U.S. Aren't we special?

● Statistics reveal that you will be sued an average of 5 times in your lifetime. . . and that number TRIPLES if you earn over $50,000. per year.

● 40 years ago a middle class family paid about 2% of its earnings to pay all taxes (income and other). . . today you work past lunch time just to pay these taxes (which are in excess of 60%). Didn't we use to call involuntary servitude SLAVERY?

Is the situation hopeless? Far from it!

Freedom Technology

Did you know that there are many ways you can protect your income and assets from lawsuits and government (including I.R.S.) seizure. . . and that you can reclaim your personal freedom as well?

Freedom Technology is the answer. . . 'the PRACTICAL means to live free, and prosper, in an increasingly unfree world'.

The more you understand the problem (above) and the solution (freedom technology). . . the more

you'll appreciate the freedom technology available through the vending and amusement business!

Do not neglect to contact FREEDOM TECH for your complimentary copy of the 'Freedom Technology Report,' if you haven't already done so. This is important, life-changing information.

In todays business and legal environment, I strongly recommend AGAINST any business organized under statutory law. This pretty much leaves only sole proprietorships, partnerships and contract trusts. The others are good only to help lawyers line their pockets. There is a much better way that ANYONE can afford:

U.B.O.'s

No, not U.F.O.'s! One such freedom technology. . . the business organization of choice. . . is without a doubt, the U.B.O: Otherwise known as the Unincorporated Business Organization, or pure contract trust (NOTE: Not all trusts are the same). This type of trust is great for both operating a business, and for holding all sorts of assets.

The rich have been using them for over 75 years to amass and protect fortunes that we can barely imagine!

A U.B.O. offers much more liability and asset protection than a corporation. . . is much more confidential. . . and is very low cost to set up and manage. You can easily do it yourself, or hire it done by a professional para-legal or attorney.

For maximum protection: Put your business in one, your house in one, all high liability items (like cars) in one, and use one or more for your other investments. NOTE: Some investments would be best to put in an offshore trust (Ask FREEDOM TECH for a complimentary Freedom Technology Report for more on this).

It's so effective. . . literally EVERYBODY who owns anything needs at least 1 U.B.O. And it's so LOW COST that everybody can AFFORD as many as they need.

I've aligned myself with some of the nations foremost U.B.O. trust experts. With all due respect, most lawyers don't know 'squat' about how to do them right. In fact, my experts are routinely solicited by lawyers from all over the country for help.

If you're interested in learning more about how you can protect your assets and yourself, and increase financial and personal privacy through the use of 1 or more very low cost trusts. . . please contact us here at FREEDOM TECHNOLOGY and ask for your complimentary copy of the Freedom Technology Report.

The Freedom Technology Report INCLUDES the trust information along with a lot of other very interesting information regarding freedom technology. There's so much more. . . you've only seen the tip of the iceberg so far.

Please do not confuse this discussion of trusts with my prior mention of 'offshore trusts' (domiciled outside the U.S.). An offshore trust has many wonderful, but different uses (described in the Freedom Technology Report).

NOTE: The publisher and author are not engaged in rendering legal, accounting, tax or other advice or services for which a professional license may be required. The author is simply sharing his personal experience, beliefs and opinions. If required, the services of a competent licensed professional should be sought.

Shipping

It's our goal to process all orders on the same day received, however, there is sometimes a little lag time waiting for funds to clear banks, transfer payments, etc. Also, Shipping time varies with each manufacturer. Some ship the day after the order is received. . . some 2 days. . some 3 days. . . some 5 days. . . and some up to 10 days or more.

For details on the standard shipping and delivery schedule for any particular machine, see the "Factory-Direct Wholesale Price List" in the Appendix, and look under individual machine "Notes".

It is very rare for any of our suppliers to be in a back-order situation, but it can happen on occasion. If a situation should arise which would cause a delay in shipping beyond the normal time provided for in our purchase agreement, we will

notify you as soon as possible, and you will have the option of a prompt refund if you do not want to wait.

Be aware that your complete shipment may come to you in more or less boxes than you may expect (not always the same as the number of machines ordered) and may not all be delivered at the same time (although they usually are).

All goods are securely packed and are delivered to U.P.S. or the freight line in good condition. While shipments almost always arrive in good condition, if there is any damage in transit you should immediately submit a claim to either U.P.S. or the freight line. Neither Freedom Tech nor the manufacturer is responsible for freight damage, but we will assist you with any claim, if necessary.

Delivery

Freight Line

Upon arrival to your freight line's local distribution center, they will normally contact you 1 or 2 days before they deliver to confirm the delivery address and make sure someone will be there to accept the shipment. The freight company driver will present you with a bill of lading showing the number of cartons (or pieces) he or she is delivering. Don't mistake this number for the actual number of items in your order. This is simply the cartons which your products are packaged in (you may have to unpack the cartons to determine the actual number of items shipped).

When you have counted all of the packages brought to you, compare that number to that shown on the bill of lading. If the number doesn't match, then confirm your count with the driver, and note the actual number received on your bill of lading. Be sure all notations are clear and legible and that you clearly state the actual number of boxes received.

Once the proper package count is known, you will want to inspect each carton for visible damage. This damage may be a crushed corner or gash in the box. Whatever the apparent damage, note it specifically on your bill of lading. Once again, bare down and write legibly. If the damage has obviously gone well into the carton and done visible harm to the products contained within, note the extent of damage on the bill of lading.

After all notations are made concerning count and shipment condition, sign and date the document. Be sure the driver signs and dates the bill of lading confirming the corrections, if any. Assure that all notations, dates and signatures have gone through all copies and that it is all legible. Depending on the drivers signature, you may want to print his or her name just below for easy recognition should it become necessary in the event of an actual claim. Retain a copy for your files.

United Parcel Service

In circumstances where it is not practical or cost effective to ship the products by common carrier, we may arrange shipment by such transports as U.P.S. In those cases, there generally is not a bill

of lading accompanying the shipment. In any case, try to get a receipt that notes any damage, or apparent possible damage.

Final Notes About Delivery

If damage is discovered after the driver leaves, don't worry. Just phone the carrier as soon as possible and inform them of the situation. They'll give you instructions as to how to file a claim.

This simple procedure will protect you in the event a claim against the carrier becomes necessary. If there has been damage to your shipment, you should notify FREEDOM TECH and submit a claim to the carrier immediately.

Please call us for help if you require aid or have any questions regarding the above.

Owners Manuals And Assembly

Machine owners manuals are shipped with the machine, if available from the manufacturer (some machines do not require manuals). See "Factory-Direct Wholesale Price List" and look under individual machine "Notes" for details on manual availability.

Most machines require very little or no assembly. Complete assembly instructions (if required) will be included with your shipment.

Route Set-Up

Upon obtaining each location it is important to set-up the machine as soon as humanly possible, but in no event more than 1 week. 1 to 3 days is best. Make sure everything is ready to go before you start locating so you can meet this objective.

If you don't place your machines promptly, you risk losing the location: Because they are more

likely to either forget about it or change their mind. And equally as important, you're sending a message to the location about your service (or lack thereof). It's not professional, and it's not good business either.

See chapter titled "Route Management".

Don't Miss Out. . . Take ACTION Now!

If you keep on doing what you've always done, you'll keep on getting what you've always got. . . IS IT ENOUGH?

Your future can be bright if you make wise choices and ACT on them today. This is an exciting, relatively low risk, and potentially high profit business. Learn it and you could RETIRE comfortably and early. . . very early!

The Facts Of Life

Source: Social Security Administration

At age 65 only 2% of the people are self-supporting:

    45% are dependent on relatives.
    30% are dependent on charity.
    23% are still working.

85 out of 100 people don't even have a paltry $250. at age 65.

Source: Harvard School of Business Study

Result of stock trading:

    97% lose money.
    2% break even.
    1% make money.

Source: Miami Herald

A small business investment beats Wall Street and real estate. 89% of people in the 50% tax bracket or above are small business owners.

Source: U.S. General Accounting Office

Of the 10,000 Americans achieving millionaire status during the past 12 months, 99% were small business owners.

Source: U.S. Department Of Commerce

Of those starting a new vending business, 92% are successful and still in business after 5 years, 90% after 10 years.

Source: LIAMA Cooperative Research

98% of those at age 65 who failed financially said is was because of the lack of a plan.

Think about it. Do you see how YOU could benefit by making a financial PLAN to start your own SMALL BUSINESS. . . a VENDING business?

We all know that money alone can't buy happiness. . . but neither can poverty! Money sure helps a lot, doesn't it? It's a wonderful life when you have the financial freedom to come and go as you like. . . to do the things you like to do. . . and to buy the things you need and want for yourself and your loved ones.

You could spend your whole life searching and never find a better opportunity than this. . . to achieve prosperity. I invite you to join us now. . . will you?

Don't Let Anything Stop You!

The more that we love security,
The more likely we will avoid risk.
And if you avoid risk,
You avoid opportunity.
Because risk is the price that you pay for opportunity.

Robert Allen, Creating Wealth

And just how much risk are we really talking about here? Not all that much. Can there really be any doubt that you can be a success in vending? YOU CAN DO IT. . . if you will!

Discover The Power In You!

If one advances confidently in the direction of his dreams, and endeavors to live the life which he has imagined, he will meet with a success unexpected in common hours. He will put something behind, will pass an invisible boundary; new, universal, and more liberal laws will begin to establish themselves around and within him, or the old laws be expanded and interpreted in his favor in a more liberal sense; and he will live with the license of a higher order of beings!

Henry David Thoreau, Walden

Remember. . . a failure is a man who decided to succeed and WISHED. A decided failure is a man who failed to decide and WAITED. A SUCCESS is a man who decided to succeed and ACTED. The time is now. Start on the road to your dreams by calling us now.

Have Questions? Contact Us. . .

Your FREEDOM TECH Support Team!

With FREEDOM TECH and our unique marketing program you're joining a team that has the potential to launch MORE vending operators on MILLION-DOLLAR careers than ALL the others! Join us part time or full time in this DYNAMIC . . . GROWING industry and you could have ALL the money you need. . . AND have the TIME to enjoy it.

FREEDOM TECH: Serving you since 1972. Written Satisfaction Guarantee!

I want to impress upon you that we are dedicated to your success in the vending business!

Please don't hesitate to contact us at any time if you have questions or if there is anything at all that we can do to serve you.

You are respected as an individual, and valued as our client. We're all looking forward to hearing from you soon. . . and to a long and mutually rewarding association.

We appreciate the confidence you show is us when you place an order. Our goal is to provide you with quality vending and amusement machines at the lowest possible cost, and offer you consulting (and other) services at little or no charge. We will do our best to show you that your confidence in us has been well placed.

Thank You,

Bill Way
And Your FREEDOM TECH Support Team.

TO YOUR GREAT SUCCESS!

See the last page of this book for FREE resources (reports, videos, etc.) including the "HOTTEST Vending Money-Makers" report!

Notes

FREE Resources: Reports, Videos, Etc.!

Valuable, hard-to-find information: See last page for details.

For FREE Resources, Questions, Or Service Contact:
FREEDOM TECH

PHONE: 970-221-9000   ●   FAX: 970-221-9696

E-MAIL: info@livefree.com

WEBSITE: (Exciting and enlightening; it's like no other!)   www.livefree.com

P.O. Box 511, Fort Collins, Colorado 80522 US
305 West Magnolia Street, Suite 255, Fort Collins, Colorado 80521 US

HOTTEST
Vending Money-Makers!

IMPORTANT: Please contact us immediately for your FREE copy of this report! We keep up on the newest and best vending and amusement opportunities! This report is an essential and integral part of the book. It is updated frequently and covers information that is not practical to print here. Don't miss it!

Please see the last page of the book for details about this and other free resources available.

Please contact us immediately for your FREE copy of this report!

In my book, Vending Success Secrets, I've shared with you some of the most FANTASTIC money-makers I've EVER found since starting business over 20 years ago. Now I'd like to share with you the 'HOTTEST Vending Money-Makers' of all!

The Very Best Opportunities. . .

4 Month Pay-Back! ● Little Time!

My personal goal (which I am achieving) is to identify the newest and best vending and/or amusement machines with the potential to pay for themselves within NO MORE than 4 to 6 months, earn AT LEAST 200% annual return or $200.00 monthly per $1,000.00 invested (gross profit) and to do this with the SMALLEST time investment possible! These are the...

HOTTEST Vending Money-Makers!

It really would be foolish to begin, or expand your business without this very valuable FREE book update and supplement.

See the last page of this book for FREE resources (reports, videos, etc.) including the "HOTTEST Vending Money-Makers" report!

Nothing Else Compares!

● $200.00+ gross monthly profit potential for each $1,000.00 invested!

● 4 to 6 month pay-back on your initial investment!

● 200% to 300% gross return on investment per year!

● Very small time investment - low servicing requirements!

● $100.00 to $200.00 gross profit per hour worked!

● Easy to locate and KEEP located! Professional Locating Service Available.

NOTE: I can not GUARANTEE any particular level of profit. You may make more or less than the average. I can ONLY make the following "Money-Back Guarantee".

Money-Back Guarantee!

I can and do sell all sorts of vending and amusement machines, and there are MANY very profitable options. But my customers make more money, and express more overall satisfaction with my 'HOTTEST Vending Money-Makers' than ANYTHING else. . . and they're also the easiest to locate, set-up, and manage! So much so that my reorders are higher than for any other machines I sell! It is for these reasons that I can offer a SPECIAL Money-Back Guarantee on the 'HOTTEST Vending Money-Makers' ONLY. (NOTE: I ALSO offer my REGULAR Money-Back Guarantee on everything else we sell, except special orders).

If after a 6 month trial period, you are dissatisfied with your machines for ANY reason, I will repurchase them from you for your full purchase price less a 30% restocking and handling fee (70% of your purchase price). And YOU KEEP ALL PROFITS earned during this trial period!

This applies on your first order only.

See Written "Satisfaction Guarantee."

What Makes Us Different?

I've written about, operated (machine routes), and sold many different types of vending and amusement machines throughout the U.S. My company, FREEDOM TECHNOLOGY, really stands out from our competition primarily due to the following:

● Guaranteed LOWEST prices or DOUBLE the difference refunded!

● NO Minimum order!

● Written Satisfaction Guarantee!

● Written MONEY-BACK Guarantee on everything we sell!

● Special additional MONEY-BACK Guarantee on my recommended 'HOTTEST Vending Money-Makers' if dissatisfied for any reason after a trial period!

● Honest and accurate information and business policies, my book 'Vending Success Secrets', and supportive consulting. We do more than anyone to help you get started on the right track, and stay there.

See written Satisfaction Guarantee.

Getting GREAT Locations!

If you like, you may choose to find your own locations for your machines. It's not at all difficult to do. . . and everything you need to know is included in this book in the chapter titled "Getting GREAT Locations!"

Professional Locating Service

Some people find that they can get off to a quicker start if they have a professional locating service get the locations. . . at least for the first order. Other people just don't want to do locating. . . ever!

Through my years of experience I've found that there are only a couple of good locating services that I would refer you to. When I receive your

order I'll send you ordering and scheduling information for my favorite ones (or contact me and I'll refer you now). They do a great job for my customers all over the country. . . and they do it at a very reasonable cost!

If you know some great locations you would like them to try and get for you, just make a list of the business names. Otherwise, the locating service will use their own judgment (which is fine if you don't want to be bothered making a list).

I believe you'll find this to be a great service and a terrific way to get off to a quick start!

Need Financing?

If you do not possess sufficient funds to start-up your vending business, I think you'd agree that it makes sense to borrow money when possible.

Any time you can invest money with the potential of making as much as 100% to 500% return. . . it certainly makes sense to borrow and pay the 12%, 15%, 18% (or even higher) interest rate you may have to pay.

The interest rate isn't too important if you have the potential to make this kind of money. . . AVAILABILITY of funds is what really matters, right? For example:

If you borrow $5,000.00 at 15% A.P.R. and pay it back over 3 years. . . you're only going to pay about $173.00 per month! Compare that with the profit you could be making! For example: $200.00

monthly return per thousand invested equals $1,000.00 per month! It can really add up, and grow fast!

Remember, I can not GUARANTEE any particular level of profit. You may make more or less than the average. . . I can ONLY make the "Money-Back Guarantee" described above.

Financing for a new start-up business CAN be difficult but there ARE some very effective ways to get it done.

The problem is that (since your business is new) you can't PROVE to a lender how much money you are (or will be) making. For this reason, most new route operators who need financing obtain it as either an 'unsecured' loan (no collateral), or secured by something OTHER than their vending machines (car, boat, house, etc.).

When you have 6 to 12 months (or more) of experience with your route, you will find it much easier to obtain 'expansion' financing because you will have 'proven yourself' a successful vending route operator.

The best sources for you to consider at this time are probably. . .

● Friends And Relatives

● Credit Cards

● Credit Unions

● Finance Companies

● Banks

● Apply to FREEDOM TECHNOLOGY

If you'd like our help in obtaining financing, simply complete the attached loan application (see "Appendix") and send it in with your order form (instead of a check). We'll review your application and FAX it to one of our lending sources (finance companies) that we think is most likely to approve it for you. We've been very effective in obtaining start-up financing for our customers.

Many very substantial businesses have been financed with credit cards or finance company loans. I've done it myself. It not only works, it works great! (Please note that, like most machine distributors, we do not accept credit cards. . . but you can obtain a cash advance against your credit line to pay for your order).

By the way, please don't be taken in by the scam financing offered by some unscrupulous promoters. The reason some of them can offer seemingly wonderful financing is because they are charging you 3 or 4 times what the machines are worth! Forget it. Get good prices and arrange for "real" financing.

If you can't get financing, just start out smaller with whatever funds you can scrape up and grow from profit alone. A business with this much profit potential can grow fast with or without financing! It'll just take a little longer.

Getting Started

The most important thing you can do right now is to contact us and ask for your free copy of my current 'HOTTEST Vending Money-Makers' report!

With this report, your next step will be absolutely crystal clear!

Please see the last page of the book for a complete list of other free resources available.

Don't Miss Out. . . Take ACTION Now!

If you keep on doing what you've always done, you'll keep on getting what you've always got. . . IS IT ENOUGH?

Your future can be bright if you make wise choices and ACT on them today. This is an exciting, relatively low risk, and potentially high profit business. Learn it and you could RETIRE comfortably and early. . . very early!

Have Questions? Contact Us. . .

Your FREEDOM TECH Support Team!

With FREEDOM TECH and my 'HOTTEST Vending Money-Makers' you're joining a team that has the potential to launch MORE vending operators on MILLION-DOLLAR careers than ALL the others! Join us part time or full time in this DYNAMIC . . . GROWING industry and you could have ALL the money you need. . . AND have the TIME to enjoy it.

FREEDOM TECH: Serving you since 1972. Written Satisfaction Guarantee!

I want to impress upon you that we are dedicated to your success in the vending business!

Please don't hesitate to contact us at any time if you have questions or if there is anything at all that we can do to serve you.

Communicating With
FREEDOM TECH

Above all else, please remember that we're here to serve you.   So feel free to communicate in whatever manner best meets your needs (phone, fax, email or mail). Having said that, let me add:

Because of our low costs, we must keep all overhead very low. For this reason we have a small staff. Small staff means that if you phone us, you may get voice mail at busy times. If this happens, please do not hang up. . . leave a detailed message. . . and we will call you back as soon as possible.

You are respected as an individual, and valued as our client. We're all looking forward to hearing from you soon. . . and to a long and mutually rewarding association.

We appreciate the confidence you show in us when you place an order. Our goal is to provide you with quality vending and amusement machines at the lowest possible cost, and offer you consulting (and other) services at little or no charge. We will do our best to show you that your confidence in us has been well placed.

Thank You,

Bill Way
And Your FREEDOM TECH Support Team.

TO YOUR GREAT SUCCESS!

FREE Resources: Reports, Videos, Etc.!
Valuable, hard-to-find information: See last page for details.

For FREE Resources, Questions, Or Service Contact:
FREEDOM TECH

PHONE: 970-221-9000 ● FAX: 970-221-9696

E-MAIL: info@livefree.com

WEBSITE: (Exciting and enlightening; it's like no other!)   www.livefree.com

P.O. Box 511, Fort Collins, Colorado 80522 US
305 West Magnolia Street, Suite 255, Fort Collins, Colorado 80521 US

Vending Resource Guide

IMPORTANT: Email and website information is available for many of the following listings. I have found it best to put this information on our website because it is difficult to keep it current in a print format. Many companies are experimenting with the internet, and their email and website information changes frequently. In this way, I can provide you with the most up-to-date information possible.

Please visit FREEDOM TECH on the net at www.livefree.com. Once there, click on "Favorite Links," and then "Vending Resource Guide." In addition to the Guide, you will find our website packed full of interesting and helpful information and links.

Visit our exciting and enlightening WEBSITE; it's like no other!   www.livefree.com

The resources mentioned throughout the book have been compiled and summarized here for your convenience. Please refer to the relevant chapter for details on how to use these resources.

Brochure Dispensing Racks (Chapter 13)

Plastic racks (free standing or stick-on) for dispensing charity brochures from machines:

Beemak Plastics, Inc.
16639 South Gramercy
Gardena, CA 90247
800-421-4393, 310-768-0750
MO-FR, 8:00am-4:30pm, PST

Charities (Chapter 13)

Charities participating in sponsorship programs:

Child Quest International
1625 The Alameda, Suite 400
San Jose, CA 95126
408-287-4673
MO-FR, 8:00am-5:00pm, PST

'Hugs Not Drugs™'
Family Life International, Inc.
1013 Lucerne Avenue, 1st Floor
Lake Worth, FL 33460
800-700-6697, 561-585-7771
MO-FR, 9:00am-5:30pm, ET

Missing Children Awareness Foundation
13094 95th Street North
Largo, FL 34643
800-741-7233, 813-584-4698
MO-TH, 9:00am-4:30pm, EST
FR, 9:00am-2:00pm, EST

Vanished Children's Alliance
2095 Park Avenue
San Jose, CA 95126
408-296-1113
MO-FR, 8:00am-4:00pm, PST

Honor Snack Tray Systems (Chapter 5)

Westgate Systems, Inc.
323 Dewey Street North
P.O. Box 0203
Eau Claire, WI 54702
715-832-6013
MO-FR, 8:00am-5:00pm, CST

Mailing Lists (Chapter 14)

Mailing lists and business data for locating machines:

American Business Information, Inc.
5711 South 86th Circle
P. O. Box 27347
Omaha, Nebraska 68127
800-555-5335, 402-592-9000
MO-FR, 8:00am-6:00pm, CST
SA, 9:00am-12:00pm, CST

Info Access, A Service Of:
American Business Information, Inc.
800-808-4636, 402-593-4650
MO-FR, 7:00am-6:00pm, CST

Miscellaneous (Chapters 5, 8)

Price stickers, miscellaneous vending parts and accessories:

WICO Corporation
6400 West Gross Point Road
Niles, IL 60714
1-800-FOR-WICO (800-367-9426)
847-647-7500
MO-FR, 7:30am-5:00pm, CST

Money Handling (Chapter 15)

Coin and currency sorting and counting appliances, and machines, plus wrapping and packing supplies:

A B C Coin
8524 Fifth Street
Frisco, TX 75034
800-752-7277, 214-377-7100
MO-FR, 8:30am-4:30pm, CST

M M F Industries
370 Alice Street
Wheeling, IL 60090
800-323-8181, 847-537-7890
MO-FR, 8:00am-5:00pm, CST

OCS (Chapter 5)

Office Coffee Service Products and information:

Coffee-Inns™
Automatic Marketing Industries, Inc
2362 West Shangri-La Road
Bldg. 200
Phoenix, AZ 85029
800-528-0552, 602-944-3396
MO-FR, 8:00am-4:00pm, MST

Westgate Systems, Inc.
323 Dewey Street North
P.O. Box 0203
Eau Claire, WI 54702
715-832-6013
MO-FR, 8:00am-5:00pm, CST

Packaging (Chapter 7)

Heat sealers and food grade poly bags for packaging bulk candy and nuts for fun-size vendors:

AR-BEE Transparent
1450 Pratt Blvd.
P. O. Box 1107
Elk Grove Village, IL 60009
800-621-6101, 847-593-0400
MO-FR, 9:00am-5:00pm, CST

Products To Vend - Major Suppliers (Chapter 9)

Bagged snacks, cookies, crackers:

Frito-Lay™
P. O. Box 660634
Dallas, TX 75266
800-352-4477, 214-334-7000
MO-FR, 9:00am-4:30pm, CST

Bakery items:

(Dolly Madison™ AND Hostess™)
Interstate Brands Corp.
12 East Armour Blvd.
P.O. Box 419627
Kansas City, MO 64141
816-502-4000
MO-FR, 8:00am-4:45pm, CST

Bulk vending:

Jerry's Nut House, Inc.
2101 Humboldt Street
Denver, CO 80205
303-861-2262
MO-FR, 8:00am-5:00pm, MST
SA, 8:00am-1:00pm, MST

Canned soda drinks:

Coca-Cola™
P. O. Drawer 1734
Atlanta, GA 30301
800-GET-COKE (800-438-2653)
404-676-2121
MO-FR, 8:30am-7:00pm, EST

Pepsi-Cola™
1 Pepsi Way
Somers, NY 10589
800-433-2652, 914-767-6000
MO-FR, 9:00am-6:00pm, EST

Packaged candy, snacks, food, canned juice and NON-soda drinks:

V S A (Vendors Supply Of America)
370 17th Street, Suite 1400
P. O. Box 17387
Denver, CO 80217
800-288-8851, 303-634-1400
MO-FR, 8:00am-5:00pm, MST

Security (Chapters 10, 15)

Tools and supplies for securing vending machines to fixed objects:

S & F Tool Company
18437 Mount Langley St., Bldg P
Fountain Valley, CA 92708
714-968-7378
MO-FR, 8:00am-4:00pm, PST

Trade Publications (Chapter 17)

'American Automatic Merchandiser Magazine' is published monthly. Covers vending and OCS only - no amusement. $6.00 sample. $40.00 year.

PTN Publishing Co., Johnson Hill Press
1233 Janesville Ave.
Fort Atkinson, WI 53538
800-547-7377, 414-563-6388
MO-FR, 8:00am-4:00pm, CST

Also publish the 'Blue Book' (buyers guide) each June. Comes free in June with subscription or available for $25.00 anytime.

Also publish the 'State Of The Industry' each August. Comes free in August with subscription or available for $6.00 anytime.

'RePlay Magazine' is published monthly. Covers amusement only - no vending. $6.00 sample. $65.00 year.

RePlay Magazine
22157 Clarendon Street
P. O. Box 2550
Woodland Hills, CA 91365
(818) 347-3820
MO-FR, 9:00am-5:00pm, PST

'Vending Times Magazine' is published monthly. Covers vending, OCS AND amusement. $5.00 sample. $35.00 year.

Vending Times Magazine
1375 Broadway, 6th Floor
New York, NY 10018
212-302-4700
MO-FR, 9:00am-5:00pm, EST

Also publish the 'International Buyers Guide' each June. Comes free in June with subscription or available for $25.00 anytime.

Also publish the 'Census Of The Industry' each August. Comes free in August with subscription or available for $25.00 anytime.

Trade Organizations And Shows (Chapter 17)

A M O A (Amusement And Music Operators Association) covers amusement only - no vending.

A M O A
401 North Michigan Avenue
Chicago, IL 60611
(312) 245-1021
MO-FR, 9:00am-5:00pm, CST
$200.00 Annual membership fee
National convention and show in September or October.

N A M A (National Automatic Merchandisers Association) covers vending only - no amusement.

N A M A
20 North Wacker Drive, Suite 3500
Chicago, IL 60606
(312) 346-0370
MO-FR, 8:45am-4:45pm, CST
$200.00 Annual membership fee
Western convention and show in April.
Eastern convention and show in October.

N B V A (National Bulk Vendors Association) covers bulk-vending only.

NBVA
200 North LaSalle Street, Suite 2100
Chicago, IL 60601
312-621-1400
MO-FR, 8:30am-4:30pm, CST
$100.00 Annual membership fee
National convention and show in April.

N C S A (National Coffee Service Association) covers OCS only.

NCSA
4000 Williamsburg Square
Fairfax, VA 22032
800-683-6272, 703-273-9008
MO-FR, 9:00am-5:00pm, EST
$350.00 Annual membership fee
National convention and show in July.

Training Materials (Chapter 13)

Sales, marketing, business management, and motivational:

Nightingale Conant
800-323-3938
MO-FR, 8:00am-9:00pm, CST
SA, 9:00am-1:00pm, CST

Vending And Amusement Machines (Chapter 3)

See chapter 3 ("A Better Way") also Trade Publications above, or contact us at FREEDOM TECHNOLOGY for a full line of machines at guaranteed lowest prices (or DOUBLE the difference refunded). See "Satisfaction Guarantee" in the Appendix under "Forms And Miscellaneous".

FREE Resources: Reports, Videos, Etc.!
Valuable, hard-to-find information: See last page for details.

For FREE Resources, Questions, Or Service Contact: FREEDOM TECH

PHONE: 970-221-9000   ●   FAX: 970-221-9696

E-MAIL: info@livefree.com

WEBSITE: (Exciting and enlightening; it's like no other!)   www.livefree.com

**P.O. Box 511, Fort Collins, Colorado 80522 US
305 West Magnolia Street, Suite 255, Fort Collins, Colorado 80521 US**

IMPORTANT: Please contact us for your FREE current 'guaranteed lowest' price list. The following price list is NOT complete nor up-to-date. I have provided this partial list which was accurate at press time only so you can get an approximate idea as to what machines should cost. This price list is updated frequently and the current version contains additional information that is not practical to print here (such as prices for the 'HOTTEST Vending Money-Makers' which I am currently recommending).

Please see the last page of the book for details about this and other free resources available.

Please contact us for your FREE current 'guaranteed lowest' price list!

Founded 1972   Bill Way's

FREEDOM
TECHNOLOGY

P.O. Box 511, Fort Collins, CO 80522 US   ●   305 West Magnolia Street, Suite 255, Fort Collins, CO 80521 US
970-221-9000   ●   FAX: 970-221-9696   ●   E-Mail: info@livefree.com   ●   WEBSITE: www.livefree.com

Wholesale Factory-Direct Costs
Vending And Amusement Machines
Operator's Wholesale Price Per Unit (4-5-99)

NO Minimum Order!
Money Back Satisfaction Guarantee!
LOWEST PRICE Guarantee - Or DOUBLE The Difference Back!

See "Important Notes"

Description	Approximate Shipping Weight	Zip Code Of Origin	Your Cost

Bulk Vendors
(Loose 'UN-packaged' candy, nut, toy capsule vendors. NON-electric mechanical operation.)

THE NORTHWESTERN CORP:

Triple Play: 3 selection bulk vendor with spill tray and elegant colonnade floor stand. Preset multi-pricing at .10¢, 25¢, or .50¢. Dimensions: 18" W, 16" round cast iron base, 45" H.

Standard: Silver & black baked-on enamel paint (green & black, red & black, tan & black, or red & white & blue available upon request)...50#.................... 60450......................$ 219.

Upgrade: Gold mottle powder coat (more durable) paint (silver mottle available upon request - not pictured). 50#....................60450......................$ 227.

OPTIONS, ACCESSORIES, & NOTES:

Excap (extra capacity back panel) specify color, EACH...............1#...................60450........................$ 7.

NOTES: Shipped in our most popular configuration, as follows, unless otherwise requested: .25¢ coin mech. (.05¢, .10¢, & .50¢ available upon request). Deep (candy/nut) product wheels (optional 1" capsule wheel in center, available upon request). Standard unit shipped in silver & black (green & black, red & black, tan & black, or red & white & blue available upon request). Upgrade unit shipped in gold mottle (silver mottle available upon request - not pictured). Stand requires minor assembly. Usually shipped within 8 business days after we receive paid order (1 to 5 additional days in transit). Shipped U.P.S. unless very large order (will ship by freight line when cost is less). In business since 1909. WARRANTY: Lifetime on parts (defects only, normal wear & tear not included). Owners manual included with first order.

U-TURN   ***Please CALL FOR PRICES - way too low to print!***

U-Turn™:   4 selection bulk vendor. Coin mech preset to .25¢.

Standard floor model: Yellow machine, black crinkle stand, powder coat (more durable) paint (colors available upon request, instead of yellow: Gold vein, silver vein, red). Dimensions: 12" W, 18" square steel base, 46" H
                                        26#.....................83401.................$ CALL.

Counter-top model: Yellow powder coat (more durable) paint (colors available upon request, instead of yellow: Gold vein, silver vein, red). Dimensions: 12" W, 22" H ....21#.................... 83401.................$ CALL.

U-Turn Eliminator™:   8 selection bulk vendor. Coin mech preset to .25¢.

Standard floor model: Yellow machine, black crinkle stand, powder coat (more durable) paint (colors available upon request, instead of yellow: Gold vein, silver vein, red). Dimensions: 12" W, 18" square steel base, 55" H
                                        38#.....................83401.................$ CALL.

Counter-top model: Yellow powder coat (more durable) paint (colors available upon request, instead of yellow: Gold vein, silver vein, red). Dimensions: 12" W, 31" H ....33#.................... 83401.................$ CALL.

U-Turn Terminator™:   8 selection bulk vendor. Coin mech preset to .25¢. Just like Eliminator™ except that the top 4 cannisters are 3-1/2" taller. Same price as Eliminator™.

Standard floor model: Yellow machine, black crinkle stand, powder coat (more durable) paint (colors available upon request, instead of yellow: Gold vein, silver vein, red). Dimensions: 12" W, 18" square steel base, 58" H
                                        38#.....................83401.................$ CALL.

Counter-top model: Yellow powder coat (more durable) paint (colors available upon request, instead of yellow: Gold vein, silver vein, red). Dimensions: 12" W, 34" H ....33#.................... 83401.................$ CALL.

OPTIONS, ACCESSORIES, & NOTES:

Pig cover instead of standard cover...NO LONGER AVAILABLE

Static product stickers: No adhesive; easy to pull off and wipe, then reapply. Available in assorted brand names such as M&M Plain, M&M Peanut, M&M Crispy, Reese's Pieces, Runts, Skittles, Hot Tamales, Mike & Ike, Fruit Tart, Jelly Belly, Boston Baked Beans, Good 'n' Plenty, Chocolate Covered Raisins, Bubble Gum, Chicle Tabs Chewing Gum, Jaw Breakers, Pistachios, Cashews, Gourmet Nuts, Gourmet Mints, Super Balls, Capsule Toys, etc. (call for current availability). Dimensions: 3-1/2" W, 2-1/2" H......83401........................50¢

NOTES: MUST BE ORDERED IN MULTIPLES OF 2 (packed 2 to a carton) double the above weight for approximate shipping weight per carton. Shipped in our most popular configuration, as follows, unless otherwise requested: .25¢ coin mech only. Candy/nut product wheel (available upon request: Gumball product wheel which also vends rubber balls and 1" toy capsules). Standard unit shipped in yellow with black crinkle stand (colors available upon request, instead of yellow: Gold vein, silver vein, red). Stand requires minor assembly. Usually shipped within 4 business days after we receive paid order (1 to 5 additional days in transit). Shipped U.P.S. unless large order (will ship by freight line when cost is less). In business since 1984. WARRANTY: 2 years on machine, 5 years on coin mech (parts only). Owners manual included with first order.

'Fun-Size' Snack Vendors
(Packaged 'fun-size' or 'bite-size' snack vendors. NON-electric mechanical operation)

Please CALL FOR INFORMATION

Packaged Snack Vendors - Mechanical
(Packaged candy/snack/pastry vendors. NON-electric mechanical operation)

AUTOMATIC MARKETING INDUSTRIES:

X-CHANGER: Low cost external bill changer for mechanical (non-electric) vendors which can not accept internal changers or bill acceptors. Changes $1. bill into EITHER all quarters OR 3 quarters, 2 dimes, & 1 nickel (you pre-set in advance). Mounts to side of most any machine (mounting bracket not necessary). Electricity required. $60. capacity. Dimensions: 6" W, 14" D, 14" H ....21#..................... 85029.....................$ 399.

> **NOTES:** Usually shipped within 5 business days after we receive paid order (1 to 5 additional days in transit). Shipped U.P.S. or Roadway Parcel Service unless very large order (will ship by freight line when cost is less). In business since 1970. WARRANTY: 1 year on parts. Owners manual included with first order.

EDINA TECHNICAL PRODUCTS:

CT-10-140: 10 selection glass front counter-top vendor. Designed to sit alone on counter-top, or on top of the F-3-83 drink vendor for a low cost, compact combo snack-drink unit. Adjustable multi-pricing to $1.00. 90 - 144 item capacity (100 items typical). Dimensions: 19" W, 21" D, 30" H.
72#.....................55442.....................$ 344.

FT-21-250: 21 selection glass front floor model vendor. Adjustable multi-pricing to $1.00. 186 - 285 item capacity (210 items typical). Dimensions: 25" W, 21" D, 54" H........151#..................... 55442.....................$ 731.

FT-27-300: 27 selection glass front floor model vendor. Adjustable multi-pricing to $1.00. 237 - 363 item capacity (275 items typical). Dimensions: 31" W, 21" D, 54" H........178#..................... 55442.....................$ 794.

> **NOTES:** Shipped in our most popular configuration with coin-mechs pre-set from .40¢ to .60¢ (adjustable). Usually shipped within 5 business days after we receive paid order (3 to 8 additional days in transit). CT-10-140 ONLY shipped U.P.S. unless very large order (will ship by freight line when cost is less). ALL others shipped by freight line. In business since 1983. WARRANTY: 1 year on parts. Owners manual included with first order.

VENDCRAFT:

FB-10: 10 selection glass front counter-top vendor. Unique "front drop" design. Designed to sit alone on counter-top, or on top of the FB-5 drink vendor for a low cost, compact combo snack-drink unit. Adjustable multi-pricing to $1.00. Up to 168 item capacity (100 items typical). Dimensions: 31" W, 22" D, 15" H.
85#.....................44144.....................$ 281.

> **NOTES:** Shipped in our most popular configuration with coin-mechs pre-set from .40¢ to .60¢ (adjustable). Usually shipped within 5 business days after we receive paid order (3 to 8 additional days in transit). FB-10 shipped U.P.S. unless very large order (will ship by freight line when cost is less). Associated with Vendors Exchange, in business since 1960. WARRANTY: 1 year on parts. Owners manual included with first order.

Packaged Snack Vendors - Electronic
(Packaged candy/snack/pastry vendors. ELECTRONIC operation.)

RADDATZ PRODUCT DEVELOPMENT CORP:

RCS-15: Very compact, 15 selection glass front counter-top vendor. Coin changer (can NOT add bill acceptor). Programmable multi-pricing to $99.95. 152 item capacity. Dimensions: 30" W, 22" D, 24" H.
120#.....................72032.................$ CALL.

RCS-20: Very compact, 20 selection glass front counter-top vendor. Coin changer (optional bill acceptor). Programmable multi-pricing to $99.95. 185 item capacity. Dimensions: 30" W, 22" D, 34" H.
165#.....................72032.................$ CALL.

RPD OPTIONS, ACCESSORIES, NOTES:

Add dollar bill acceptor when ordering vendor OR anytime (RCS-20 ONLY) ....72032.................$ CALL.

Floor stand, with lockable storage ....70#...................72032.................$ CALL.

SLAVE COLD DRINK VENDOR: RCD-5: Very compact, 5 selection floor model vendor, 12 oz. cold canned drinks. 130 can capacity. SLAVES off RCS-15 or RCS-20 snack vendor. (SLAVE vendors will NOT operate alone. Coin changer & controller board on snack vendor runs cold drink vendor). Dimensions: 30" W, 26" D, 35" H...230#.....................72032.................$ CALL.

NOTES: Usually shipped within 13 business days after we receive paid order (3 to 8 additional days in transit). Shipped by freight line. In business since 1990 (Relatively new company, but owner, Dick Raddatz, has 20 years prior experience with Coinco and CEO of Polyvend). WARRANTY: 1 year on parts. Owners manual included with first order.

SAVAMCO INC:

FM-345: 25 selection floor model vendor. Lighted product display. Coin changer (optional bill acceptor) Programmable multi-pricing to $99.95. Up to 396 item capacity (245 items standard). Dimensions: 33" W, 27" D, 62" H ....300#..................... 55760.................$ 1,675.

SAVAMCO OPTIONS, ACCESSORIES, NOTES:

Add dollar bill acceptor when ordering vendor OR anytime......................................55760.....................$ 406.

SLAVE COLD DRINK VENDOR: CD-300-5 SLAVE: 5 selection floor model vendor, 12 oz. cold canned drinks. 300 can capacity. SLAVES off FM-345 snack vendor. (SLAVE vendors will NOT operate alone. Coin changer & controller board on snack vendor runs cold drink vendor). Dimensions: 32" W, 28" D, 61" H ....360#..................... 55760.................$ 1,287.

NOTES: Usually shipped within 13 business days after we receive paid order (3 to 8 additional days in transit). Shipped by freight line. In business since 1968. WARRANTY: 90 days on keypad, 1 year on all other parts. Owners manual included with first order.

Cold Drink Vendors - Mechanical
(12 ounce cold canned drink vendors. NON-electric mechanical operation. Electric refrigeration.)

AUTOMATIC MARKETING INDUSTRIES:

X-CHANGER: Low cost external bill changer for mechanical (non-electric) vendors which can not accept internal changers or bill acceptors. Changes $1. bill into EITHER all quarters OR 3 quarters, 2 dimes, & 1 nickel (you pre-set in advance). Mounts to side of most any machine (mounting bracket not necessary). Electricity required. $60. capacity. Dimensions: 6" W, 14" D, 14" H ....21#....................85029.....................$ 399.

NOTES: Usually shipped within 5 business days after we receive paid order (1 to 5 additional days in transit). Shipped U.P.S. or Roadway Parcel Service unless very large order (will ship by freight line when cost is less). In business since 1970. WARRANTY: 1 year on parts. Owners manual included with first order.

EDINA TECHNICAL PRODUCTS:

F-3-83: 3 selection floor model drink vendor. Designed to stand alone, or stack the CT-10-140 snack vendor on top for a low cost, compact combo snack-drink unit. Adjustable multi-pricing to $1.00. 83 can capacity. Dimensions: 19" W, 22" D, 32" H.............................122#.....................55442.....................$ 656.

FMR-8-200: 8 selection floor model drink vendor. Adjustable multi-pricing to $1.00. 200 can capacity. Dimensions: 28" W, 26" D, 55" H.............................246#.....................55442.................$ 1,031.

NOTES: Shipped in our most popular configuration with coin-mechs pre-set from .55¢ to .75¢ (adjustable). Usually shipped within 5 business days after we receive paid order (3 to 8 additional days in transit). F-3-83 ONLY shipped U.P.S. unless very large order (will ship by freight line when cost is less). FMR-8-200 shipped by freight line. In business since 1983. WARRANTY: 1 year on parts. Owners manual included with first order.

VENDCRAFT:

FB-5: 5 selection floor model drink vendor. Designed to stand alone, or stack the FB-10 snack vendor on top for a low cost, compact combo snack-drink unit. Adjustable multi-pricing to $1.00. 175 can capacity. Dimensions: 31" W, 25" D, 37" H..230#....................44144....................$ 831.

NOTES: Shipped in our most popular configuration with coin-mechs pre-set from .55¢ to .75¢ (adjustable). Usually shipped within 5 business days after we receive paid order (3 to 8 additional days in transit). Shipped by freight line. In business since 1960. WARRANTY: 1 year on parts. Owners manual included with first order.

Cold Drinks - Electronic
(12 ounce cold canned drink vendors. ELECTRONIC Operation)

SAVAMCO INC:

CD-300-5: 5 selection floor model drink vendor. Coin changer (optional bill acceptor) Programmable multi-pricing to $99.95. 300 can capacity. Dimensions: 32" W, 28" D, 61" H.
360#....................55760....................$ 1,537.

SAVAMCO OPTIONS, ACCESSORIES, NOTES:

Add dollar bill acceptor when ordering vendor OR anytime....................................55760....................$ 406.

NOTES: Usually shipped within 13 business days after we receive paid order (3 to 8 additional days in transit). Shipped by freight line. In business since 1968. WARRANTY: 90 days on keypad, 1 year on all other parts. Owners manual included with first order.

Cold Drinks - Electronic SLAVES
(12 ounce cold canned drink vendors. ELECTRONIC Operation)
(SLAVE vendors will NOT operate alone. Coin changer & controller board on snack vendor runs cold drink vendor)

RADDATZ PRODUCT DEVELOPMENT CORP:

RCD-5 SLAVE: Very compact, 5-selection floor model vendor, 12 oz. cold canned drinks. 130 can capacity. SLAVES off RCS-15 or RCS-20 snack vendor (see "Packaged Snack Vendors - Electronic"). Dimensions: 30" W, 26" D, 35" H ....230#....................72032....................$ CALL.

NOTES: Usually shipped within 13 business days after we receive paid order (3 to 8 additional days in transit). Shipped by freight line. In business since 1990 (Relatively new company, but owner, Dick Raddatz, has 20 years prior experience with Coinco and CEO of Polyvend). WARRANTY: 1 year on parts. Owners manual included with first order.

SAVAMCO INC:

CD-300-5 SLAVE: 5 selection floor model vendor, 12 oz. cold canned drinks. 300 can capacity. SLAVES off FM-345 snack vendor (see "Packaged Snack Vendors - Electronic"). Dimensions: 32" W, 28" D, 61" H.
360#....................55760....................$ 1,287.

NOTES: Usually shipped within 13 business days after we receive paid order (3 to 8 additional days in transit). Shipped by freight line. In business since 1968. WARRANTY: 1 year on parts. Owners manual included with first order.

Amusement

MAYONI ENTERPRISES: New Generation **COMPUVEND** Impulse machines: Programmable for 1 or 2 quarters only (.25¢ or .50¢). Various other programming options. All offer LED light display and sound effects (ONLY Talking Gypsy talks). Large coin box now standard, holds $500.00. Dimensions: 9" W, 10" D, 15" H (On stand 52" H).

SUGGESTED START-UP COMBOS: Order as: "Mayoni Combo #___", as follows:

#1: TALKING GYPSY: With PD-100 stand ....60#..................... 91331 ....$ 978.

#2: TALKING GYPSY & LOVE METER: With PD-100 stand, PL-200 mounting plate, and EP-300 easy plug
90#.....................91331...................$ 1,612.

#3: TALKING GYPSY & STRESS TEST: With PD-100 stand, PL-200 mounting plate, and EP-300 easy plug
90#.....................91331...................$ 1,612.

#4: TALKING GYPSY & MEMORY QUIZ: With PD-100 stand, PL-200 mounting plate, and EP-300 easy plug
90#.....................91331...................$ 1,612.

#5: TALKING GYPSY & PHYSICAL FITNESS: With PD-100 stand, PL-200 mounting plate, and EP-300 easy plug...90#.....................91331...................$ 1,612.

MAKING COMBOS WITH HOTTEST PRODUCERS (My recommendations): 'A'=best, 'B'=excellent, 'C'=very good ('C'=secondary piece does great with 'A' or 'B', but do not put alone) 'D'=fair to good (D=secondary piece goes with 'A' or 'B', but do not put alone - except Lucky Lotto). Put any 'A' or 'B' alone or in any combination with each other. Add 'C' or 'D' as a second or third piece (except Lucky Lotto may stand alone). Use only PD-100 pedestal stand (no pole stands). Instead of expensive carousel stand in malls, use 2 to 4 pedestal stands with 2 or 3 machines (arrange back to back, in triangle, or in square) looks great. Make up your own combos from below.

A TALKING GYPSY.

B LOVE METER (SEX REACTOR will do a little better but some locations object to "sex". LOVE METER is same machine - different graphics), STRESS TEST.

C MEMORY QUIZ, PHYSICAL FITNESS (don't put with Stress Test), PERSONALITY ANALYZER.

D Heart Rate, Bio Rhythm, NON-Talking Gypsy, Lucky Lotto (only if lotto tickets sold at location), perfect match.

STRESS TEST, MEMORY QUIZ, HEART RATE, PHYSICAL FITNESS, SEX REACTOR, or **LOVE METER**..20#..................... 91331 ....$ 584.

BIO RHYTHM, or **NON-TALKING GYPSY**...............................20#..................... 91331 ....$ 791.

TALKING GYPSY, LUCKY LOTTO, PERFECT MATCH, or **PERSONALITY ANALYZER.**
20#.....................91331....................$ 869.

MAYONI COMPUVEND OPTIONS, ACCESSORIES, NOTES:

PO-101 Pole stand (supports 1 machine ONLY)......................22#..................... 91331 ....$ 75.

PD-100 Pedestal stand (most attractive) supports 1 to 3 machines. Needs mounting plate for 2 or 3 machines ....40#..................... 91331 ....$ 109.

PL-200 2-unit mounting plate...5#..................... 91331 ....$ 25.

PL-205 3-unit mounting plate...7#..................... 91331 ....$ 35.

SB-400 Safety bracket: EXTRA security. Strengthens door & allows padlocking (standard unit already includes quality barrel lock)..9#..................... 91331 ....$ 42.

AT-900   Anti-theft bracket: Fastening point for security cable............................91331.....................$ 6.

RL-150   4 rubber legs: For counter-top set-up...91331.....................$ 5.

EP-300   Easy plug: Consolidates 2-3 machines on 1 cord..........5#....................91331.....................$ 25.

CS-900   Carousel stand: Accommodates 6 machines on hexagon stand.
                                                                    Call....................91331...................$ 1,875.

NOTES: Usually shipped within 5 business days after we receive paid order (1 to 5 additional days in transit). Shipped U.P.S. unless very large order (will ship by freight line when cost is less). In business since 1983. WARRANTY: 1 year on parts and labor. Owners manual not available and not required (instruction sheet included on some models, and phone support available).

Call for current prices on other equipment not listed.

Important Notes

NO Minimum Order! Samples Available!

Order a sample if you'd like. Then get started with as few or as many machines as you like. After you PROVE to yourself that you are doing the RIGHT thing. . . then EXPAND at whatever rate you are COMFORTABLE with (even one machine at a time).

As a practical matter, if you're just getting started, I'd suggest you start out with at least 5 machines if you can (3 minimum). Some people want to try only 1, but that's really not a very good market test. Whether the experience is good or bad, 1 is just not a good representative sample.

Money-Back Guarantee!

You may order a single sample or carton of any machine we offer. . . examine it at your leisure for up to 10 days. . . and if you like, YOU MAY RETURN IT TO US for a FULL REFUND! See "Satisfaction Guarantee" in the Appendix under "Forms And Miscellaneous" for details.

LOWEST PRICE Guarantee. . . Or DOUBLE The Difference Back!

As a national wholesale factory-direct distributor of vending and amusement machines, we strive to offer the absolute LOWEST PRICES possible on QUALITY machines. In the VERY UNLIKELY event that you should find the same machines you purchased from us available through another distributor at a lower price. We'll promptly send you a CASH REFUND for DOUBLE the difference you paid! See "Satisfaction Guarantee"

in the Appendix under "Forms And Miscellaneous" for details.

Freight Costs

All prices are F.O.B. (freight collect) from FREEDOM TECH's place of shipment in the continental United States. Freight is very reasonable. Freight estimates can be easily obtained. See "Freight Quotes Made Easy" in the Appendix (or call us for help):

Miscellaneous

1. Our most popular products offered are listed above. Other machines, equipment, supplies, parts, services and materials are variously priced and will be provided upon request.

2. All information contained herein deemed reliable but not guaranteed.

3. All prices are subject to change without notice or obligation.

4. See Purchase Agreement for complete purchase terms.

5. Warranties are abbreviated in product notes. See manufacturers written warranty for complete warranty details.

6. Please see: "Freight Quotes Made Easy" and "Ordering Factory-Direct" in the Appendix for more details.

Thank You For Your Business

You are respected as an individual, and valued as our client. We're all looking forward to hearing

from you. . . and to a long and mutually rewarding association. Thank you for the confidence you have shown is us by placing an order. Our goal is to provide you with quality vending and amusement machines at the lowest possible cost, and offer you optional consulting (and other) services at little or no charge. We will do our best to show you that your confidence in us has been well placed.
Thanks Again,

Bill Way
And Your FREEDOM TECH Support Staff.

TO YOUR GREAT SUCCESS!

FREE Resources: Reports, Videos, Etc.!
Valuable, hard-to-find information: See last page for details.

For FREE Resources, Questions, Or Service Contact: FREEDOM TECH

PHONE: 970-221-9000 ● FAX: 970-221-9696

E-MAIL: info@livefree.com

WEBSITE: (Exciting and enlightening; it's like no other!)   www.livefree.com

P.O. Box 511, Fort Collins, Colorado 80522 US
305 West Magnolia Street, Suite 255, Fort Collins, Colorado 80521 US

Freight Quotes Made Easy

All prices are F.O.B. (freight collect) from FREEDOM TECH's place of shipment in the continental United States. Freight is very reasonable. Freight estimates can be easily obtained as follows (or contact us for help):

In general, all SMALL MACHINES are shipped U.P.S. (United Parcel Service) whenever possible because they are usually less costly than freight lines on SMALL ORDERS. On very large orders, a freight line is less costly. And MANY machines are too LARGE or too HEAVY for U.P.S.

U.P.S. will not accept any individual parcel over 150 pounds, or over their size restrictions (width X 2, + depth X 2, + height X 1 must not total over 130 inches).

You don't have to try and figure out which products may be shipped U.P.S. At the end of each product description there are "NOTES" which will tell you how the product may be shipped.

Choose the item(s) above that you would like a shipping estimate for. You will need a separate shipping estimate for each manufacturer (for example, one estimate for all items to be shipped from U. S. Vend Technology).

Make A Note Of The Following:

Add up the "approximate shipping weight" (listed in the first column of the "Wholesale Factory-Direct Costs") for each item ordered = total shipping weight.

The "zip code of origin," listed in the second column, is the postal zip code for the city that the factory is located in, and/or where your machine(s) will be shipped from.

The "zip code of destination" (your own zip code).

At the end of each product description there are "NOTES" which will tell you if the product is shipped by U.P.S. or Freight Line. Make a note of this information as well.

U.P.S. Shipments

If the item is shipped by U.P.S. (United Parcel Service) call U.P.S. as follows:

U. P. S.
800-742-5877
MO-SA, 7:30am-8:00pm, all time zones

Tell U.P.S. that you would like a freight estimate.

Tell them up front that ALL items are within their "maximum SIZE guidelines", and that NO items will be subject to their "minimum charge guidelines" (that way, you won't have to bother telling them the dimensions of each item).

Give them the shipping weight of EACH individual item.

Be sure to tell them the total number of cartons (don't just multiply the number of cartons times the rate for one carton) because there is a special "hundred weight" rate for large orders being delivered to a single address.

Give them the "zip code of origin" (where the machines are being shipped from - see above) as well as the "zip code of destination" (your own zip code).

They will give you a reasonably close estimate for the total shipment. That's all there is to it.

The actual shipping cost may vary somewhat due to precise shipping weight shipped, amount of insurance required, other misc., etc.

Freight Line Shipments

If the item is shipped by freight line, call the Roadway Express automated quote system anytime, 24 hours a day, 7 days a week, from a TOUCH TONE phone, as follows:

Roadway Express
1-800-762-3929
24 hours a day, 7 days a week

You will be fully prompted by a recorded voice as to how to proceed with each step. You do not have to wait for each recording to be completed, and may enter the information requested at ANY time.

Press '3', for "easy rate quotations".

Enter the 5 digit "origin zip code" (where the machines are being shipped from - see above) followed by the '#' sign.

Enter the 5 digit "destination zip code" (your zip code), followed by the '#' sign.

Enter the freight classification number '125' (vending machines are class 125 freight), followed by the '#' sign.

Enter the TOTAL shipping weight for the ENTIRE order, followed by the '#' sign.

Press '2', followed by the '#' sign, for total charges.

Follow prompts for more information if you want, or simply hang up.

DEDUCT a 35% DISCOUNT from whatever the total freight quote is.

This will give you a reasonably close estimate for the entire shipment (don't forget to deduct the 35% discount). Although Roadway Express is used a lot, each manufacturer reserves the right to use whatever freight line they want. All the freight lines have very similar pricing, and the final price after discounts would be similar. For simplicity, I find it easier to just use the Roadway Express automated quotation system for all freight quotes. These estimates are about as close you can "estimate".

The actual shipping cost may vary somewhat due to actual freight line used, actual discount applied, precise shipping weight shipped, amount of insurance required, other misc., etc.

FREE Resources: Reports, Videos, Etc.!

Valuable, hard-to-find information: See last page for details.

For FREE Resources, Questions, Or Service Contact:
FREEDOM TECH

PHONE: 970-221-9000 ● FAX: 970-221-9696

E-MAIL: info@livefree.com

WEBSITE: (Exciting and enlightening; it's like no other!)   www.livefree.com

P.O. Box 511, Fort Collins, Colorado 80522 US
305 West Magnolia Street, Suite 255, Fort Collins, Colorado 80521 US

Ordering Factory-Direct
How To Place Your Order

Lets Get Started!

The vending business offers you one of the most spectacular opportunities for financial independence ever! And for a relatively small investment of your time and money. Why wait? Order now!

How To Order

You will find a Purchase Agreement in the "Forms And Miscellaneous" section of the Appendix. Ordering is simple. Here's all there is to it:

Fill in the requested information in the two boxes at the top of the form.

Now fill in your machine order, including the quantity, description, unit price, and total amount for each different item ordered.

After listing all the items you're ordering, total the "Amount" column and enter that figure at the bottom of the column (where it says "Total Purchase Price").

"Total Purchase Price" lists the total you are paying for this order. Purchase a BANK CASHIERS CHECK ONLY for this amount (no money orders, personal checks, or credit cards) payable to "BILL WAY" (NOT to Bill Way's Freedom Technology).

Sign and date the order at the bottom of the page.

Forward 1 copy of the Purchase Agreement together with the check mentioned above, to us at the address on the Purchase Agreement.

That's it. . . you're done!

In a rush? If you like you can FAX us your order, and wire transfer payment. If this interests you, contact us for wire transfer instructions.

FAST Service!!

It is our goal to process all orders on the same day received, and most of our manufacturers ship within just a few days.

Upon our receipt we will send you a confirmation that your order has been received and processed. You can expect the shipping date and transit time to be approximately as indicated in the product "Notes" following the description of the machines you purchased (listed on the "Wholesale Factory-Direct Price List").

No further communication will go out unless there is some sort of delay in the normal shipping process. If you do not receive your order within the time frame indicated, please contact us and we will confirm the shipping date, information, and track the shipment if necessary.

Please Do NOT Contact The Manufacturer Directly

Our job as a distributor is to handle routine communications with you. The manufacturer does not want to be in the position of doing our job for us, and is not being paid to do so. Therefore, I ask that you do not contact the manufacturer directly regarding the processing or shipping of your order. If you have any questions or concerns, please contact us here at FREEDOM TECH. After receipt of your order, you may contact the manufacturer for the purposes of obtaining parts, or for technical support.

Please note that the violation of this request may cause us to reject future orders from you!

Communicating With FREEDOM TECH

Above all else, please remember that we're here to serve you. So feel free to communicate in whatever manner best meets your needs (phone, fax, email or mail). Having said that, let me add:

Because of our low costs, we must keep all overhead very low. For this reason we have a small staff. Small staff means that if you phone us, you may get voice mail at busy times. If this happens, please do not hang up. . . leave a detailed message. . . and we will call you back as soon as possible.

Have Questions? Contact Us. . .

Your FREEDOM TECH Support Team!

With FREEDOM TECH and our unique marketing program you're joining a team that has the potential to launch MORE vending operators on MILLION-DOLLAR careers than ALL the others!   Join us part time or full time in this DYNAMIC . . . GROWING industry and you could have ALL the money you need. . . AND have the TIME to enjoy it.

FREEDOM TECH: Serving you since 1972. Written Satisfaction Guarantee!

I want to impress upon you that we are dedicated to your success in the vending business!

Please don't hesitate to contact us at any time if you have questions or if there is anything at all that we can do to serve you.

You are respected as an individual, and valued as our client. We're all looking forward to hearing from you soon. . . and to a long and mutually rewarding association.

We appreciate the confidence you show is us when you place an order. Our goal is to provide you with quality vending and amusement machines at the lowest possible cost, and offer you consulting (and other) services at little or no charge. We will do our best to show you that your confidence in us has been well placed.

Thank You,

Bill Way
And Your FREEDOM TECH Support Team.

TO YOUR GREAT SUCCESS!

FREE Resources: Reports, Videos, Etc.!

Valuable, hard-to-find information: See last page for details.

For FREE Resources, Questions, Or Service Contact:
FREEDOM TECH

PHONE: 970-221-9000   ●   FAX: 970-221-9696

E-MAIL: info@livefree.com

WEBSITE: (Exciting and enlightening; it's like no other!)   www.livefree.com

**P.O. Box 511, Fort Collins, Colorado 80522 US
305 West Magnolia Street, Suite 255, Fort Collins, Colorado 80521 US**

Consulting Services Available

Have Questions? Contact Us!

We are totally committed to our customers. That's why we offer well-trained and talented vending consultants. . . to help assure your success in the vending business.

I invite you to call us at FREEDOM TECHNOLOGY for a FREE consultation to review the options that might best fit your needs, wants, and available funds. . . and to discuss other matters, plans and questions you may have regarding your new (or established) venture.

There is no charge for the initial consultation, nor for brief future consultations. Those who have read this book generally require very little or no consultation and often just send in an order and get started. We do charge in situations where consultation is substantial, because my machine prices are just so low that we must charge separately for this.

Do You Really Need Consulting?

Information is dispensed inexpensively through this book, which generally informs our clients of most everything they need to know to get started in vending, usually without having to pay for any consulting at all. It is my goal to answer all your questions in this book and eliminate your need to spend any money on consulting. . . however, that is not always possible for everyone in every situation.

When we get questions that are not answered in this book, I modify the book and include the answer. We print in low numbers, so we can keep the information current. For most people, the book is enough. . . with little or no private consulting required. If you do need consulting it is available by telephone, e-mail, FAX, or mail for a relatively low fee.

Most of our new clients simply read this book and find they are comfortable getting started in vending at that point. They choose what type of vending interests them most. They order one or more machines (following the simple instructions in the Appendix on "Ordering Factory Direct"). Next, they locate and service their machines as I advise in this book. They find that things work out about like they expect, so they are very happy. Then they continue ordering more machines on a regular basis. It's that simple. Little or no consulting is usually necessary.

This method keeps our cost so low that nobody can beat our prices. . . and the material in this book makes it all possible because otherwise it would be too time consuming and expensive for you to learn what you need to know (it's not easy to find accurate information). My business is supported by a lot of people who order a little bit each month or two.

I invite you to contact us with your questions, machine information requests, or how to order. We will try to answer brief inquiries at no charge (at our sole discretion). . . and of course, we expect routine communications regarding the placing and processing of orders. But for anything more than that, I must ask you to set up a consulting account and pay our nominal consulting fees.

As you know, we are essentially a mail order catalog house, or discount distributor. We do not have extensive 'free' consulting or support figured into our price structure. While we do offer this optional consulting and support for those who want it, we must charge extra for this or we would have to raise our prices for everyone. I hope you understand. (Please see chapter titled "A Better Way" for more details on this.)

To Keep Your Costs Down. . . Be Prepared

Read 'VENDING SUCCESS SECRETS' very carefully. Highlight the parts that seem important to you. And write down your questions as you go.

As you read, you will find that all or most of your questions will be answered. So check them off.

When you're all finished, if any questions remain, then you may need consulting assistance (if you feel the remaining questions are of importance) or if you feel that you will need support during the start up phase.

To keep your charges as low as possible, WRITE down your inquiry as concisely as possible, and send it to us together with a bank cashiers check and the completed form below. We will respond in the method you indicate below.

If you have no need for consulting at this time, but want it to be available to you if and when you need it, then I suggest that you open your consulting account now.

Consulting Policies And Rates

Effective January 1, 1996

Our consulting services are very simple, informal, and relatively low cost. To consult with one of our consultants regarding any issue, our policies and rates are currently as follows (subject to change at any time with prior notice). No exceptions can be made except for brief inquiries (at our sole discretion).

● These policies and rates apply to all communications with you except routine communications regarding the placing and processing of orders, and other brief inquiries (at our sole discretion).

● A consulting rate of only $60.00 per hour, pro-rated at $1.00 per minute, with a 15 minute minimum charge ($15.00) per consultation.

● For telephone consulting, you pay for the call. If we are returning your call long distance, we add an additional flat rate long distance charge of $15.00 per hour, pro-rated at .25¢ per minute, with a 3 minute minimum charge (.75¢) per consultation.

If we are able to respond by e-mail, FAX, or mail there are no additional charges over and above the consulting fee, which is only for the time it takes us to respond to your request.

This is usually a lower cost method of consulting. For one thing, you save long distance phone charges. Also, most inquiries can be handled for a much lower total charge because it is a much more efficient method of response for us. This is because very often information can be copied from our computer files and pasted into our response to you, which is then e-mailed, FAXed, or mailed. To transmit the same information verbally would take much more time.

Whenever PRACTICAL, try to make a concise WRITTEN inquiry by e-mail, FAX, or mail. . . instead of the telephone. . . and specify a similar method of response.

When contacting us, please be sure to let us know the preferred method of response (telephone, e-mail, FAX, or mail).

● To receive consulting services you must first open a consulting account by completing a "Consulting Services Agreement" (available in the Appendix under "Forms And Miscellaneous") and mailing it to us together with a BANK CASHIERS CHECK ONLY (no money orders, personal checks, or credit cards) payable to BILL WAY (NOT to Bill Way's Freedom Technology). This check shall be in an amount not less than $60.00, which will be credited to your consulting account.

● When, and if, your credit is used up, you will then be billed for all future consultations, if any. Payment shall be made by BANK CASHIERS CHECK ONLY, as indicated above. Any bill which remains unpaid for more than 10 days may result in a suspension of consultations.

● Payments credited to your consulting account are not refundable, however, upon your request we will terminate your consulting account and apply any remaining balance to your primary account at FREEDOM TECHNOLOGY, which may then be used for future machine orders. FREEDOM TECHNOLOGY reserves the right to terminate your consulting account at any time, in which case any credit balance will be refunded to you.

● All fees are due for consulting services and long distance charges (if any) regardless as to the degree of success (or lack thereof) of the consultation. If you feel that our consulting services are not necessary or helpful to you, you are free to terminate your consulting account at any time, and any remaining credit left on your account will be applied as mentioned above.

● Consulting services are sold with the understanding that Bill Way, Bill Way's FREEDOM TECHNOLOGY, and his agents and/or employees are are not engaged in rendering legal, accounting, tax or other advice or services for which a professional license may be required. Consultants are simply sharing their personal experience, beliefs and opinions. If required, the services of a competent licensed professional should be sought.

After we receive your initial check and completed form, all future inquiries may be made my telephone, e-mail, FAX, or mail, as you prefer.

As I've already said, it is my goal to make this book so complete that little or no consultations are necessary. After years of perfecting it, I think I have come pretty close, but this is still a 'work-in-progress'. It's in a constant state of being updated and may never be finished. Our consulting services do help fill the gap.

Have Questions? Contact Us. . .

Your FREEDOM TECH Support Team!

With FREEDOM TECH and our unique marketing program you're joining a team that has the potential to launch MORE vending operators on MILLION-DOLLAR careers than ALL the others! Join us part time or full time in this DYNAMIC . . . GROWING industry and you could have ALL the money you need. . . AND have the TIME to enjoy it.

FREEDOM TECH: Serving you since 1972. Written Satisfaction Guarantee!

I want to impress upon you that we are dedicated to your success in the vending business!

Please don't hesitate to contact us at any time if you have questions or if there is anything at all that we can do to serve you.

You are respected as an individual, and valued as our client. We're all looking forward to hearing from you soon. . . and to a long and mutually rewarding association.

We appreciate the confidence you show is us when you place an order. Our goal is to provide you with quality vending and amusement machines at the lowest possible cost, and offer you consulting (and other) services at little or no charge. We will do our best to show you that your confidence in us has been well placed.

Thank You,

Bill Way
And Your FREEDOM TECH Support Team.

TO YOUR GREAT SUCCESS!

FREE Resources: Reports, Videos, Etc.!
Valuable, hard-to-find information: See last page for details.

For FREE Resources, Questions, Or Service Contact:
FREEDOM TECH

PHONE: 970-221-9000 ● FAX: 970-221-9696

E-MAIL: info@livefree.com

WEBSITE: (Exciting and enlightening; it's like no other!)   www.livefree.com

P.O. Box 511, Fort Collins, Colorado 80522 US
305 West Magnolia Street, Suite 255, Fort Collins, Colorado 80521 US

Notes

Complete and send to FREEDOM TECHNOLOGY with initial payment to open your consulting account.

Consulting Services Agreement

I am fully aware of your written "Consulting Policies And Rates Effective January 1, 1996", and agree to them, as evidenced by my signature below.

I understand that Bill Way, Bill Way's FREEDOM TECHNOLOGY, and his agents and/or employees are not engaged in rendering legal, accounting, tax or other advice or services for which a professional license may be required. Consultants are simply sharing their personal experience, beliefs and opinions. If required, the services of a competent licensed professional should be sought.

Enclosed is a BANK CASHIERS CHECK ONLY (no money orders, personal checks, or credit cards) payable to BILL WAY (NOT to Bill Way's Freedom Technology) in an amount not less than $60.00, which shall be credited to my consultation account. Either party may cancel this agreement at any time, in accordance with your consulting policies mentioned above.

Print Name   Signature   Date

E-mail Address (If available)   FAX# (If available)   Phone# (Voice)

Mailing Address   City, State, Zip Code

$_____

Initial payment enclosed for my consulting account in an amount not less than $60.00. BANK CASHIERS CHECK ONLY, (no money orders, personal checks, or credit cards) payable to BILL WAY (NOT to Bill Way's Freedom Technology).

Method Of Our Reply

Please indicate the preferred method of reply. This will be the method of reply for this inquiry (if any) and for future inquiries unless you specify otherwise (at some future time). Circle all that are acceptable to you:

E-mail   FAX   U.S. Postal Service   Telephone

Initial Inquiry (If Any)

If applicable, please write down your initial inquiry below, or on attached sheets (Or if you prefer, you may contact us by e-mail, FAX, U.S. Postal Service, or telephone at some future time. . . in which case your account will already be set up and ready to go):

Selected Machines - Photos

Following are photos and specifications of selected machines that may be of particular interest to you for various reasons. Some are not recommended, some are okay, and some are great! Please refer to the relevant section of this book for recommendations, or contact us.

You may also find it interesting and helpful to refer to the "Wholesale Factory-Direct Costs" (listed in the "Appendix") for comparative price data.

Please note that NOT ALL the machines listed in the "Wholesale Factory-Direct Costs" are pictured in the pages that follow. However. . .

For a FREE COLOR BROCHURE featuring any machine pictured, or listed in the "Wholesale Factory-Direct Costs," please contact us as directed below. (NOTE: Brochures subject to availability.)

FREE Resources: Reports, Videos, Etc.!
Valuable, hard-to-find information: See last page for details.

For FREE Resources, Questions, Or Service Contact:
FREEDOM TECH

PHONE: 970-221-9000 ● FAX: 970-221-9696

E-MAIL: info@livefree.com

WEBSITE: (Exciting and enlightening; it's like no other!)   **www.livefree.com**

P.O. Box 511, Fort Collins, Colorado 80522 US
305 West Magnolia Street, Suite 255, Fort Collins, Colorado 80521 US

Notes

Dear Friend,

The mission of our company is to offer the very finest vending equipment in the industry, the finest service, prompt delivery, to give service beyond what is expected and to make your new venture one of enjoyment and prosperity.

Thank you for your interest in the finest bulk candy machine on the market, named the U-Turn. The name describes the machine perfectly, however, it could properly be named "THE MONEY MACHINE" as well.

The lid of our U-Turn serves several functions: (1) it features a screw-down lock that provides high security; (2) it provides a positive seal to keep the product fresh; and (3) its pyramid-like shape prevents it from becoming used as an ashtray or a place for empty pop cans and coffee cups. Because of its shape, heavy objects cannot be placed upon it. In addition, we have cut a coin slot in the lid making it a separate coin box for the purpose of charitable giving. We ask your customers to make a donation to a charity of your choice and deposit it in the lid. This keeps charity donations and candy sales separate, and leaves no question about how much money goes to charity. Only our U-Turn is mounted on a square base. This not only makes the U-Turn very stable, but also custodial people love us, as they can clean right up to the U-Turn base.

The U-Turn features four or eight selections. From any angle nearly all selections are visible and create a very attractive and colorful display. Vending is an impulse—stimulated business. Our U-Turn triggers the impulse. The canisters have a molded inventory gauge for inventory control and serving convenience. The vending tumbler has ten adjustment settings rather than the very few adjustment settings that are common in the industry. It also helps maintain control on number of product pieces vended. Each coin mechanism has its own coin box, making it easy to track proceeds and, if used properly, will discourage dishonesty. The coin mechanisms are made from M-90 Celcon (Delrin) and have a special fall-through feature which accepts pennies, nickels and dimes without activating the mechanism.

The U-Turn is made of steel and is finished with a scratch-resistant, baked-on powder coating. It turns on steel bearings, is simple to assemble (less than 5 minutes) and will stand the test of time on location. Candy vends completely and is kept sanitary and clean because of our very steep vending chute and spring-loaded chute door. Optional: Twenty-five cent stickers are available.

The U-Turn is guaranteed for two full years. Our company pays for a five year maintenance policy protecting you against loss by malicious mischief, vandalism, or outright theft. All you need to do is send us an official loss report and $100 deductible for U-Turn or $150 deductible for Eliminator.

In short, with up to 600 inches of product display, several eye-catching colors, up to 8 removable canisters, the finest coin mechanism in the industry, and a five year warrantee, we have earned our nickname, "The Money Machine."

Call us - we'll answer your questions. We're excited about our U-Turn products and the vending business. We're committed to your success since your success is our success!

Sincerely yours,
Your Vending Support Team

FACTS* YOU SHOULD KNOW ABOUT VENDING

*Average Hourly Income of Office Worker $4.85
*Average Hourly Income of Factory Worker.....$7.04
*Average Hourly Income of Salesman.............$8.16
*Average Hourly Income of Plumber..............$12.00

*Average Hourly Income
of Snack Vender Owner/Operator.................$70.58

HOW DOES YOUR PRESENT INCOME COMPARE WITH THE ABOVE???

*Compiled from Dept. of Labor Statistics

ASK YOURSELF?

WHAT OTHER BUSINESS OFFERS THE FOLLOWING with a National Firm backing you every step of the way!

• No Selling Experience Needed
• No Technical Experience Required
• High Income Potential
• Automatic Repeat Business Which Creates Lifetime Income
• Not Seasonal
• No Fixed Equipment
• No Credit Risks
• Comprehensive Company Support

RECESSION PROOF   INFLATION PROOF

Questions & Answers

1. **Why the U-Turn Bulk Candy Vendor?**
   Eye appeal, the U-Turn described offers total flexibility and reliability, made out of the finest materials available, the most innovative, state-of-the art bulk candy machine on the market today!

2. **How do I find locations?**
   You can choose to locate the machines yourself. A list of suggested business types and a telephone script are available for your use. Or, for a nominal fee, a professional locator will assist you in finding profitable locations. It is best to give him/her addresses and phone numbers to work with.

3. **How much time is required to service a location?**
   Usually about 10 minutes to clean the machine and refill the candy. Servicing is very simple.

4. **Is vending considered a small business?**
   Yes. It has all the advantages of any business: a) you can deduct car or van expenses used in business; b) some expenses for your home can be deducted; and c) retirement plan contributions to a defined plan.

5. **What is the competition?**
   Normally you aren't competing with other same-name brand products. U-Turn vending machines are unique and have high visibility that most machines don't have, therefore, attracting customers to your machines. U-Turn vending machines also have the advantage of 4 or 8 segments which offers the consumer a wider selection.

6. **Who owns vending machines?**
   65 percent are owned by small investors with an average of 197 machines each.

7. **Will I need employees?**
   Probably not. Vending is an ideal family business. 100 machines can be serviced in one or two weekends per month. Your U-Turn vending machine is on duty 24 hrs. a day, 365 days a year, and never gets tired.

8. **Where do I buy candy?**
   We will supply you names, addresses and phone numbers of suppliers for your candy

9. **Will I receive proper support after my purchase?**
   Yes. We have a support center to help you with any questions or needs that you might have and we help with your expansion program. Just call!

10. **How soon after my purchase can I start earning money?**
    You can expect to start earning money within two weeks after your purchase.

11. **How can I get started?**
    By calling your company representative. He/she can walk you through the few simple steps of starting your vending business. He/she will line you up with professional locators, candy suppliers, bookkeeping systems, suggested settings, locations for your candy machines, and professional advice.

Read what some of our customers say about *UTurn* and our company.

The above are only case examples of our customers, and should not be construed as a promise or implication of earnings from U-Turn.

Call Now To Order!

Specifications and Features

| UTurn Candy Vendor | UTurn Eliminator |

Specifications:

Model:	UT-BC-110 (Electric Yellow) UT-BC-210 (The Silver Collection)	UT-E-130 (Electric Yellow) UT-E-230 (The Silver Collection)
Type:	Free standing - Bulk Candy, Nuts.	Free standing - Bulk Candy, Nuts.
Weight:	Approximately 26 lbs.	Approximately 38 lbs.
Height:	Approximately 46" high.	Approximately 55" high.
Capacity:	6 - 8 lbs. per canister	4 - 6 lbs. per canister
Optional Dividers:	Divides canister to reduce inventory.	Divides canister to reduce inventory.
Selections:	4 selections	8 selections
Decor:	Yellow or Silver with black coin mechanisms, silver vein pole and base for all models.	
Paint:	Powder coat finish on metal parts.	Powder coat finish on metal parts.
Complete Stand:	Finished in powder coat silver vein.	Finished in powder coat silver vein.
Lock:	High Security Lock.	High Security Lock.
Options:	Vend prices adjustable to fit various products. Same for all models.	
Color Option:	Color may be changed in large quantities with a nominal fee. See Optional Colors below.	

Features:

Display:	400 sq. in. of product. 4 selections.	600 sq. in. of product. 8 selections.
Donation Slot:	*Donation slot in steel lid. Allows for higher profits. No out of pocket payout to charity.*	*Donation slot in steel lid. Allows for higher profits. No out of pocket payout to charity.*
Canister:	High Impact Polystyrene.	High Impact Polystyrene.
Pole:	14 gauge cold rolled steel tubing.	14 gauge cold rolled steel tubing.
Base:	10 gauge cold rolled steel.	10 gauge cold rolled steel.
Turntable:	All steel turntable.	All steel turntable.
Body:	14 gauge cold rolled steel.	14 gauge cold rolled steel.
Coin Mechanisms:	M-90 Celcon (Delrin) Does not corrode. "Keeps odd coins--nickels, pennies, dimes." Has a fall through - mechanism that eliminates jams. Spring loaded door.	
Coin Boxes:	One for each coin mechanism (better controls on money). Simple to service! Easy to Track Money!	
Space Needed:	Takes approximately 1 1/2 square feet of space. Base 18" square. Same for all models.	
Gasketed Lid:	Gasketed Lid preserves freshness and prevents spillovers from one segment to another on all models.	
All Mechanical:	Since there is no need for electricity, the machine can be located almost any place. Same for all models.	
Bindicators:	Each canister has inventory control numbered lines. Same inventory control is used for all models.	
Reliable:	The all mechanical design of the machine results in more trouble free operation than electronic models.	
Maintenance:	Maintenance is simple for all models!	Maintenance is simple for all models!
Economical:	Costs much less than machines with comparable features.	

Keeps merchandise fresh by rotating its own stock: First in/First out. Same for all models.

Warranted to be free from defects in materials and workmanship under normal use for a period of two years, to the original purchaser. 5 years warrantee on the coin mechanism.

5 Year Maintenance: Covers the machines against theft or vandalism. Complete replacement of machine with proper police report and/or its equivalent and $100 for the U-Turn or $150 for the Eliminitor.

Patented   **Made in the U.S.A.**   © Copyright 1996

We Ship Internationally!

- **Red**
- **Yellow**
- **Blue**
- **White**
- **Hunter Green**
- **Forest Green**
- **Black**
- **Teal**
- **Brass**
- **Silver Vein**
- **Chrome**
- **Pink**

Don't Delay A Prosperous Future!

COMPACT SNACK & REFRIGERATED DRINK VENDOR

Fast Features

- **"Positive Front Drop" Delivery System**
  Better merchandises products, for increased sales.

- **"Quick Change" Coin Mechanisms**
  Individual coin mechanisms for each selection can be changed on location in seconds.

- **Award Winning Graphics**
  This is sure to lead to spontaneous sales of product.

- **Anti-Theft Push Door**
  Inhibits "Reach Up Theft"

- **Reliable, Mechanical Design**
  The mechanical design results in more trouble free operation than electronic models, maintenance is simple.

- **Versatile**
  Vends candybars, gum, crackers, cookies, nuts, bagged chips, pastries, popcorn, sodas, juices and much more!

Fast Facts

Models:	SNACK	FB-10
	DRINK	FB-5
		R134A Refrigerant/CFC Free
Size:	SNACK	15"H x 31"W x 22.5"D 85 lbs.
	DRINK	37"H x 31"W x 25" D 230 lbs.
Capacity:	SNACK	Up to 168 Items
	DRINK	175 Cans
Selections:	SNACK	Up to 12 Selections
	DRINK	5 Selections
Options:	Stand	
	Dollar Bill Changer	

**COMPACT COMBINATION
SNACK AND DRINK VENDOR**

SNACK MACHINE Specifications	DRINK MACHINE Specifications
MODEL CT-10	**MODEL** F-3
SIZE 30" high x 19" wide x 21" deep (Unboxed)	**SIZE** 32-1/2" high x 19" wide x 20" deep (Unboxed)
CAPACITY 90 to 144 items	**CAPACITY** 83 12 oz. cans
SHIPPING WEIGHT 72 lbs.	**SHIPPING WEIGHT** 122 lbs.

FEATURES

SMALL FOOTPRINT   Only 2.90 square feet.

RELIABLE   All mechanical design results in more trouble-free operation than electronic models.

COIN MECHANISMS   Individual coin mechs are easily removed for vend price changes or service by operator.

QUALITY   CSA and UL approved. Occasional defrosting of drink machine is required.

OPTIONS   Clamp set available to attach units.

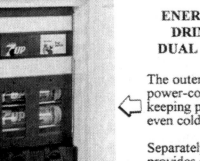

ENERGY EFFICIENT DRINK MACHINE DUAL DOOR SYSTEM

The outer door allows low power-consumption while keeping product at a more even cold temperature.

Separately locked inner door provides easy access for the operator to load product. Coin tray remains secure with independent lock.

Individually mounted
coin mechs; No need to
remove all coin mechs
to change or repair one

Pull-out product trays
cut stocking time by 25%

Riveted steel construction –
lifetime of reliable operation

Entire unit UL/CSA approved
(Not just components of system)

Energy efficient –
Costs pennies per day

Nationwide service centers
provide on-location calls
for refrigerated units

29 Selection Soda/Snack Combo

8 SELECT 12oz. CAN VENDOR   21 SELECT SNACK VENDOR

SPECIFICATIONS

MODEL FMR-8-200.

TYPE Refrigerated 8 column drink merchandiser.

SIZE 55" high x 28" wide x 26 1/2" deep unboxed.

WEIGHT 246 lbs. shipping weight.

CAPACITY Up to 200 - 12 ounce cans.

OPERATION Completely non-electrical vend mechanism for dependability. UL listed refrigeration system, 115 volts - 60 hz. - 5.0 amps.

SPECIFICATIONS

MODEL FT-21-250.

TYPE Glass front candy and chip merchandiser.

SIZE 54 1/4" high x 24 3/4" wide x 21 1/4" deep unboxed.

WEIGHT 151 lbs. shipping weight.

CAPACITY 186 to 285 items.

EASY LOADING Pull out product tray speeds servicing.

COIL SIZES Small diameter - 11, 14 and 18 space - fit the twelve 2 inch trays. Large diameter - 6, 7 and 9 space - fit the nine 4 inch trays.

ENERGY EFFICIENT DUAL DOOR SYSTEM

The outer door allows low power consumption while keeping product at a more even cold temperature. Simple, yet attractive eye pleasing design fits any decor.

Separately locked inner product doors provide easy access for the operator to load product.

COMPACT FULL FEATURE VENDING SYSTEMS

RCS20EP/RCD5SU
Snack and Slave Cold Can Merchandiser

The ideal vending system for small to medium locations. Features 20 snack selections, 5 cold can selection, bill validator capable, durable and ultra compact size that will meet your offices needs now and in the future.

FEATURES

RCS20EP Snack Vendor
- 20 selections – 10 chip, 10 candy
- Large 185 piece capacity
- Electronic controller
- L.E.D. Credit Display
- Individual selection pricing to $99.95
- Uses latest changer
- Bill validator capable
- 24 VDC Vend Motors
- Durable all steel construction – powder coat paint
- 2 point locking system
- Anti-theft system

RCD5SU Slave Cold Can Vendor
- Slaves off electronics and changer in the snack vendor
- 5 selection of 12oz. cold cans
- 160 cans vendable – slant shelf
- 130 cans vendable – serpentine
- Individual selection pricing through snack vendor
- 24 VDC motorized vend system
- Reliable cooling system
- All steel construction

SPECIFICATIONS

SIZE: 30⅝"W x 69½"H x 26½"D
WEIGHT: 390 lbs.
115 VAC-2 AMP / 5 AMP

OPTIONS

Bill Validator
4 Count Vend Tray

RPD
Raddatz Product Development Corporation

COLD DRINK
DISPENSER AND ELECTRONIC
SNACK MERCHANDISER

THE 300 SERIES COMBO

THE 300 SERIES COMBO COLD DRINK DISPENSER AND FM 345 ELECTRONIC SNACK MERCHANDISER
1 CONTROLLER BOARD, 1 COIN MECHANISM, 2 MACHINES

CD-300-5
COLD DRINK MERCHANDISER

- Five slant shelf columns
- 300 12 oz can capacity, plus over 24 cans cold storage
- Multiple pricing — 5¢ to $99.95
- Baked enamel finish for superior durability
- High profile backlit graphic for spontaneous sales

- **Size:** 61" high, 32 1/2" wide, 28" deep
       154 CM 79 CM   76 CM
- **Shipping Weight:** Approximately 360 Pounds / 163 Kilos

FM 345
SNACK MERCHANDISER

- 25 selections as shown
- Individual motor drives—If one fails the rest continue to operate
- LED read-out for:
       Credit display
       Alternate selection light
       Price light
- Tilt down top shelf
- 3 point high security locking door
- Separate locked money area
- Various shelving configurations available

- **Size:** 62 1/2" high, 33" wide, 27" deep
       160 CM   80 CM   68 CM
- **Shipping Weight:** Approximately 300 pounds / 135 Kilos
- **Options:** Dollar bill acceptance, 70 Sel Multinational Controller board
- **Foreign Market Options:** 220 V. Transformers, 7 language scroll display,
                 Coinco or Mars coin mechanism interface

ST 1000   STRESS

HR 1100   HEART RATE

PF 1600   PHYSICAL FITNESS

GP 1800   NON-TALKING GYPSY

TG 2100   TALKING GYPSY

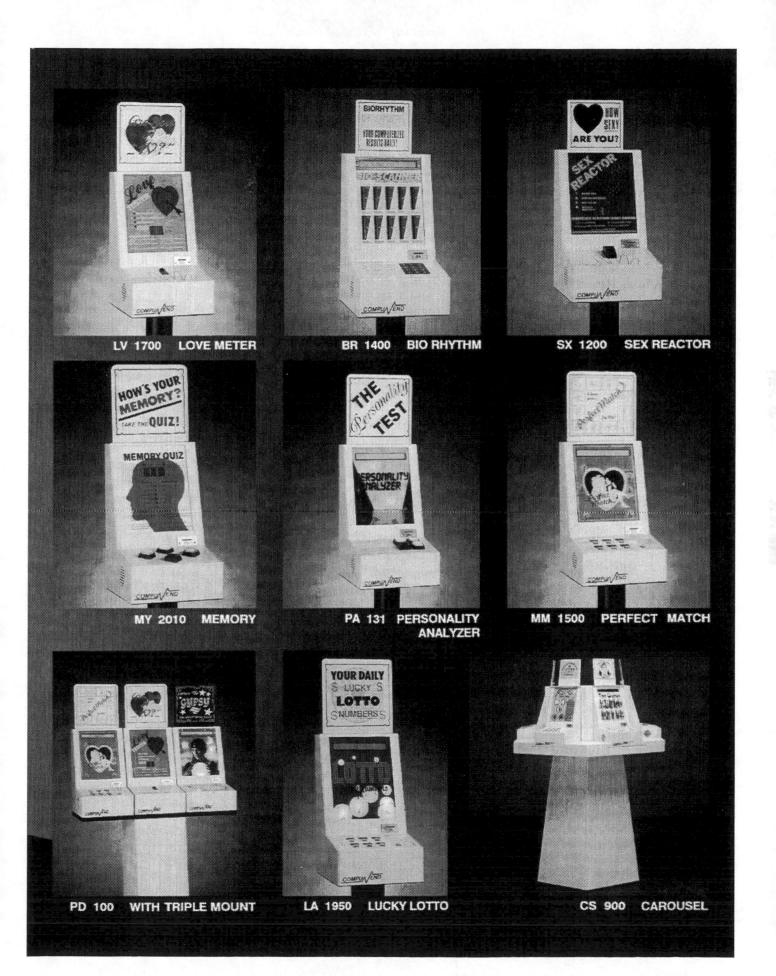

LV 1700   LOVE METER   BR 1400   BIO RHYTHM   SX 1200   SEX REACTOR

MY 2010   MEMORY   PA 131   PERSONALITY ANALYZER   MM 1500   PERFECT MATCH

PD 100   WITH TRIPLE MOUNT   LA 1950   LUCKY LOTTO   CS 900   CAROUSEL

NEW Generation

ACCESSORIES

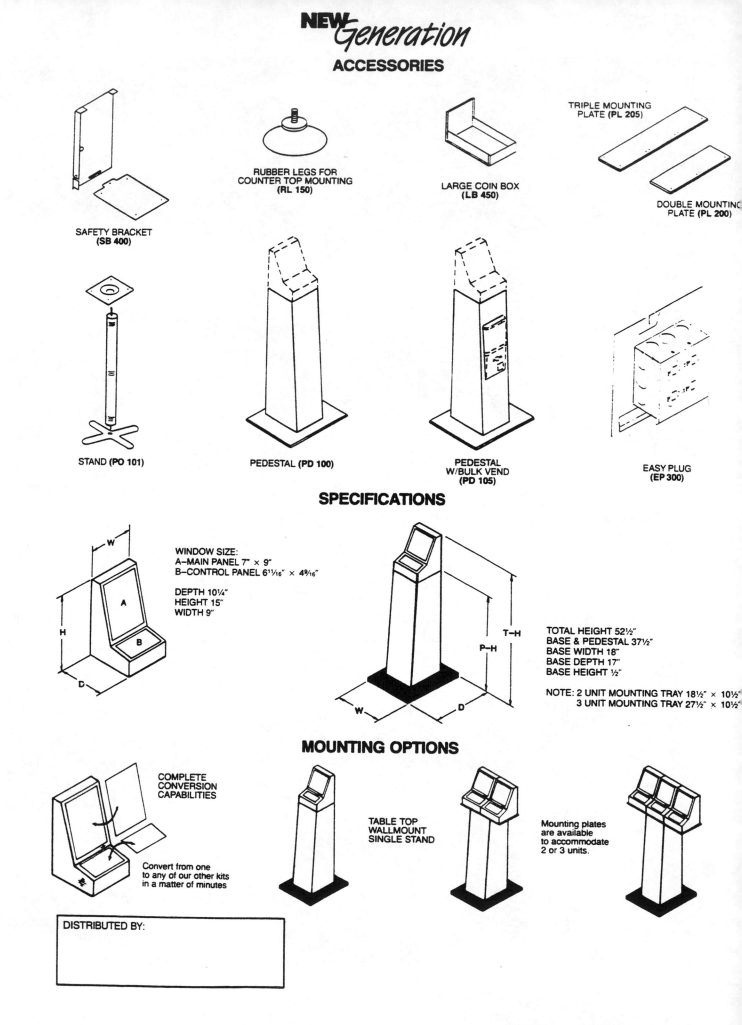

SAFETY BRACKET (SB 400)

RUBBER LEGS FOR COUNTER TOP MOUNTING (RL 150)

LARGE COIN BOX (LB 450)

TRIPLE MOUNTING PLATE (PL 205)

DOUBLE MOUNTING PLATE (PL 200)

STAND (PO 101)

PEDESTAL (PD 100)

PEDESTAL W/BULK VEND (PD 105)

EASY PLUG (EP 300)

SPECIFICATIONS

WINDOW SIZE:
A—MAIN PANEL 7" × 9"
B—CONTROL PANEL 6¹¹⁄₁₆" × 4⁹⁄₁₆"

DEPTH 10¼"
HEIGHT 15"
WIDTH 9"

TOTAL HEIGHT 52½"
BASE & PEDESTAL 37½"
BASE WIDTH 18"
BASE DEPTH 17"
BASE HEIGHT ½"

NOTE: 2 UNIT MOUNTING TRAY 18½" × 10½"
3 UNIT MOUNTING TRAY 27½" × 10½"

MOUNTING OPTIONS

COMPLETE CONVERSION CAPABILITIES

Convert from one to any of our other kits in a matter of minutes

TABLE TOP WALLMOUNT SINGLE STAND

Mounting plates are available to accommodate 2 or 3 units.

DISTRIBUTED BY:

Quality Snacks. . .
For You And Your People

+ Attractive convenience

+ We service regularly

+ Costs you nothing except for snacks purchased

+ Fresh and clean

+ Takes very little space

Fresh Products. . .
20 - 30% Health Oriented Snacks

Cookies	Brownies
Nuts	Raisens
Chips	Crackers
Candy	Granola Bars

Name Brands. . .

Frito Lay	Nabisco
Dolly Madison	Hostess
Snickers	Planters
M & M Mars	Quaker Oats
Hershey	Reeses

Other items as available from suppliers. Selections are based upon sales and availability.

For Prompt Service Please Call:

Snack Shoppe ™   QUALITY SNACKS

Bob Smith
SMITH VENDING SYSTEMS
(555) 555-5555

Placement Agreement

Date: _____

Vendor: Location:

Machine Description:

General Terms:

The vendor will maintain all service requirements of the machine(s) placed on location. The Location agrees to provide space and power (if required) and use reasonable effort to protect the machine(s) from external damage and theft.

Titled to the machine(s) shall remain in the name of the Vendor, and the Vendor or Vendor's agent may at any time take possession of and remove the machine(s) without legal process and liability of any nature to either party.

This agreement may be terminated at any time by notice from either party. At termination of agreement, the machine(s) will be picked up by the Vendor within a reasonable time.

Miscellaneous Provisions:

Whereas, the Location is the owner or lessee of the Premises in which the Machine(s) is (are) to be installed, and:

Whereas, the Vendor is in the business of installing and operating vending and amusement machines:

The parties have executed this Agreement the day and year first written above.

Vendor, by: Location, by:

_____   _____
Signature   Signature

_____   _____
PRINT Name And Title   PRINT Name And Title

Route Report - Route #: _____, Location #: _____, Equipment: _____, Key #'s: _____
Location: _____, Address: _____, Contact Person: _____
Notes: _____

Service		Product (If Any)			Sales (& Analysis)					Commission (If Any)			Notes
Service Date	# Days Between Service	Prod. Pos. #	Prod. # Added	Prod. Amount Added	Vend Price	# Vends Sold	Avg. # Vends Per Mo.	Gross Sales	Avg. Mo. Gross Sales	Comm. Amount Due	Date Comm. Paid	How Comm. Paid	

Service		Product (If Any)			Sales (& Analysis)					Commission (If Any)			Notes
Service Date	# Days Between Service	Prod. Pos. #	Prod. # Added	Prod. Amount Added	Vend Price	# Vends Sold	Avg. # Vends Per Mo.	Gross Sales	Avg. Mo. Gross Sales	Comm. Amount Due	Date Comm. Paid	How Comm. Paid	

Computing Loan Payments

Monthly Payment Per $1,000.00 Financed

Interest Rate	10.%	11.%	12.%	13.%	14.%	15.%	16.%	17.%	18.%	19.%
12 Months	87.92	88.38	88.85	89.32	89.79	90.26	90.73	91.20	91.68	92.16
24 Months	46.14	46.61	47.07	47.54	48.01	48.49	48.96	49.44	49.92	50.41
36 Months	32.27	32.74	33.21	33.69	34.18	34.67	35.16	35.65	36.15	36.66
48 Months	25.36	25.85	26.33	26.83	27.33	27.83	28.34	28.86	29.37	29.90
60 Months	21.25	21.74	22.24	22.75	23.27	23.79	24.32	24.85	25.39	25.94

Credit Application

I was referred to your company by: _____
Amount requested: $ _____
Loan purpose: _____
Date: _____

Type of credit:
- □ Individual credit
- □ Joint credit
- □ Unsecured credit
- □ Secured credit

A married applicant may apply for Individual credit.

APPLICANT

FIRST NAME | MIDDLE INITIAL | LAST NAME

DATE OF BIRTH | SOCIAL SECURITY NO. | HOME PHONE

COMPLETE MARITAL STATUS SECTION ONLY IF APPLICATION IS FOR SECURED CREDIT, JOINT CREDIT OR IF APPLICANT RESIDES IN A COMMUNITY PROPERTY STATE.

□ MARRIED   □ SEPARATED   □ UNMARRIED

DEPENDENTS   NO.   AGES

STREET ADDRESS   DATE MOVED IN MO: YR:

CITY   STATE   ZIP

□ OWN/BUY   □ PARENTS   PAYMENT   PAYMENT MADE TO:
□ RENT   □ OTHER $

ADDRESS   CITY   STATE   ZIP

PREVIOUS ADDRESS (IF AT PRESENT ADDRESS LESS THAN 4 YEARS)   DATE MOVED IN MO: YR:

EMPLOYER   OCCUPATION

EMPLOYER'S ADDRESS   BUSINESS PHONE

DATE STARTED   NET MONTHLY INCOME*
MO: YR: $

PREVIOUS EMPLOYER (IF EMPLOYED IN CURRENT POSITION LESS THAN 2 YRS.)   DATE STARTED MO: YR:

PREVIOUS EMPLOYER'S ADDRESS

MONTHLY AMOUNT AND SOURCE OF OTHER INCOME*—INCLUDE ALIMONY, CHILD SUPPORT OR SEPARATE MAINTENANCE ONLY IF YOU WISH TO HAVE IT RELIED UPON FOR THIS APPLICATION $

HAVE YOU HAD ANY JUDGMENTS AGAINST YOU? □ NO □ YES
HAVE YOU EVER FILED BANKRUPTCY? □ NO □ YES
DO YOU OWE ANY BACK TAXES? □ NO □ YES
WILL ANY INCOME BE REDUCED DURING LOAN TERM? □ NO □ YES
(IF YES TO ANY OF THE QUESTIONS, PLEASE GIVE DETAILS ON REVERSE)

CO-APPLICANT OR SPOUSE

COMPLETE AS APPLICABLE: 1) FOR CO-APPLICANT, IF APPLYING FOR JOINT CREDIT; 2) FOR SPOUSE, IF MARRIED AND RESIDING IN OR SECURITY LOCATED IN A COMMUNITY PROPERTY STATE; 3) FOR SPOUSE OR FORMER SPOUSE, IF RELYING ON ALIMONY, CHILD SUPPORT, OR SEPARATE MAINTENANCE PAYMENTS. (#2 AND #3 NOT OBLIGATED ON LOAN)

FIRST NAME   MIDDLE INITIAL   LAST NAME

SOCIAL SECURITY NO.   RELATIONSHIP   DATE OF BIRTH

EMPLOYER   OCCUPATION   DATE STARTED MO: YR: NET MONTHLY INCOME* $

EMPLOYER'S ADDRESS   BUSINESS PHONE

PREVIOUS EMPLOYER (IF EMPLOYED IN CURRENT POSITION LESS THAN 2 YEARS)

ASSETS—DESCRIPTION

MARKET VALUE	Description		
$	CASH ON HAND AND IN BANKS □ CHECKING	BANK NAME	ADDRESS	ACCOUNT NO.
	□ SAVINGS	BANK NAME	ADDRESS	ACCOUNT NO.
$	AUTO (YR., MAKE, MODEL)		
$	AUTO (YR., MAKE, MODEL)		
$	STOCKS AND BONDS		
$	RESIDENCE	PURCHASE PRICE $	DOWN PAYMENT $
$	OTHER REAL ESTATE (TYPE OF PROPERTY AND ADDRESS; TITLE IN NAME OF; PURCHASE PRICE) (PLEASE GIVE DETAILS ON REVERSE IF NECESSARY)		
$	LIFE INSURANCE	FACE VALUE $	
$	OTHER ASSETS AND PERSONAL PROPERTY (PLEASE GIVE DETAILS ON REVERSE)		
$	**TOTAL ASSETS**		

LIABILITIES—NAME AND ADDRESS OF CREDITOR

BALANCE OWED	MONTHLY PAYMENT	Creditor
$	$	SECURITY PACIFIC ACCOUNT NO.
$	$	PERSONAL LOAN
$	$	PERSONAL LOAN
$	$	CREDIT CARDS □ VISA □ MASTERCARD □ AMERICAN EXPRESS □ DINERS □ CARTE BLANCHE
$	$	AUTO LOAN
$	$	AUTO LOAN
$	$	INSTALLMENT PURCHASE
$	$	INSTALLMENT PURCHASE
$	$	INSTALLMENT PURCHASE
$	$	MORTGAGE OR LIENS ON RESIDENCE
		OTHER MORTGAGES OR LIENS ON REAL ESTATE (PROPERTY DESCRIPTION) (PLEASE GIVE DETAILS ON REVERSE)
$	$	CREDITOR'S NAME
$	$	ALL OTHER INDEBTEDNESS INCLUDING CHARGE CARDS NOT LISTED ABOVE AND BACK TAXES (PLEASE GIVE DETAILS ON REVERSE)
$	$	CO-SIGNER, GUARANTOR OR ENDORSER
	$	AMOUNT YOU PAY FOR ALIMONY OR CHILD SUPPORT
$	$	**TOTAL LIABILITIES**

See reverse side.

010483-0388

Additional Comments / Explanations: _____

_____

_____

_____

_____

_____

_____

_____

_____

State Notices

CALIFORNIA—A married applicant may apply for a separate account.

NEW YORK—A Consumer Report (credit report) may be requested in connection with this application. Upon request, you will be informed whether or not a Consumer Report was requested and the name and address of the consumer reporting agency.

OHIO—The Ohio laws against discrimination require that all creditors make credit equally available to all credit worthy customers, and that credit reporting agencies maintain separate credit histories on each individual upon request. The Ohio Civil Rights Commission administers compliance with this law.

I authorize Security Pacific and/or its affiliates to investigate my and, if lawful, my spouse's credit record in granting, renewing, or collecting this credit, or in the future for marketing purposes. I authorize any person to release such information to you as requested by you. This application is correct to the best of my knowledge, will be relied upon by you, and may be kept whether or not approved.

Date Signed _____ 19 _____ (Sign Here) _____

_____ (Sign Here)

If the application was taken by telephone, the customer was advised of and verbally approved the necessary credit checks.

☐ YES   INITIALS _____

FREEDOM
TECHNOLOGY

Bill Way's FREEDOM TECHNOLOGY
305 West Magnolia Street, Suite 255
Fort Collins, CO 80521 U.S.A.
Voice & FAX: 970-221-9000

PURCHASE AGREEMENT

BUYER _____

_____

_____

SHIP TO _____

_____

_____

DATE _____

ACCOUNT # _____

HOME PHONE # ( ) _____

WORK PHONE # ( ) _____

FAX PHONE # ( ) _____

E-Mail _____

FREEDOM TECHNOLOGY agrees to supply the above named BUYER with the following equipment, supplies and services in accordance with the terms and conditions of this agreement:

QUANTITY	DESCRIPTION	UNIT PRICE	AMOUNT
		$	$

TOTAL PURCHASE PRICE:
Federal, State and local taxes BUYERS' responsibility
BANK CASHIERS CHECK PAYABLE TO: "BILL WAY" $

Thank You

The BUYER acknowledges that he/she has read the terms and conditions of sale on both sides of this agreement, and agrees to be bound by all of the terms and conditions.

BUYERS' ACCEPTANCE _____ DATE _____

BUYERS' ACCEPTANCE _____ DATE _____

FREEDOM TECHNOLOGY REPRESENTATIVE _____ DATE _____

BILL WAYS' OR AUTHORIZED AGENTS' ACCEPTANCE _____ DATE _____

This agreement is effective only when accepted by BILL WAY or his authorized agent.

IMPORTANT - THE TERMS AND CONDITIONS OF THIS AGREEMENT ARE AS FOLLOWS:

1. PARTIES: This agreement is entered into between BILL WAY, doing business as Bill Way's FREEDOM TECHNOLOGY, and the BUYER(s) shown on the face of this document, as attested to by the signatures of acceptance by both parties. This agreement constitutes the entire contract and both parties have read and agreed to the terms set forth herein.

2. PAYMENT: All payments are to be made by bank cashiers check only (no money orders or personal checks) payable to "BILL WAY".

3. SHIPPING: FREEDOM TECHNOLOGY shall cause the products purchased by the BUYER to be shipped within 30 days or less after the entire balance is paid and checks have cleared. All products purchased will be shipped FOB (freight collect) from FREEDOM TECHNOLOGY's place of shipment in the continental United States. Upon receipt by commercial carrier, all products shall be deemed to belong to BUYER, and damage claims shall be the responsibility of the BUYER in any event.

4. TRAINING: FREEDOM TECHNOLOGY agrees to supply training materials to BUYER for the purpose of servicing and maintenance of equipment purchased, in the form of an owners manual, when available from the manufacturer.

FREEDOM TECHNOLOGY publishes a book titled "VENDING SUCCESS SECRETS" which will be shipped to the BUYER at no charge IF it has not been previously purchased by the BUYER or shipped with a prior order.

Optional private consulting may be made available for the BUYER from FREEDOM TECHNOLOGY upon request, and for an additional fee (see "Consulting Services Request" agreement).

5. LOCATING AND SPONSORSHIP: BUYER is solely responsible for physical placement and location of equipment. The purchase price does not include fees for placing any equipment under this agreement. FREEDOM TECHNOLOGY may provide the names of professional locators to the BUYER for the purpose of obtaining locations for said equipment, but neither warrants the quality of locations nor endorses the locator or locating company contracted by the BUYER. The BUYER agrees that any contract entered into by the BUYER with a locating service is solely between the BUYER and said service, and that FREEDOM TECHNOLOGY has no responsibilities or liabilities in connection with such agreement. The BUYER further agrees that any questions regarding locator services contracted for will be directed to the locator the BUYER contracted with, who is solely responsible for any locating agreement.

Upon request by BUYER, FREEDOM TECHNOLOGY will assert its' best effort to make available to the BUYER an opportunity to contract with a national charity for a sponsorship agreement.

6. WARRANTY: Products purchased may be warranted by the manufacturer in accordance with the terms of that particular manufacturers written warranty. No other warranty is expressed or implied. It is understood by the BUYER that this warranty covers only original manufacturers defects in products and not subsequent damage due to shipping, vandalism, or misuse.

7. REPRESENTATIONS AND WARRANTS: The Satisfaction Guarantee printed in the FREEDOM TECHNOLOGY marketing materials shall be considered part of this agreement.

It is understood that this is not a franchise nor a security offering and the BUYER shall function as an independent contractor and is solely responsible for his taxes, insurance, license and the acts and omissions of his agents or employees. BUYER is not required to pay any fee or royalty to FREEDOM TECHNOLOGY other than the charges for the purchase price of products specifically contracted for in writing. It is further understood that this agreement DOES NOT constitute the BUYER, the agent or legal representative of FREEDOM TECHNOLOGY for any purpose whatsoever. BUYER is not granted any right or authority to assume or to create any obligation or responsibility, expressed or implied on behalf of or in the name of FREEDOM TECHNOLOGY, or to bind FREEDOM TECHNOLOGY in any manner.

BUYER also acknowledges and agrees that no representations or warranties are made by FREEDOM TECHNOLOGY or any other person, either expressed or implied, regarding income, expenses or profits, repurchase of products sold by FREEDOM TECHNOLOGY (except as may be provided for in the Satisfaction Guarantee mentioned above) or any security agreement.

The BUYER hereby indemnifies and holds FREEDOM TECHNOLOGY harmless from any and all claims and liability which may arise out of any activities of FREEDOM TECHNOLOGY in furtherance of this contract, from any acts or omissions of its agents or employees, or from the operation of its equipment. BUYER accepts all responsibility and liability for all products vended from the equipment purchased, for all location liabilities and arrangements, and for all claims of any sort arising from the operation and/or use of all FREEDOM TECHNOLOGY equipment or other products sold.

8. MODIFICATION - INTERPRETATION: This agreement shall not be modified or amended in any manner, except by an instrument in writing executed by both parties hereto. This Agreement encompasses all of the promises, terms, conditions and representations made by either party hereto.

9. ACCEPTANCE: This Agreement shall be effective only upon written acceptance by Bill Way or an authorized agent of FREEDOM TECHNOLOGY. In the event of non-acceptance by FREEDOM TECHNOLOGY all monies tendered by the BUYER shall be returned within 5 (five) business days by FREEDOM TECHNOLOGY.

10. ARBITRATION: It is hereby understood that any controversy, dispute or question arising out of, in connection with, or in relation to this Agreement or its interpretation, performance or non-performance, or any breach thereof shall be determined by arbitration conducted in Larimer County Colorado in accordance with the rules of the American Arbitration Association. Both parties agree that they will not be liable for legal fees other than their own, should any dispute arise, and regardless of the outcome of such dispute. The award of the Arbitrator shall be final and binding. This Agreement and any dispute relating thereto shall be construed under common law.

FREEDOM
TECHNOLOGY

Bill Way's FREEDOM TECHNOLOGY
305 West Magnolia Street, Suite 255
Fort Collins, CO 80521 U.S.A.
Voice & FAX: 970-221-9000

PURCHASE AGREEMENT

BUYER _____

_____

_____

SHIP TO _____

_____

_____

DATE _____

ACCOUNT # _____

HOME PHONE #   (   ) _____

WORK PHONE #   (   ) _____

FAX PHONE #   (   ) _____

E-Mail _____

FREEDOM TECHNOLOGY agrees to supply the above named BUYER with the following equipment, supplies and services in accordance with the terms and conditions of this agreement:

QUANTITY	DESCRIPTION	UNIT PRICE	AMOUNT
		$	$

TOTAL PURCHASE PRICE:
Federal, State and local taxes BUYERS' responsibility
BANK CASHIERS CHECK PAYABLE TO: "BILL WAY" $ _____

Thank You

The BUYER acknowledges that he/she has read the terms and conditions of sale on both sides of this agreement, and agrees to be bound by all of the terms and conditions.

_____   DATE _____   _____   DATE _____
BUYERS' ACCEPTANCE   BUYERS' ACCEPTANCE

_____   DATE _____   _____   DATE _____
FREEDOM TECHNOLOGY REPRESENTATIVE   BILL WAYS' OR AUTHORIZED AGENTS' ACCEPTANCE

This agreement is effective only when accepted by BILL WAY or his authorized agent.

IMPORTANT - THE TERMS AND CONDITIONS OF THIS AGREEMENT ARE AS FOLLOWS:

1. PARTIES: This agreement is entered into between BILL WAY, doing business as Bill Way's FREEDOM TECHNOLOGY, and the BUYER(s) shown on the face of this document, as attested to by the signatures of acceptance by both parties. This agreement constitutes the entire contract and both parties have read and agreed to the terms set forth herein.

2. PAYMENT: All payments are to be made by bank cashiers check only (no money orders or personal checks) payable to "BILL WAY".

3. SHIPPING: FREEDOM TECHNOLOGY shall cause the products purchased by the BUYER to be shipped within 30 days or less after the entire balance is paid and checks have cleared. All products purchased will be shipped FOB (freight collect) from FREEDOM TECHNOLOGY's place of shipment in the continental United States. Upon receipt by commercial carrier, all products shall be deemed to belong to BUYER, and damage claims shall be the responsibility of the BUYER in any event.

4. TRAINING: FREEDOM TECHNOLOGY agrees to supply training materials to BUYER for the purpose of servicing and maintenance of equipment purchased, in the form of an owners manual, when available from the manufacturer.

FREEDOM TECHNOLOGY publishes a book titled "VENDING SUCCESS SECRETS" which will be shipped to the BUYER at no charge IF it has not been previously purchased by the BUYER or shipped with a prior order.

Optional private consulting may be made available for the BUYER from FREEDOM TECHNOLOGY upon request, and for an additional fee (see "Consulting Services Request" agreement).

5. LOCATING AND SPONSORSHIP: BUYER is solely responsible for physical placement and location of equipment. The purchase price does not include fees for placing any equipment under this agreement. FREEDOM TECHNOLOGY may provide the names of professional locators to the BUYER for the purpose of obtaining locations for said equipment, but neither warrants the quality of locations nor endorses the locator or locating company contracted by the BUYER. The BUYER agrees that any contract entered into by the BUYER with a locating service is solely between the BUYER and said service, and that FREEDOM TECHNOLOGY has no responsibilities or liabilities in connection with such agreement. The BUYER further agrees that any questions regarding locator services contracted for will be directed to the locator the BUYER contracted with, who is solely responsible for any locating agreement.

Upon request by BUYER, FREEDOM TECHNOLOGY will assert its' best effort to make available to the BUYER an opportunity to contract with a national charity for a sponsorship agreement.

6. WARRANTY: Products purchased may be warranted by the manufacturer in accordance with the terms of that particular manufacturers written warranty. No other warranty is expressed or implied. It is understood by the BUYER that this warranty covers only original manufacturers defects in products and not subsequent damage due to shipping, vandalism, or misuse.

7. REPRESENTATIONS AND WARRANTS: The Satisfaction Guarantee printed in the FREEDOM TECHNOLOGY marketing materials shall be considered part of this agreement.

It is understood that this is not a franchise nor a security offering and the BUYER shall function as an independent contractor and is solely responsible for his taxes, insurance, license and the acts and omissions of his agents or employees. BUYER is not required to pay any fee or royalty to FREEDOM TECHNOLOGY other than the charges for the purchase price of products specifically contracted for in writing. It is further understood that this agreement DOES NOT constitute the BUYER, the agent or legal representative of FREEDOM TECHNOLOGY for any purpose whatsoever. BUYER is not granted any right or authority to assume or to create any obligation or responsibility, expressed or implied on behalf of or in the name of FREEDOM TECHNOLOGY, or to bind FREEDOM TECHNOLOGY in any manner.

BUYER also acknowledges and agrees that no representations or warranties are made by FREEDOM TECHNOLOGY or any other person, either expressed or implied, regarding income, expenses or profits, repurchase of products sold by FREEDOM TECHNOLOGY (except as may be provided for in the Satisfaction Guarantee mentioned above) or any security agreement.

The BUYER hereby indemnifies and holds FREEDOM TECHNOLOGY harmless from any and all claims and liability which may arise out of any activities of FREEDOM TECHNOLOGY in furtherance of this contract, from any acts or omissions of its agents or employees, or from the operation of its equipment. BUYER accepts all responsibility and liability for all products vended from the equipment purchased, for all location liabilities and arrangements, and for all claims of any sort arising from the operation and/or use of all FREEDOM TECHNOLOGY equipment or other products sold.

8. MODIFICATION - INTERPRETATION: This agreement shall not be modified or amended in any manner, except by an instrument in writing executed by both parties hereto. This Agreement encompasses all of the promises, terms, conditions and representations made by either party hereto.

9. ACCEPTANCE: This Agreement shall be effective only upon written acceptance by Bill Way or an authorized agent of FREEDOM TECHNOLOGY. In the event of non-acceptance by FREEDOM TECHNOLOGY all monies tendered by the BUYER shall be returned within 5 (five) business days by FREEDOM TECHNOLOGY.

10. ARBITRATION: It is hereby understood that any controversy, dispute or question arising out of, in connection with, or in relation to this Agreement or its interpretation, performance or non-performance, or any breach thereof shall be determined by arbitration conducted in Larimer County Colorado in accordance with the rules of the American Arbitration Association. Both parties agree that they will not be liable for legal fees other than their own, should any dispute arise, and regardless of the outcome of such dispute. The award of the Arbitrator shall be final and binding. This Agreement and any dispute relating thereto shall be construed under common law.

Satisfaction Guarantee!

We at FREEDOM TECHNOLOGY are totally committed to your success and satisfaction in the vending and amusement business, offering you:

NO MINIMUM ORDER. . . NO RISK MONEY BACK GUARANTEE. . . LOWEST PRICE GUARANTEE. . . CONSULTING services and ongoing SUPPORT! What other company offers you this kind of OPPORTUNITY. . . . SECURITY. . . and SUPPORT? You'll soon find that no other company can compare! FREEDOM TECHNOLOGY. . . serving you, our valued customer and partner in success. . . since 1972.

NO RISK Money Back Guarantee!

You may order a single sample or carton of any machine we offer. . . examine it at your leisure for up to 10 days. . . and if you like, YOU MAY RETURN IT TO US for a FULL REFUND!

SPECIAL GUARANTEE on our HOTTEST machines (machines recommended in my 'HOTTEST Vending Money-Makers' report ONLY): At any time after 6 months, but before 9 months from your receipt of the machines you purchased, if you decide that for ANY reason you do not want them, at YOUR SOLE OPTION, we will repurchase them for the full purchase price you paid, less a 30% restocking and handling fee (70% of the purchase price). And YOU KEEP ALL PROFITS EARNED during this time! This offer applies only on your first order of the specific machines described above, and only on an order of $30,000.00 or less. Free merchandise provided (if any) must be returned as well.

PLUS. . . If you should EVER decide that you want to sell your machine route for ANY reason (like moving, retiring, etc.) we offer you FREE marketing consulting services to help you sell your route (ask us for details). And remember, an established route is generally worth MUCH MORE than just the cost of the machines! Many route operators make a VERY SUBSTANTIAL PROFIT upon the sale of their routes!

LOWEST PRICE Guarantee - Or DOUBLE The Difference Back!

As a national factory-direct wholesale distributor of vending and amusement machines, we strive to offer the absolute LOWEST PRICES possible on QUALITY machines. In the VERY UNLIKELY event that you should find the same machines you purchased from us available through another distributor at a lower price, just send us a copy of their published price list within 30 days of your purchase. We'll promptly send you a CASH REFUND for DOUBLE the difference you paid!

Return Procedure And Important Notes:

All returns will be processed within 30 days of receipt or less. Prior to returning any machines, you must write us for a "return authorization number" (RA#) which must be marked on each carton returned. Cartons received by us with no RA# will not be accepted. Your request for a RA# must be in writing, shall include a copy of your shipper's delivery receipt (or shippers verification of delivery date) and postmarked within the time period stated above. No returns accepted on special order, used or reconditioned machines.

All items returned must be shipped to our designated warehouse in the continental United States, in the original packing materials, freight prepaid, in good and resalable condition (subject only to normal wear and tear, except samples which may not be placed into service and must be returned in new condition) within 10 days after issuance of the RA#. Promptly after shipment, you must send us the shippers name, address, phone number, bill of lading number or tracking number, and date of shipment (so we can track shipment and confirm delivery). Any machines returned to us in substandard condition will warrant a fair and reasonable adjustment in the credit you will receive, or if you notify us within 10 days that you do not want to accept the credit offered, they will be returned to you freight collect.

The following applies only to our HOTTEST machines returned during the 9 month trial period: You must give the machines a fair try by actually placing them into service and operating them for at least 6 months. You must keep route records showing that you serviced your machines at least once a month; and listing your service date gross receipts, business name, address, and phone number for each machine location serviced. . . ALL GOOD BUSINESS PRACTICES. You must send us a copy of these route records at the time you request a RA#.

Offer void where prohibited by law.

P. O. Box 511, Fort Collins, CO 80522 US ● 305 West Magnolia Street, Suite 255, Fort Collins, CO 80521 US
970-221-9000 FAX: 970-221-9696 ● EMAIL: mail@livefree.com ● WEB SITE: www.livefree.com

FREE Resources: Reports, Videos, Etc.!
Valuable, hard-to-find information!

HOTTEST Vending Money-Makers! (Free Report)
Updated frequently! Learn about the newest and best vending and amusement opportunities!
See page 161 for details.

Vending - Making It Work! (Free Video)
Turn your dreams into reality! Get this 'must-see' video now!

Price List & Catalog - Vending & Amusement Machines (Free)
Get our complete current "GUARANTEED LOWEST" price list (Guaranteed lowest price or DOUBLE the difference refunded - see written 'Satisfaction Guarantee'). Photos, color brochure included.

Vending Machine Locating Companies (Free List)
A select list of the best machine placement companies I've found to date. Each company listed is 'PERFORMANCE RATED.' Updated frequently.

Millionaire's Secrets! (Free Report)
Learn THE SINGLE MOST IMPORTANT WEALTH RULE: Master it and you cannot help but grow wealthy, no matter what your situation; fail to learn it and your chances of becoming wealthy drop to 1 in 10 million! Learn THE INFINITE BOOTSTRAP PRINCIPLE: How to apply whatever limited resources you have to become financially independent in 6-12 months!

Freedom Technology Report (Free Report)
BREAK-THRU! Your personal freedom and wealth absolutely EXPLODES with this exciting new cutting-edge growth industry, 'FREEDOM TECHNOLOGY!' Defined as the PRACTICAL means to live free, and prosper, in an increasingly unfree world. You're being robbed by excessive taxes, regulation, and privacy invasion! Turn adversity into opportunity now!

Financial Privacy, Asset Protection, Alternative Banking
(Free Report)
How anyone (this means you) can increase privacy, lower taxes, and protect assets! Learn about little-known low cost domestic and offshore banking alternatives; domestic and offshore trusts; U.B.O.'s (Unincorporated Business Organizations); I.B.C.'S (International Business Corporations).   Solutions as low as $60.00, $200.00, $450.00, etc.

Global Wealth - International Offshore Opportunities! (Free Report)
Huge tax-sheltered income potential! Offshore Major Credit Card! (No credit check or social security number required; guaranteed approval!) Offshore bank account! Privacy! Asset protection! Investments! Also an opportunity to start your own international offshore business! Membership just $200! FREE report.

Right Way L.A.W. (Free Report)
Your knowledge of L.A.W. can set you free! Learn And Win! A non-profit organization founded to help people learn the law and overcome problems that may arise without the need for expensive and sometimes incorrect biased legal advice from attorneys. Learn to protect yourself from the frauds perpetrated upon you causing loss of wealth and liberty! What taxes you have to pay and what taxes are voluntary! Property rights! Civil and criminal actions. Criminal defenses not used by attorneys; find out WHY! Plus much more!

Virtual Office (Free Report)
The future of telecommunications: Integrates telephone, fax, computer & internet! Your electronic assistant runs your business for you while you live, work, or play anywhere in the world! Improve your image! No special equipment needed (not even a computer)! Only $30.00 month!

FREE Resources: Reports, Videos, Etc.!
Valuable, hard-to-find information!
(Continued - See Prior Page)

All Of The Above!
Just ask us for your complete package of FREE RESOURCES.

Ordering Instructions:

When requesting free resources please provide your name, mailing address, phone number, and email address (or state that you do not have an email address). The above is subject to availability and may be discontinued at any time. Some of the above may be available only in electronic format (email or internet). Some of the above may not be available outside the US and Canada. Please contact us for current information.

FREE Resources: Reports, Videos, Etc.!
Valuable, hard-to-find information: See other side of this page for details.

For FREE Resources, Questions, Or Service Contact:
FREEDOM TECH

PHONE: 970-221-9000 ● FAX: 970-221-9696

E-MAIL: info@livefree.com

WEBSITE: (Exciting and enlightening; it's like no other!)   **www.livefree.com**

P.O. Box 511, Fort Collins, Colorado 80522 US
305 West Magnolia Street, Suite 255, Fort Collins, Colorado 80521 US

Grow Rich In America's Best Cash Business!

How would you like to make up to $200.00 per hour in a very simple business where you could earn 100% return of your investment in as little as 4 months?

Learn the truth about who really is getting rich with vending and amusement machines. How, what, and why?

You'll Learn How Easy It Is To...

★ Get started on a shoestring...and with a money back guarantee!

★ How to make up to $200.00 gross profit per hour!

★ Earn your initial investment back in as little as 4 months!

★ Earn up to 500% gross return on investment per year!

★ Quickly turn $2,500.00 into at least $5,000.00 monthly income...working part-time only a few fun hours a month!

★ Do all this with no selling or selling experience required!

★ Learn the pitfalls, risks and rip-offs in vending... yes, there are scams and fatal mistakes you must learn to avoid!

★ Buy ALL the BEST vending and amusement machines at the factory-direct WHOLESALE cost, and save up to 75%.

★ Get great locations without selling!

★ Also, route management, machine selection, financing, getting started.

★ Receive ready-to-use forms, and a simple route record-keeping system.

★ What trade magazines to get, what associations to join, what conventions and shows to attend...

★ PLUS much more. PLEASE...take the time to read this carefully. It could be worth a fortune to you!

Bill Way started his business on a shoestring in 1972, at the age of 21, with just a $300.00 loan. Within 6 years he had built a million dollar company! He's both a successful vending route operator, and an authorized distributor for some of the largest and most respected vending equipment manufacturers in the U.S. He's helped countless others start their own highly profitable vending business.

"This book is an ABSOLUTE MUST for anyone considering getting into vending. IT COVERS IT ALL!"
— *B. M. of Big River, California*

"I found it EASY TO FIND LOCATIONS for my equipment. My (32) machines never leave their locations and just KEEP ON MAKING MONEY."
— *G. B. of Dallas, Texas*

"The machines are well made and require little, if any service. I consider them to be the BEST INVESTMENT I EVER MADE."
— *E. H. of Sunnyvale, California*

"ANYONE CAN BE SUCCESSFUL IN VENDING WITHOUT RISKING A FORTUNE TO DO SO. My compliments to BILL WAY for helping me get started."
— *K. B. of Denver, Colorado*

"It's hard to believe so much income can be generated with so little time!"
— *R.C. of Seattle, Washington*

"We started a few months ago with great success. ALL OUR MACHINES WILL BE PAID FOR IN MUCH LESS THAN 12 MONTHS."
— *T. V. of Orange County, California*

"BILL WAY saved my vending business. With Bill's help I increased my sales volume by 5 times in just 3 months. I was able to purchase vending machines at less than half the price I had been paying. BILL WAY is (someone) you can count on for fair prices and sound advice."
— *R. Z. of Fort Collins, Colorado*

ISBN 0-9658227-0-2

9 780965 822701

$24.95

Vending Success Secrets

How Anyone Can Grow Rich
In America's Best Cash Business!

By Bill Way

Third edition, completely revised

Published By: **FREEDOM TECH PRESS**
P.O. Box 511, Fort Collins, CO 80522 US
305 West Magnolia Street, Suite 255, Fort Collins, CO 80521 US
970-221-9000 ● FAX: 970-221-9696 ● E-MAIL: info@livefree.com ● WEBSITE: www.livefree.com

Cover By: Robert Howard

Library of Congress Catalog Card Number 97-60132

ISBN 0-9658227-0-2

Vending Success Secrets

How Anyone Can Grow Rich
In America's Best Cash Business!

By Bill Way

Third edition, completely revised

Published By: FREEDOM TECH PRESS

"WOW, I love my (electronic games) and the revenue they produce! (Owns 28). Because of their size they are SO EASY TO LOCATE. The quality, workmanship and styling are second to none!"

K.H. of Richland, Washington

"I've been surprised at the money we've been able to make with a minimal amount of effort!"

B.W. of Bakersfield, California

"I personally like the price, reliability, and the ease in which the (electronic games) can be placed. I certainly intend on purchasing more games as my business expands."

B.D. of Canada

"I have had no breakdowns. Thanks for shipping my last 10 machines so fast. Though the Lauderdale area is quite competitive with game machines, with the versatility, and small size, I AM ABLE TO FIND MANY GOOD LOCATIONS."

G.D. of Fort Lauderdale, Florida

"The machines are virtually maintenance free and are providing excellent income. They are producing a 100% RETURN ON INVESTMENT in less than one year, after paying a commission to the location! Enclosed please find order for 5 more machines. I will be buying more of these machines as fast as my budget allows!"

L.L. of Missouri

"We started a few months ago with great success. ALL OUR MACHINES WILL BE PAID FOR IN MUCH LESS THAN 12 MONTHS!"

T.V. of Orange County, California

"BILL WAY saved my vending business. With the help of BILL WAY I increased my sales volume by 5 times in just 3 months. I was able to purchase (packaged snack, drink, and bulk) vending machines at less than half the price I had been paying. BILL WAY is (someone) you can count on for fair prices and sound advice."

R.Z. of Fort Collins, Colorado

"I have known Bill for approximately 22 years. You will find Bill to be a person with great integrity and a genuine desire to perform to the best of his ability. He is an individual of the utmost honesty and integrity."

D.C. of Greeley, Colorado

"You were very honest and caring and that seems to be a rare quality in people now days. We were concerned about handling this long distance but everything worked out fine. We'll be in Fort Collins over July 4th. I would like to meet you if you're in the office."

B.M. of Silver Lake, Kansas

"I have been personally acquainted with Bill Way for the past two and one half years. During this time our company has conducted business of a contractual nature on a continuing basis with Mr. Way. Our experiences in this regard. . . have been completely satisfactory. (I) believe him to be very capable, conscientious and sincere in his dealings with others. He possesses an unusually high degree of technical understanding of his specialized field and is fortunate to also have a good grasp of the many other facts of the business world that play such an important role in making any business venture or endeavor successful."

P.R. of Greeley, Colorado

"Mr. Way has banked with (our bank) since May, 1973. He has always handled his accounts in a satisfactory manner. Mr. Way is an extremely conscientious and sincere person. He can be counted on to fulfill whatever obligations he undertakes."

R.W. (V.P. of Bank) of Greeley, Colorado

What Others Are Saying. . .

About Bill Way and vending or amusement machines he suggests:

"This book is an ABSOLUTE MUST for anyone considering getting into vending. IT COVERS IT ALL!"

B.M. of Big River, California

"I'M THRILLED WITH THE PROFIT. I've just ordered another shipment."

C.B. of San Francisco, California

"I've had the pleasure of doing business with BILL WAY for several years now, and some of his vending systems offer the most incredible profit potential I've seen yet. Based upon total investment required, it's possible to earn an ANNUAL RETURN OF WELL OVER 900%!"

T.Y. of Fort Collins, Colorado

"I'VE EARNED BACK MY INITIAL INVESTMENT IN 8 MONTHS! My 10 machines take about 10 hours of my time per month. It's hard to believe so much income can be generated with so little time!"

R.C. of Seattle, Washington

"In July I 'celebrated' the end of my first full year in vending. I can only marvel at your willingness to help a rank neophyte such as myself. Among the vending people I've met - equipment salespeople, manufacturing reps (etc.) - YOU STAND HEAD AND SHOULDERS ABOVE THEM ALL!"

"Your unselfish sharing of your time, and your knowledge represent rarities to be cherished in the business world today. Your willingness to stand behind the products you sell is exemplary. It's a real pleasure to find someone whose word is as good as his 'paper' in todays marketplace. I would unhesitatingly recommend BILL WAY. . . to anyone interested in pursuing vending as a business."

H.H. of Albuquerque, New Mexico

"For some time I've wanted to send you a letter of appreciation. I found it EASY TO FIND LOCATIONS for my equipment. My (32) machines never leave their locations and just KEEP ON MAKING MONEY."

G.B. of Dallas, Texas

"The machines are well made and require little, if any service. I consider them to be the BEST INVESTMENT I EVER MADE."

E.H. of Sunnyvale, California

"I have 200 (bulk vend) machines now, and will expand to 500 machines. (Bulk-vend) is the ONLY WAY TO GO!"

P.O. of San Diego, California

"I've been in the vending business for years and (BULK-VEND) MACHINES ARE MY TOP PRODUCERS."

W.M. of Orlando, Florida

"Not only are the PROFIT MARGINS VERY HIGH, but the (packaged snack) machines are relatively trouble free and indestructible. ANYONE CAN BE SUCCESSFUL IN VENDING WITHOUT RISKING A FORTUNE TO DO SO."

"I appreciate the fact that FREEDOM TECHNOLOGY is a local, family-run business. My compliments to BILL WAY for helping me get started. I look forward to ordering more machines in the near future."

K.B. of Denver, Colorado

"I was associated with your products for some years, both in Australia and Europe which resulted in several hundred GAMES being acquired. . . We are pleased to advise you of EXTREMELY TROUBLE FREE years of operation."

K.R. of Bentley, Australia

"Within just a couple of weeks, I had placed all 25 (electronic games). Individually they are grossing from $40. to $140. cash each week!"

G.S. of Ohio